Harmony Korine: Interviews

Conversations with Filmmakers Series
Gerald Peary, General Editor

Harmony Korine

INTERVIEWS

Edited by Eric Kohn

University Press of Mississippi / Jackson

www.upress.state.ms.us

The University Press of Mississippi is a member
of the Association of American University Presses.

Copyright © 2015 by University Press of Mississippi
Manufactured in the United States of America

First printing 2015
∞
Library of Congress Cataloging-in-Publication Data

Korine, Harmony.
  Harmony Korine: interviews / edited by Eric Kohn. — Conversations
with filmmakers series
    pages cm
  Includes index.
  Includes filmography.
  ISBN 978-1-62846-160-2 (cloth : alk. paper) — ISBN 978-1-62846-161-9 (ebook)
  1. Korine, Harmony—Interviews. 2. Motion picture producers and directors—United
States—Interviews. I. Kohn, Eric, editor. II. Title.
  PN1998.3.K675A5 2014
  791.4302'33092—dc23   2014024116

British Library Cataloging-in-Publication Data available

Contents

Introduction

So many artists have staked a claim to creating "subversive" work over the years that the term has practically lost its value. But that's hardly the case for Harmony Korine, still one of the most prominent subversive filmmakers in America.

Ever since erupting onto the independent film scene as the irrepressible prodigy who wrote the screenplay for Larry Clark's *Kids* in 1992, Korine has retained his stature as the ultimate cinematic provocateur: He both intelligently observes modern social milieus and gleefully thumbs his nose at them at the same time. Now approaching middle age and arguably more influential than ever, Korine remains a knowingly sensationalistic and innovative creative mind.

But it's been a bumpy ride. In 1995, Korine came out nowhere and became an overnight media darling, stealing the spotlight from *Kids* director Larry Clark and quickly taking advantage of the attention to project his bad boy image across the world. Korine's origin story, the tale of a disillusioned NYU dropout discovered by Clark while skating around Washington Square Park, quickly overshadowed the sheer determination involved in his first completed screenplay. A serious film geek raised by a documentary filmmaker in Nashville, Korine turned Clark's idea for a movie about promiscuous teenagers whose antics ultimately lead to an AIDS dilemma into a full-fledged screenplay over the course of three weeks. The young writer recorded conversations with his friends as the basis for a highly naturalistic flow of dialogue, resulting in a seminal portrait of New York's underground youth culture. The movie portrayed a dark, depraved world, but it was especially haunting because it maintained a stark realism throughout.

A hit at Sundance and Cannes, *Kids* transcended the perceived limitations of its NC-17 rating and grossed $20 million at the box office, effectively turning Korine into a major pop culture figure. That same year, he appeared on *Late Night with David Letterman* and mystified a nation with a combination of wide-eyed innocence and scrappy demeanor. The media loved Korine's playful behavior and foul mouth. He expressed adoration for vaudeville and certainly put on a good show, tap dancing for one interviewer and harassing pedestrians while hanging out with another. He was practically an auteur before even directing his first film.

The next few years unfolded in a whirlwind of creativity and scandalous gestures. Korine's directorial debut, *Gummo*, was shot in rundown Nashville neighborhoods on 16mm, eschewing plot for bizarre asides and eccentric character sketches. The *New York Times'* Janet Maslin infamously called it the worst movie of the year, an assertion that *Gummo's* producers considered placing on its poster. There's no doubting the potency of a movie so dense with images and information, which dances a line between experimental documentary and lyrical portrait of an alienated lower class with such riveting intensity that it transcends any easy categorization.

Set in a decrepit neighborhood ravished by a tornado, *Gummo* contains an ensemble of pariahs, including a mute boy who wanders about town wearing bunny ears, a pair of boxing skinhead siblings, a gay dwarf, and two young rebels who kill stray cats for cash—one of whom, Solomon (Jacob Reynolds), receives questionable advice from his tap-dancing mother (Linda Manz). A kaleidoscopic peek into America's marginalized inhabitants, *Gummo* tossed aside traditional plot in favor of freewheeling images and vignettes. It mystified even the viewers who loved it.

Next, Korine was invited to join the vaunted brotherhood of Dogme 95, the DIY movement kickstarted by Danish filmmakers Lars Von Trier and Thomas Vinterberg that required all participants to adhere to a set of arbitrary rules, like shooting on video with natural lights and no special effects. The sole American participant in the project, Korine's effort (which admittedly broke some of the Dogme rules) was unsurprisingly brash, but also far more focused than his previous effort. The story of a schizophrenic man and his maniacal relatives (based on Korine's uncle), *Julian Donkey-Boy* delivered a brutal, transgressive form of dramatic storytelling littered with eccentric digressions. Characterized by an ultragrainy DV look and abrupt editing techniques, the film was anchored by Ewen Bremmer's disturbing performance. It also owed much to German New Wave legend Werner Herzog—now one of Korine's major advocates—in the role of the boy's crazed father. Critics were once again divided on the merits of Korine's output, but there was no doubting that the attention to his burgeoning artistry continued to increase.

In the wake of *Julian Donkey-Boy*, he kicked off an ill-fated project called *Fight* in which hidden cameramen (including colleagues David Blaine and Leonardo DiCaprio) watched as Korine attempted to engage random street characters in violent brawls. After suffering major injuries and a handful of arrests, Korine abandoned the project; the completed footage has never screened publicly, and has become a central ingredient in the filmmaker's irascible reputation, even once he cleaned up his act.

Korine was rarely sober when he made *Fight*, but drugs could hardly mollify the impact of fame and expectations barreling down on him from every direction. His much-publicized relationship with actress Chloe Sevigny, who had appeared in all of his completed features up until that point, ended badly. By the end of the decade, Korine abruptly vanished from the public eye, heading out to Europe for a depraved three-year interlude in his career that remains largely undocumented. This period culminated in 2003 with his admission to a methadone clinic.

With help from advocates of his earlier work, including the fashion magnate agnès b., Korine gradually put his life back together. In 2005, he directed a television documentary about his old pal David Blaine. By then, Korine had quietly resettled in Nashville, where he fell in love with a local waitress, got married, and bought a house. In 2008, he unveiled the agnès b.–produced *Mister Lonely*, arguably his softest, most accessible work—a delightfully surreal tale about a Michael Jackson impersonator (Diego Luna) who discovers a commune filled with other outcasts playing dress up, which takes place in parallel to another offbeat story involving Werner Herzog as a priest. The next year, Korine was making the rounds with *Trash Humpers*, a scrappy production shot on lo-grade video featuring the titular characters (including one played by Korine) wandering around murky regions of Nashville and engaging in the eponymous sex act. But they also share poetry and tender monologues about the spiritual dimensions of being a pariah, statements that suggested the movie served as Korine's mantra. Consolidating the aesthetics of his earlier films with more sophisticated pontifications, *Trash Humpers* is arguably Korine's most personal work.

Korine started work on *Spring Breakers* the next year. The apotheosis of his attempts to subvert pop culture, the movie's trim plot involved a group of college girls who rob a diner to fuel a hedonistic voyage to the center of the party scene in St. Petersburg, Florida. Filmed with an alarmingly bright palette and occasional shadowy interludes, set to a combination of pulsating electronic melodies and an ominous score by Cliff Martinez, *Spring Breakers*' biggest coup was its cast: Pop star Selena Gomez led an ensemble of well-known faces as the women at the helm of the gleeful adventure, which abruptly shifts tones when they wind up arrested.

Rescued by a messianic pimp named Alien played with memorable exuberance by James Franco, the girls wind up thrust into a nightmarish inversion of the pleasure they initially sought. But the ones who choose to stick around for this next stage find themselves entranced by an even greater height of rebellion. Hence the true shock value of *Spring Breakers*: rather than moralizing, Korine celebrates the dogma-fueling criminal antics for their capacity to undermine the rigidity of social mores. Describing this outlook as "gangster mysticism" in interviews, Korine proved he could maintain his outsider perspective even while creating a more commercial film.

The response to the movie seemed to validate his ambition. *Spring Breakers* grossed more in its limited opening weekend release than any of his previous films in their entire theatrical runs, landed on numerous critics' top-ten lists, and even led to a serious awards campaign for Franco. Korine was no longer a rebel at odds with the establishment; he had successfully invaded it without selling out.

The irony of Korine's reputation as a kind of twisted cultural insurgent is that he came from a relatively low-key background. Born in a commune in Salinas, California, Korine grew up in Nashville under the guidance of his documentarian father, who taught him how to make movies. In high school, encouraged by a teacher who liked his writing, Korine made a remarkable black-and-white short film called *A Bundle of Minutes* that featured an angry loner wandering about town, committing robberies and ranting about his life. It ultimately helped him gain acceptance to NYU and convinced Clark to hire him to write *Kids*. Viewed in retrospect, *A Bundle of Minutes* outlines much of the restless excitement for deconstructing traditional storytelling methods visible in all of Korine's work. At one point, fuming about the limitations of his world, the movie's protagonist rants that he's "the world's most stupid genius." That may well remain Korine's means of self-justification: His movies cherish striking images and the flow of shocking events over cohesive ideas. He lets his unvarnished inspiration lead the way, which may be why he has always wrestled with the challenge of explaining himself to the public.

Yet it's through the process of speaking to various journalists that he may have crafted his most intricate achievement. Throughout twenty years of interviews, Korine has developed into one of the great fabulists of our time, his storytelling antics extending beyond a handful of distinctive feature films and permeating the discourse surrounding them.

For that reason, his inclusion in the venerable Conversations with Filmmakers Series makes for a unique opportunity: Korine is one of the youngest filmmakers to receive this treatment and perhaps its most elusive subject.

For much of his career, Korine has actively played with the media's attempt to comprehend his output and has invented stories to shroud the true nature of his origins as well as his creative inspiration. As a result of those tendencies, this collection provides not only an amusingly offbeat perspective on his character but an overview of his distinctly scatter-shot approach to narrative invention. In many cases, especially during the early stages of Korine's career, journalists were made into unwitting collaborators in Korine's decade-spanning cross-media attempt to construct his true artistic identity with the same eccentric elements found in his movies.

Interviewers willing to engage with the aesthetic qualities of his work have found that Korine will gladly indulge them by exploring the themes percolating throughout it. Others, either unwilling or incapable of analyzing it beyond superficial details (or merely interested in his tabloid history), find themselves venturing further down the rabbit hole of his fictions. When Korine invents stories in interviews, he's feeding his mythology. There's a natural downside to this charade: Not since Orson Welles has a filmmaker's persona so heavily threatened to subsume the attention to his work. Even these days, sober and settled, the forty-year-old Korine's bad boy reputation continues to haunt him.

Despite this, many of his influences are indeed well-documented: his admiration for Herzog's films and poetic narratives of Terrence Malick result in a distinctly grimy form of lyricism. Korine's inspirations stretch far beyond cinema, however, as demonstrated by his predilection for photographers like William Eggleston and fine artists like Mike Kelly. Yet his main reference point is his own head: He will explain, for example, his interest in filmmaker Alan Clark's depiction of violence, but that doesn't make the violence in Korine's films into a form of pastiche. Instead, like his rambling interviews, Korine goes wherever his mind wanders, a proclivity that he has repeatedly and accurately labeled "mistakist art." That process naturally extends to his means of explaining the process of filmmaking for him.

The first time I interviewed Korine, I nearly fell prey to one of his usual tricks. During a conversation after the North American premiere of *Mister Lonely* at the Toronto International Film Festival, I naively asked Korine about the delay between that notable change of pace and his earlier output. Though he directed a David Blaine documentary in 2005 as a work-for-hire effort, *Mister Lonely* was his first narrative feature in nearly a decade. Instead of delving into the details of his previously destructive lifestyle, a flameout that culminated in self-imposed exile to Europe and eventual time spent in methadone clinics, he unloaded an exotic tale regurgitated to several journalists at the time.

This fantasy, which I later confronted him about in the 2008 *Indiewire* interview included in this volume, finds Korine venturing to South America and joining a fictitious tribe tellingly called the Malingerers as they searched for a mythological fish. Absurd as it sounds, however, the Malingerers yarn was the epitome of Korine's apocryphal style, in which outlandish ingredients point to deeper truths. Korine later admitted to me that, in spite of this fabrication, "there are some ways of saying things without actually saying them." Korine's journey with the Malingerers story is a clear-cut and rather beautiful abstraction of his literal experiences with addiction and impractical decision-making that led him astray before he rediscovered faith in his creativity.

At the same time, as Korine has matured, so too has his capacity to grapple with the process of explaining his radical aesthetics. Early on, Korine managed to confront the brash publicity machine that welcomed his talent while validating the efforts of critics and scholars who strove to find an intellectual foundation beneath his various provocations. Korine's unbridled energy, and the way it was eventually impacted by drug abuse and emotional exhaustion, has become entwined with his means of alternately elucidating and obscuring the ideas in his work. As his films have shown increasing calculation, so has his means of seriously discussing them. The chronology of this book is a de facto narrative of Korine growing up.

When I met with Korine while he was working on post-production for *Spring Breakers*, I shared with him a mountain of interviews I had already amassed from various archives, pointing out their variability, as many interviews told different sides of the same story. "I always knew someone would do this," he said with a chuckle. Though somewhat inarticulate about his motivations, Korine recalled how he treated each interview as a creative experiment ("it was kind of a game for me," he said more than once); even now, while less bizarrely irreverent when discussing his films, Korine leaves much to interpretation and evades the challenge of explaining his intentions aside from pointing out the ephemeral phenomena that drive his productivity.

Because Korine tends to discuss his films casually and avoids self-analysis, he has been criticized as an empty rebel with no intellectual foundation for his work. As a performance artist for whom the media apparatus is a natural stage, Korine allows himself to be misunderstood. However, the interviews in this book have been selected to downplay the tabloid aspects of Korine's early career and instead elucidate his legitimate filmmaking sensibilities. But they also speak to his broader ambition to work as a mixed-media artist; along with feature-length films, Korine has created paintings, prose, installation art, and music videos. Collectively, they underscore his ongoing rebellion against conventional narrative modes.

Like many filmmakers asked to explain their work, Korine tends to repeat the same reasons behind his motives. However, trenchant interviewers have been able to get him to open up. The 2003 interview from *Les Inrockuptibles*, generously translated into English by the illustrious French subtitler Henri Behar, marks one of the few instances in which Korine provides candid details about the creative breakdown he suffered after the release of *Julian Donkey-Boy*. Elsewhere, Korine drops his playful, dodgy routine in a prolonged discussion from *ANP Quarterly* with longtime friend Aaron Rose (who included the filmmaker in his perceptive documentary *Beautiful Losers*). At home in Nashville, Korine provides a laid-back but incredibly detailed overview of his artistic progress.

Korine's ability to slip between allegorical and literal discussion of his intentions mirrors the process of viewing his films. He spotlights objects and people we're often afraid to recognize or unwilling to understand. With each film, that process has grown increasingly controlled. Similarly, his interviews have adopted a tamer quality notable for their introspection. The concluding installments of this book find him on the rise once again, basking in the success of *Spring Breakers* and on the brink of a new project.

While many Korine interviews are available by way of a handy Google search, the majority of the ones included in this volume are not. Only about a third of the interviews that I have selected have also been posted on the exhaustive unofficial fan site Harmony-Korine.com, which has been steadily curated by Korine devotee Scott Nolan for several years.

This project would not have come together without the assistance of my good friend Livia Bloom, an editor of the must-read Errol Morris installment of this series, who encouraged me to consider a contribution of my own. Nick Dawson, who edited wonderful volumes for this series on Hal Ashby and Dennis Hopper, also provided essential guidance. At the University Press of Mississippi, Leila Salisbury was kind enough to accept this proposal and deal with my questions as the book came to-gether. My colleagues at *Indiewire* provided me with words of encourage-ment, as they do on a regular basis—and so did Janet and John Pierson, Scott Macaulay, and Henri Behar.

Nolan, the committed proprietor of Harmony-Korine.com, helped me map out a path in my search of more obscure interviews. Korine's ceaselessly hardworking assistant at the time, Scott Pierce, was an essen-tial partner-in-crime during my trip to Nashville and beyond. Above all, my partner Liz Bloomfield is the best support system in everything I do, personally and professionally, so I dedicate this book to her.

Of course, nobody deserves greater credit for the completion of this project than the endlessly inventive and innovative creative force known as Harmony Korine, whose fascinating trajectory has encom-passed more advanced personal and artistic challenges than many cre-ators face in their entire careers. And he's just getting started.

EK

Chronology

1973   Korine born to Eve and Sol Korine in Bolinas, California. Korine would later describe these early living conditions as a "hippy commune." Sol Korine is a documentary filmmaker and produces several features for PBS.

1975   Korine and his family move to Nashville, Tennessee.

1990   Korine receives a grant from the Nashville public school system to produce his first short film, *A Bundle of Minutes*.

1992   Korine is accepted in early admission to NYU's Dramatic Writing program at the Tisch School of the Arts. He enrolls the next year.

1993   Korine meets photographer Larry Clark in Washington Square Park. After Korine shares his short film with Clark, he's hired to write *Kids* and later *Ken Park*. A few months later, he drops out of school. Meets future girlfriend Chloe Sevigny.

1994   Korine travels to Los Angeles to meet with Hollywood agents and decides not to hire any of them. He returns to New York for the production of *Kids*.

1995   *Kids* premieres in a secret midnight slot at the Sundance Film Festival, generating major buzz for both Clark and Korine. The film screens in competition at the Cannes Film Festival, where Korine publicly states his intention of making "films like nobody has ever seen before." He makes first of three appearances on *Late Night with David Letterman*.

1997   Completes first directorial effort, *Gummo*, in hometown Nashville after intentions of shooting in Xenia, Ohio, don't pan out. The film premieres at the Telluride Film Festival to mixed response, but garners acclaim from Werner Herzog.

1998   Korine is contacted by Thomas Vinterberg about creating a project for the Dogme '95 movement. He chooses the script he has written for *Julien-Donkey Boy*. Publishes *The Bad Son* in conjunction with Tokyo gallery Taka Ishii, a collection of photographs featuring Macaulay Culkin. Publishes experimental novel *A*

Crackup at the Race Riots, frequently described as an attempt to write "the Great American Choose Your Own Adventure Novel."

1999   Completes his second feature, *Julien-Donkey Boy*, which screens at several festivals and garners significantly more critical acclaim than *Gummo* while remaining fairly divisive. Scheduled fourth appearance on *Letterman* cancelled mid-show when Letterman allegedly discovers Korine backstage rifling through fellow guest Meryl Streep's purse. Attempts to make a documentary about his attempts to get into fights. David Blaine and Leonardo DiCaprio split duties with the camerawork. After getting jailed and seriously injured multiple times, Korine abandons the project, titled *Fight*. Collaborates with Gang Gang Dance frontman Brian Degrow on album *SSAB Songs*.

2000   In April, the Patrick Painter Gallery in Los Angeles hosts an exhibition entitled *The Sigil of the Cloven Hoof Marks They Path*, featuring large-size images of black metal icons as well as the soon-to-be-infamous video installation *The Devil, The Sinner and His Journey*, in which Korine wore black face and pretended to be O. J. Simpson and acted alongside Johnny Depp as Kato Kalin.

2001   Allegedly loses two homes and most of his possessions in sudden fires within a two-month period. Among the material lost in these fires: a screenplay for a feature entitled *What Makes Pistachio Nuts?* Two weeks after 9/11, he flees to London.

2002   Releases photography collection *Pass the Bitch Chicken* in collaboration with Christopher Wool.

2003   Future producing partner agnès b. hosts gallery exhibition of Korine's photographs in Paris. Strapped for cash, Korine stabilizes himself by directing a documentary about friend David Blaine for British network Channel 4. Returns to Nashville.

2007   *Mister Lonely*, Korine's first narrative feature in eight years, premieres at the Cannes Film Festival to considerable acclaim. It is purchased by IFC Films soon afterward and later screens at the Toronto International Film Festival. Marries Rachel Simon, former Nashville waitress and bit player in *Mister Lonely* ensemble. Appears in artist profile documentary *Beautiful Losers*.

2008   Drag City publishes *The Collected Fanzines*, which contains zines from the early nineties Korine published with Mark Gonzalez.

2009   Collaborates with Vanderbilt University for *Pigxote* exhibition, a collection of Korine's private photographs. Premieres *Trash Humpers* at the Toronto International Film Festival. It is later acquired by Drag City and released early the next week. Documentary festival CPH: DOX, in Copenhagen, gives it a top award in spite of its fictional ingredients.

2010   Rachel gives birth to a daughter, Lefty.

2011   Releases short film *Umshimi Wan*, which premieres at the SXSW Film Festival, as well as Proenza Schouler–sponsored short *Snowballs*. Travels to Florida to research and write the screenplay for *Spring Breakers*.

2012   Films *Spring Breakers* in Florida, later it calling "the hardest shoot of my life." It premieres at the Venice Film Festival, where Annapurna Pictures acquires it. The company later splits the distribution efforts with upstart distributor A24.

2013   Drag City republishes *A Crackup at the Race Riots* at roughly the same time that *Spring Breakers* hits theaters. *Spring Breakers* opens in limited release on March 15 ahead of its nationwide expansion. It grosses $5 million in three days, more than any of Korine's previous films grossed during their entire theatrical runs. A few weeks later, news that Korine will make another midsize crime movie with Annapurna Pictures begins to circulate.

Filmography

Though he has only directed five features over the course of a career spanning two decades, Harmony Korine's moving image artwork also includes installation work, music videos, and commercials, all of which reflect his distinct creative interests. Below is a fairly comprehensive selection of his major filmed works, including the two screenplays he did not direct. For more information, we recommend consulting Harmony-Korine.com and the Internet Movie Database.

A BUNDLE OF MINUTES (short film) (1991)
Director/Editor/Cinematographer/Narrator: **Harmony Korine**
Cast: Sol Korine, Harmony Korine
16mm, black and white, 5 minutes

KIDS (1995)
Miramax/Excalibur Films
Producers: Leigh Blake, Michael Chambers, Cathy Konrad, Patrick Panzarella, Christine Vachon, Gus Van Sant, Cary Woods, Lauren Zalaznick
Director: Larry Clark
Screenplay: **Harmony Korine**
Cinematography: Eric Alan Edwards
Original Music: Lou Barlow, John Davis
Editing: Christopher Tellefsen
Cast: Leo Fitzpatrick, Sajan Bhagat, Billy Valdes, Alex Glen, Justin Pierce, Chloe Sevigny, Rosario Dawson, Harold Hunter, Jon Abrahams, Jeff Pang, Michele Lockwood, Carisa Glucksman, Yakira Peguero
35mm, color, 91 minutes

CASPER (music video for Daniel Johnston, unreleased) (1995)
Director: **Harmony Korine**
Original Music: Daniel Johnston
Super 8mm, color, 2 minutes

VISUAL MAFIA (MTV spot) (1995)
MTV
Director/Star/Editor: **Harmony Korine**
Producer: Aaron Rose
Video, color, 1 minute

GUMMO (1997)
New Line Cinema
Director/Screenplay: **Harmony Korine**
Producers: Stephen Chin, Scott Macaulay, Robin O'Hara, Ruth Vitale,
Cary Woods
Cinematography: Jean-Yves Escoffier
Editing: Christopher Tellefsen
Production Design: David Doerenberg
Costume Design: Chloe Sevigny
Cast: Jacob Sewell, Nick Sutton, Jacob Reynolds, Darby Dougherty,
Chloe Sevigny, Linda Manz
35mm, 16mm, and Super 8mm, color, 89 minutes

THE DIARY OF ANNE FRANK PT II (video installation) (1997)
Director: **Harmony Korine**
16mm, Super 8mm, and video, color, 40 minutes
Note: Footage predominantly culled from unused *Gummo* material

SUNDAY (Sonic Youth music video) (1998)
Director: **Harmony Korine**
Original Music: Sonic Youth
Cast: Macaulay Culkin, Rachel Miner
Video, color, 4 minutes

JULIEN DONKEY-BOY (1999)
Fine Line Features
Director/Screenplay: **Harmony Korine**
Producers: Jim Czarnecki, Scott Macaulay, Robin O'Hara, Cary Woods
Cinematography: Anthony Dod Mantle
Editing: Valdis Oskarsdottir
Cast: Ewen Bremner, Chloe Sevigny, Werner Herzog, Evan Neumann
Video, color, 94 minutes

FIGHT HARM (unfinished) (1999)
Director/Star: **Harmony Korine**
Cinematography: Leonardo DiCaprio, David Blaine
Video, color, 30 minutes

WHAT MAKES PISTACHIO NUTS? (unproduced screenplay) (1999)
Screenplay: **Harmony Korine**

THE DEVIL, THE SINNER AND HIS JOURNEY (video installation)
(2000)
Director: **Harmony Korine**
Cast: **Harmony Korine**, Johnny Depp
Video, color, 10 minutes

KORINE TAP (short video) (2000)
Director: **Harmony Korine**
Video, color, 1 minute
JOKES (anthology film, unfinished) (2000)
Director: Gus Van Sant (completed segment, titled EASTER; uncompleted segments titled HERPES and SLIPPERS)
Cinematography: Anthony Dod Mantle
Screenplay/Producer: **Harmony Korine**
Video, color, 33 minutes (EASTER)

KEN PARK (2002)
Vitagraph Films
Director: Larry Clark
Screenplay: **Harmony Korine**
Producers: Pascal Breton, Olivier Bremond, Victoria Goodall, Kees
Kasander, Jean-Louis Piel, Wan Wei
Cinematography: Edward Lachman, Larry Clark
Cast: Adam Chubbuck, James Bullard, James Ransone, Stephen Jasso,
Tiffany Limos, Maeve Quinlan
35mm, color, 96 minutes

DAVID BLAINE: ABOVE THE BELOW (TV special) (2003)
BBC Television
Directors: **Harmony Korine**, Steve Smith
Producers: Simon Mills, Mike Montgomery, Jo Pilkington, Hazel

Stewart, Katie Taylor
Cinematography: Gary Beckerman, Crighton Bone, Dave Emery, Alan Haddow, Adrian Kelly
Cast: David Blaine
Video, color, 81 minutes

NO MORE WORKHORSE BLUES (Bonnie "Prince" Billy Music Video) (2004)
Director: **Harmony Korine**
Video, color, 3 minutes

LIVING PROOF (Cat Power music video) (2006)
Director: **Harmony Korine**
Producer: Margaret Brown
Cinematography: Lee Daniel
Video, color, 3 minutes

BLACKBERRY WINTER (short film) (2006)
O'Salvation
Director/Screenplay/Cinematography: Brent Stewart
Producers: **Harmony Korine**, Nadja Romain
Sound Mix: K. K. Proffitt
Cast: Chris Bower
35mm, black and white, 47 minutes

ALUMINUM FOWL (documentary short) (2006)
O'Salvation
Director: James Clauer
Producers: **Harmony Korine**, Nadja Romaine
Video, color, 13 minutes

MISTER LONELY (2007)
IFC Films
Director/Screenplay: **Harmony Korine**
Producers: Charles-Marie Anthonioz, agnès b., Adam Bohling, Ann Carli, James Flynn, **Harmony Korine**, Richard Mansell, Hengameh Panahi, David Reid, Nadja Romain, Peter Watson
Cinematography: Marcei Zyskind
Editing: Paul Zucker, Valdis Oskarsdottir

Original Music: Jason Spaceman, The Sun City Girls
Cast: Diego Luna, Werner Herzog, Denis Lavant, Leos Carax, Samantha Morton
35mm, color, 112 minutes

STUCK (Thorntons chocolate commercial) (2007)
2AM Films
Director: **Harmony Korine**
Creative Directors: Tom Ewart, Dave Sullivan
Music: Corker/Conboy, Derailer
Video, color, 1 minute

TRUE DEDICATION (four-part Budweiser advertisement) (2008)
Director: **Harmony Korine**
Agency: Fallon, London
Creative Director: Richard Flintham
Editing: Leo Scott
Cast: Dave Cloud
Video, color, 30 seconds each

THE DIRTY ONES (short film series) (2008)
O'Salvation
Director/Screenplay: Brent Stewart
Producer: **Harmony Korine**
Cinematography: Roger Pistole
Cast: Rachel Korine, Raven Dunn
Video, color, 11 minutes

CRUTCHNAP (short film produced for *One Dream Rush* project) (2009)
Director/Camera: **Harmony Korine**
Video, color, 43 seconds

TRASH HUMPERS (2009)
Drag City
Director/Cinematography: **Harmony Korine**
Producers: Charles-Marie Anthonioz, agnès b., Amina Dasmal, Robin C. Fox
Editing: Leo Scott

Cast: Rachel Korine, Brian Kotzur, Travis Nicholson, **Harmony Korine**
Video, color, 78 minutes

ACT DA FOOL (short film commissioned by Proenza Schouler) (2010)
Director: **Harmony Korine**
Cast: Michelrica Hughes, Miileah Morrison, Elizabeth Smith, Kiara Smith
Video, color, 4 minutes

CURB DANCE (short film dedicated to Jonas Mekas) (2011)
Director/Star: **Harmony Korine**
Editing: Michael Carter
Cinematography: Scott Pierce
Original Music: Brian Kotzur

UMSHINI WAN (short film) (2011)
Director: **Harmony Korine**
Producers: Charles-Marie Anthonioz, agnès b., Ben Conrad, The Mill, Ryan Zacarias
Cinematography: Alexis Zabe
Editing: Leo Scott
Original Music: Justin De Nobrega
Cast: Die Antwoord (Ninja and Yolandi Visser)
Video, color, 15 minutes

REBEL (short film) (2011)
Director: **Harmony Korine**
Cast: James Franco
Video, color, 6 minutes

THE FOURTH DIMENSION (anthology film) (2012)
Director/Screenplay: **Harmony Korine** (Segment: LOTUS COMMU-NITY WORKSHOP)
Producers: Charles-Marie Anthonioz, agnès b.
Cinematography: Chris Blauvelt
Editing: Leo Scott
Original Music: Val Kilmer
Cast: Val Kilmer, Rachel Korine
Video, color, 30 minutes

GOLD ON THE CEILING (music video for The Black Keys) (2012)
Director: **Harmony Korine**
Cast: Dan Auerbach, Patrick Carney, the ATL Twins

SPRING BREAKERS (2013)
A24/Annapurna Pictures
Director/Screenplay: **Harmony Korine**
Producers: Charles-Marie Anthonioz, agnès b., Vikram Chatwal, Chris
Contogouris, Megan Ellison, Ted Field, Jonathan Fong, Jordan Gertner,
Chris Hanley, Jane Holzer, Vince Jolivette, Susan Kirr, Miles Levy
Cinematography: Benoit Debie
Editing: Douglas Crise
Original Music: Cliff Martinez, Skrillex
Cast: Selena Gomez, Ashley Benson, James Franco, Vanessa Hudgens,
Rachel Korine
35mm, color, 94 minutes

Harmony Korine: Interviews

Nashville. Harmony's House. Present Day. Part I.

Eric Kohn / 2013

Interview conducted January 11, 2013. Previously unpublished.

Eric Kohn: Your first interview was for *Sassy* in 1993. Do you remember what it was like to do that?

Harmony Korine: Yeah. I think I had just written *Kids*. Chloe Sevigny wasn't even my girlfriend at that point; we were friends. She was an intern at that magazine. I think that's how they heard of me.

EK: What did you make of that early interest in your work?

HK: It seemed like a game for me. It was way pre-Internet. It seemed like nobody even read it. It felt like it wasn't much different than doing some interview with a high school newspaper. It was fun. At the very beginning, with those interviews, you have to remember: A year earlier, I was getting grounded, wrecking cars, running stop signs. It wasn't like not knowing what you're in store for. It was just a game.

EK: How did your family feel about the early stirrings of your career ambition?

HK: They were definitely supportive of me wanting to be a director. When my dad found out I wanted to make movies, it wasn't a big surprise to him. He probably helped me. I made my first film when I was a sophomore in high school.

EK: How did that come about?

HK: I was a sophomore or junior at Hillsborough High School taking a creative writing course in 1990. My teacher's name was Miss Bradshaw. She's still around. She's still teaching. Until that point, I was a pretty mediocre student. I had never been given any type of encouragement by a

3

teacher before. In public schools, teachers really don't have that much time to pay any attention to you. It's more like you're cattle. At schools before that, I went to a place where if you were late teachers would smack you. So I was coming out of that whole thing, so I didn't trust teachers so much. They were the same thing as police or something.

But in this class, I wrote a short story and she said she liked it. She thanked everyone for their assignments but said there was this one special piece of writing. I was falling asleep, dreaming about girls. Then she said my name and I was like, "What the fuck?" And she asked me to read it. I thought it was completely retarded but she saw some merit in it. She asked me to stay behind after class and asked me what I wanted to do. I said I really wanted to make movies. She gave me this story I wrote and asked if I could turn it into a script. I said, "Of course," but had no idea what it took to write a script. She said, "I could probably get you a grant, a couple thousand dollars from the school board." I somehow broke down the story into some type of shooting script and she took it and got something like $2,000 from the school system. Then my dad showed me how to work a 16mm Bolex film camera. He showed me how to edit. And this guy named Coke Sams, who [worked on] all the *Ernest* movies, like *Ernest Goes to Camp*—my dad knew him and I see him all the time now [in Nashville]. My dad asked him if we could use his machines to edit and he was cool with it. So we would go in there at night.

EK: What was your script about?
HK: It was called *A Bundle a Minute* and about this kid, a runaway. If you saw it, I think you could probably see a type of thematic relationship to what I'm doing now. I had this jazz soundtrack and me talking on top of it. It was only five minutes long, this Cassavetes, Woody Allen thing, except shot in the South. I put on a fake accent and sounded like W. C. Fields. So I finished this thing and it was a surprise to everyone. My dad helped on the technical side and then I played around with the equipment and figured the rest out. I'd watched movies so I thought I knew what I was doing. I probably had read a couple of things. I don't remember at that point what was available, even.

EK: When did you see the results?
HK: I shot some of it in New York, where we finished it, where my grandma lived. My dad and sister acted in it. We shot in Manhattan, on the Lower East Side. I remember I had it processed at Duart. I was like fifteen or sixteen at this point. I went to go pick up the film and the guy

there—I've never said this to anyone, but I'm remembering it now—the guy handed me the roll of film and said, "You're pretty young." He thought I was just a runner. I said, "No, this is my thing, I can't wait to see it." He asked me if I wanted to see it projected. I was like, "What?" And he said, "Let me show you what it looks like." He was encouraging me. He said, "I saw it. It looks really beautiful." And this was just some guy there. So I saw it in some screening room all alone as he projected it. This was the first time I had ever seen any footage I had ever shot. It was unbelievable. I couldn't believe it was even in focus. It was the greatest. I asked him to rewind it three or four times. I sat there for like an hour. This was raw footage. I don't remember how long it was, maybe forty-five minutes, but it was just unbelievable. I saw the camera moving. Things were working. There was no sound, no sync, but I remember thinking, "I can do this." It didn't look too far off from other movies I had watched. It didn't look too far off from *She's Gotta Have It*, which I remember seeing recently. My dad had rented a VHS copy of that. It had snowed and we were out of school. He rented it for himself. He was in his mid-thirties then. By the time my parents were my age now, I was already in college. Actually, by the time they were my age now, I had done *Kids* already. It's pretty crazy to think about that now. It just blew my mind that it worked—I could somehow translate my ideas visually.

EK: And did the film open further doors for you?
HK: So because I wasn't a particularly great student, here's what that did: The only college I wanted to go to was NYU, mostly because I wanted to live in the city but also because at that point there was something romantic about that school. I applied and sent that film. They offered me a scholarship and I didn't want to apply anywhere else. I remember my dad was trying to push me to apply elsewhere. I had wanted to go to the film school, originally, because the idea was that I'd go somewhere and find all these like-minded movie kids who wanted to do what you wanted to do. You think in your mind that they're all going to be waiting to start some kind of movement or something. That couldn't be further from my experience. My dad said something good. I had already started making films in high school on my camcorder. He said, "Why do you want to go learn things you already know? Why don't you learn to be a writer?" I didn't read all that much. I was a skateboarder. There were books that changed my life, like S. E. Hinton and Jim Carroll books, but mostly I wasn't a huge reader. So the idea of being a writer seemed really foreign to me. But I realized there was a point in that as far back as I

could remember, I didn't want to be dependent on anyone else for anything creative. The idea that I would have to wait for someone to write something for me was horrible. Back then, I was thinking about movies in different ways. So I realized maybe I should go to the writing program, the dramatic writing undergraduate program. I only went to college for one year since I wrote *Kids* in my first semester.

EK: What was it like to transition into college mode?

HK: I didn't have any money. I moved in with my grandmother. My dad wouldn't pay for anything, so I lived with her in Queens, commuting from Flushing into the city every day on the F train. I graduated high school in 1992 so this was right after that. It was the best. For me that was the time of my life. I had been coming there for years as a skater and even before that so I already loved it. My experience in college was closer to high school. I wasn't in dorms. If I had a class in the morning and then nothing until the afternoon, I had to take a bus and a train, which would take at least an hour. So I couldn't go back and forth; I'd just stay in the city all day. When everyone else went back to their dorms, I would just stay out and watch movies. There were specific places I would go alone and spend all day there. I'd go to Avery Fischer Media Hall and watch movies in the library. They would have those huge catalogs of VHS tapes. For me it was amazing, watching three or four films in a row. When I didn't go there, I'd go to theaters. My favorite was a place on St. Marks Street, which would show double features every day. It's been gone for ten years or more now. But they'd have, like, Marx brothers movies playing there back to back for like two dollars. There'd be dope fiends in there nodding off the whole time. It was incredible, that place.

EK: How often did you go to classes?

HK: I went to all of them. Pretty much right away I realized that while there were a couple of nice kids there, it didn't have any relationship to what I was doing at all. Nothing. Not even the teachers. There was one kid who became a close friend of mine and we'd go see movies together. I don't know what happened to him. His name was Jared. He was really, really smart and had insane taste in things. He and I would walk around and watch movies, go to music shops and bookstores, stuff like that. But outside of him, I had no relationship to anyone there. Not to sound mean, but a lot of it was crummy, what I would hear people talking about, it just wasn't interesting. Now having said that, remember I only went for a very short period of time. Because up until that point I knew nothing about writing scripts, the very first year there, they just taught fundamentals of narrative. Even though my films are not narrative, it was very important for me to understand those fundamentals. They set up the rules for me, you know?

EK: You mean structure?
HK: Structure, yeah—beginning, middle, and end, traditional three-act structure. After school I went wild and pissed all over it—but it was helpful for me that I knew the rules going in.

EK: What sort of texts did you read?
HK: The classics. All the Greeks, Aristotle, *Poetics*. That was really helpful for me.

EK: That would explain the literary references in early interviews, catching journalists who expected more crass responses by surprise.
HK: At that point, when you're that young, nobody really expects anything from you. You go in with the most base expectations so even though a lot of what I was saying at that point was half-baked, people were still surprised that there was something else there.

EK: Your entire career took off during a three-month period in the fall of 1992.
HK: Exactly. That was when I met Larry Clark in the park. My first assignment [that semester] was to write a twenty-page script. In between classes I used to hang out in Washington Square Park with all the skaters there, just smoke weed and hang out. I was pretty motivated. I knew at a young age that I'd make movies and that I probably wouldn't go to college for all of it. I don't remember what I told my parents. In my mind, I knew I wasn't going to go through with it. I was just like, "Fuck that." It was boring.

EK: Did you still harbor aspirations of being a professional skater?
HK: By that point I'd already quit skateboarding. I used to write for some skateboard company and I'd grown bored of it. They used to send me sponsored skateboards. I realized at some point I'd never be that great. I wanted to make films. I remember I had a package sent to my house around my sophomore year [of high school] and I just called all my friends and said, "Here, take everything I have, I'm not going to do it any more. I'm going to make movies." I gave everything away.

EK: So the story of Clark discovering you "skateboarding in the park" isn't entirely true . . .

HK: No, I wasn't literally skateboarding, but the skaters were my friends—like Harold and Justin, those people who were in the movie. Harold was a legendary skater by that point. There was this company in New York called SHUT that had all my favorite skateboarders riding with it. I got pretty close with them and some others. So when I moved up there we would still hang out.

EK: At what point in your semester did you meet Clark?

HK: Maybe two months in. I had written a script about a kid who on his thirteenth birthday, his dad takes him to a prostitute. I was hustling—when I was a kid, I wanted to make films. I didn't want to wait. It's hard to explain it. It was impossible to shut my brain down. It's still hard now, but back then I couldn't be subdued. All I wanted to do was make things. I'd just sit in my grandma's house and paint all day. I'd cut things up, make collages, sing into tape recorders, play the banjo into my answering machine. I'll tell you how obsessive I was: I would literally change my answering machine message like once every hour at my grandma's house. No one would ever call me. But I kept changing it. I would write a poem or sing a song or record something off the television. Then I'd stick it in the answering machine and hope someone would call it. I can't explain to you . . . it was wild, man. I felt like I was around all these influences at that time and I was voracious. There will never be a time that will compare with that.

EK: You were firing on all cylinders creatively and then suddenly Clark asked you to write a screenplay.

HK: Yeah, and I didn't even know what that meant. I could barely tie my shoes. My grandma would feed me, she'd come in with plates of fruit because I'd forget to eat. I can't explain what was happening at that point, but I felt like I was on fire. I'd go to sleep at night and my mind would be racing, dreaming things up.

EK: How quickly did your collaboration with Clark come together?

HK: So I would take those films that I made in high school—this was before cellphones, so I had a pager. I'd stick my pager number and my grandma's number on the tapes of my films. Anytime I saw someone that I recognized, I would just run up to them. Like one time I saw that band Salt 'n' Pepper. I'd seen them on *Yo! MTV Raps*. I handed them a videotape of my films. They called me the next day and were like, "This is really good." I remember calling my parents and saying, "Salt 'n' Pepper are calling me." They were like, "Who?" They asked me if I wanted to do a music video. I never did it, but I was so excited to have anybody tell me they liked what I did. I came from a culture where everybody only tells you how horrible you are—skateboarding in the eighties, people spitting on you, getting in fights.

My parents always encouraged me, because I was such a pain in the ass, so they encouraged me to do anything that was away from them, but that was encouragement for me. I felt like I knew I was good, but I just didn't think the rest of the world would think that. I used to walk around with these tapes, and the famous story was that Larry came up and started taking photos of me and some of the other skaters. We started talking to him and he asked me what I do. I said I was at NYU and wanted to make movies. He said, "I'm a photographer, and I'm going to make movies someday, too." I handed him that tape and never thought anything else about it. The next day he called me and said, "That's pretty good. Why don't you come over here?" So it's pretty amazing that the film Miss Bradshaw got me a couple thousand dollars to make got me started.

I go over to his house. I didn't know who he was or anything to do with the art world at that point. He had all these penises on the wall and Hermann Nietzsche books everywhere, Mike Kelley paintings and collages everywhere. It just so happened that I explained to him what my [treatment] was about. His eyes lit up and he asked to read it. Then he called me and said, "This is pretty good." That's when it started. I remember I told my teacher, "This guy wants me to write a script with him." The teacher put me on the phone with her agent. [Clark] was still pretty underground at that point so I don't know if they knew who he was. You know when I knew when it was real? I remember Gus Van Sant walked into Larry's apartment. I was like, "OK, this shit's legit."

EK: How long after you met Clark did you write the feature-length script?
HK: We talked about it for a long time, for weeks or something. Mostly we talked about movies I liked. I was really into a lot of movies then. I'd go to Kim's Video on St. Mark's. It's funny—I was talking to Todd Phillips recently. I saw him while I was in Los Angeles [editing *Spring Breakers*]. We were talking about that era and he worked at Kim's. I have memories of renting from him when he was a clerk. For me, that place was the most important out of everything. The young people there were curating the

place, so they'd have notes about the directors and explanations about the films. That was the greatest. I'd go in there and rent three or four things a day, watch them all night and return them the next day. At that point, I was really into watching youth films, so *Kids* is like a lot of that. I had no interest in actors. I loved Bowery Boys movies, Huntz Hall.

EK: So that's why you started telling people he was your grandfather.
HK: (laughs) Maybe, right? More than anything I think *Pixote*, the Héctor Babenco film, was the biggest deal to me. Also, *Los Olvidados* and *Zero for Conduct*.

EK: Any American movies?
HK: There were some, like *Over the Edge*, the [Jonathan] Kaplan movie, I just loved, as well as *Rumblefish*, *The Outsider*. They were huge for me.

EK: Did Clark encourage you to use these references?
HK: Right. He had had this really broad idea of making the film. Christine Vachon was his producer and the idea was that AIDS, which was a big deal back then (laughs) . . . that's such a funny sentence: "AIDS was a big deal." But it was something like they were going to give a million dollars to various directors to make a movie with an AIDS theme. I didn't know anything about AIDS except that I didn't want to get it. So I used AIDS as you might in a horror film, like the shark in *Jaws*: AIDS is going to get you. Larry's one directive was that he wanted to make a movie about a virgin surgeon—a teenager who deflowers girls, that's his thing. That was half of an idea. We talked about it for a while. I went back to my grandma's house during Christmas break.

EK: Did he pay you anything at that point?
HK: I don't remember. I think we traded a couple photographs for the script. He didn't have a lot of money back then. And the idea of this turning into an actual film wasn't real to me. Thinking back on it, it really just seemed like a strange dream. I didn't really know screenwriters back then. I'd probably read Paul Schrader books or something. I remember writing my first script, which I just found the other day, and it looks like it was written on a word processor. The format looks like the person who wrote it had some type of brain injury. Everything was misspelled. I didn't know anything about punctuation. It was like a caveman with a crayon. I just had ideas. By that point, I remember I had a Mac with a

screenplay program that I used to write *Kids*. I figured a week was what it would take to write a script, so I set a deadline. I probably wrote ten pages a day. I knew from that first semester of school that one page equaled one minute. But mostly what I knew came from watching films. I wrote it in my grandma's basement in a week. I kept audio recordings of all these kids' speech patterns. It was very important to me at that point that the dialogue was authentic.

Also, I was always good at remembering the rhythms of the way people talked—it was more about pauses and the actual cadences. I wanted it to be authentic. I was making up all the dialogue. I just imagined it. But I wanted it to seem like it was exact, so I wrote it as exact as I could. It's pretty strange to think about it, but I don't think I had any notes. It was just a stream of consciousness. I can honestly say that I had no idea how the movie was going to end until I got there. I was making it up as I was going along. When I got to the end of the script, I remember staring up at the ceiling on my bed, thinking, "Wouldn't it be a good twist if Caspar rapes her?" Not good in the moral sense but in terms of the story. (laughs) I remember when I was at the Angelika Cinema with Chloe. She gets raped on the couch, right? So I was like, "What if we bought a couch and you just sat by the exit of the door with your legs spread, passed out, so that everyone exiting the film could just walk past you?" I remember trying to convince her to do that. The whole script took a week and there were no rewrites. Clark was like, "Whoa, this is good!" That was the craziest thing of all for me. That's when the phones started to ring.

EK: Did you get an agent?

HK: So within a week of when the movie got financed, I got a call from someone who worked for Scorsese, saying that Scorsese loved it and wants to do it or something. Larry went and met with Scorsese. Literally, within a couple of days after that, I was told I had to come to Los Angeles and get an agent. This lady I knew set up a meeting for me and I flew out there. I met with all the agencies. There was a lot of crazy shit. At the end of it, I just said no to everybody. I didn't want it. I had met Cary Woods, who went on to produce *Kids* and *Gummo*. He saw that I couldn't figure it out. I was having difficulty processing all that stuff. Remember, I wanted to make movies, but I did not care about a community. It was not important to me to become part of a film community. I did not care about going off to Los Angeles and transitioning into that corporate, Hollywood zone.

EK: How did agencies pitch themselves to you?

HK: It was everything. You would meet with them and they would say, "Can you ever imagine doing this, or doing that?" I was only a little kid. I couldn't even shave at that point and I was going in and meeting all these big agencies. It made me uncomfortable and I told them that. On the one hand, I was very excited and flattered by it, because it represented this idea that I could soon be making my own films. Past that, it felt like it was a strange dance with the devil. I didn't have a reference for anything. I remember that the director of *Scent of a Woman*, Martin Brest, picked me up at the airport. He had somehow read the script. He drove me around and explained to me what was going to happen, what people were going to say to me. He didn't want anything from me. Then he dropped me off at my hotel and that helped me a little bit.

EK: How did Cary help you?

HK: He had read the script and wanted to produce it. He had been Gus's first agent in the eighties. He had gotten the money for *Drugstore Cowboy*. I liked Cary because he's a character. All those agencies were very corporate. Money wasn't a big thing for me at that point. I just wanted to be free to make specific types of films. I told that to Cary. He was wild. He was more like a throwback producer. I remember he called Gus with me and we all spoke. Cary said, "Don't take an agent and I'll produce all your movies. You can go home and live your life the way you want to live it. Don't worry about it. If all you want to do is make films, then we'll do it that way."

EK: He saved you.

HK: Yeah, I mean, he saved me at that point. I said no to everybody and said I wouldn't be represented at that time. And I went back to my life. Eventually, I would get an agent, but at that point . . . you know, agents would ask me what I wanted. I would tell them, "I want to fuck Drew Barrymore. I want to look at Drew Barrymore's ass." I wanted to see what they would do. And they would actually try to help me. I remember this one guy just goes, "Consider it done." That was actually exciting. But I didn't really care about Drew Barrymore's ass. Everything was still fun for me at that point. I didn't have anything to lose.

EK: After *Kids* started to get noticed on the festival circuit, do you remember realizing that the media was interested in your story?

HK: This hits on something at the core of everything. I've always seen everything as one thing, a unified aesthetic. Although movies are what I'm most known for, I've never cared to differentiate between anything I do. I try not to give any more or less significance to anything else. It's all part of one thing. From the very beginning, the films were tied into the books I was writing, which were tied into the art I was making and the way that I spoke to people. I just wanted to say things from different sides. I wanted sounds and images to fall from the sky. Those songs I sang into the answering machines when I was a kid were coming from the same source as the movies. I felt like answering questions [from the press] were very much tied to the artwork.

EK: Did anyone coach you?
HK: No, no one could. People did try to tell me stuff. I remember times when studio people would get angry at me. If I remember correctly, the first thing like that was doing the press conference at Cannes for *Kids*. It got pretty heated. I remember talking about dicks and stuff. I just remember the studio was not happy with that at all.

EK: What was it like to go to Sundance?
HK: That was the first time anyone had seen the movie. I remember people coming out and feeling like it wasn't normal. A lot of people reacted strongly both for and against. It had an impact. That was fun. It was fun for me to mess with grownups. That was a great sense of joy for me—and it still is, to this day. When people would come to me and ask how I could do this or that, it was great. I enjoyed that. I didn't give a fuck. In fact, while I wouldn't say the films were pure provocations . . . well, some of them are provocations.

EK: How did the popularity of *Kids* impact your aspirations?
HK: It happened very quickly—I was on *Letterman* and all those things. Pretty quickly I knew I'd be able to make my own movie. As soon as I knew that, I knew I didn't want to write anymore for anyone else.

EK: Is Letterman still a fan?
HK: You'd have to ask him. I heard I was thrown off the show for shoving Meryl Streep.

EK: Did that really happen?

HK: You know, that's a good question. (laughs) No, I'm being dead serious. I could not tell you one way or the other. The last time I was on, I was bumped. In hindsight, it was a good decision that they bumped me. For some reason, I wanted to go out there and do some damage. You could go out there and be horrible and that's what you're known for. It could've changed everything forever.

EK: Going back to the aftermath of *Kids* . . .
HK: *Kids* was made for Larry. If he hadn't asked me to write it, I probably wouldn't have ever written it or made a movie like that. It was a movie written for him. I knew that now was my chance to make a film the way I imagined films. I knew, even if the script was going to be inscrutable, that if I was ever going to make that movie, it was at that point. I had enough good will and enough money had been made off *Kids* that I could make the film I wanted to make: *Gummo*.

EK: How long had you been thinking about *Gummo*?
HK: I shot that movie a mile or two away from here. *Gummo* was a collection of things. It wasn't dreamt up in a conventional way. I just started compiling images in my mind, images I wanted to see based on characters I'd seen growing up around here. I had a series of scenes, scenarios. I used to videotape things off the television and then watch them, these collage-like compilations. The things I was interested in were things you could imagine seeing on YouTube now. That's kind of how I started imagining the movie.

EK: At what point during all this did you write *Ken Park*?
HK: I wrote that before. *Ken Park* was written before *Gummo*. Larry realized I was a pretty good writer and he was doing this film with Ed Lachman. Before we even got the financing he said he had this other idea. *Ken Park* was the beginning for me of experimenting with narrative. It was my first semester at NYU. I have the first thirty pages of the script that I turned into my professor. He was like, "What the fuck is this?" Larry wanted to see five things. He wrote them down in red ink on a napkin. He said, "Turn these into a movie." So it would be like, "Kid jerks off while being strangled," or "Kid in his underwear stabs his grandparents." It was like that.

EK: So by the time you were facing the press, you had already gone through a whole year of writing screenplays, going to college, leaving college, and meeting agents.

HK: Yes. That was 1994. I told Cary, "Now I'm ready to make my own movie."

One to Watch

Andrea Linett / 1994

From *Sassy* magazine, 1994. Reprinted by permission of the author.

Harmony looks like your basic scruffy New York City street kid, wearing humongous Levi's cords barely held up by an old belt, a pilling ski sweater with primary-colored stripes, old-man shoes from Chinatown and, of course, a beeper. A nineteen-year-old sophomore at NYU's Tisch School of the Arts, he's already written his first feature film, *Kids*, which should be out this month. "I'm a self-proclaimed genius," he told me. "I came to that rationalization [I think he means *realization*] when I was pretty young. Like, I used to try and fly and stuff." He lived in Bolinas, California ("kind of a small hippie place above San Francisco"), with his mom, dad, younger brother, and sister until he was about five, then moved to NYC, which was "the best place" and a source of inspiration for him since "there's so many characters." Now he lives in Brooklyn with a grandma who "cuts me fruit. That's what I really like about her." Harmony (who, despite this comment, is actually quite charming in a boyish way) has always wanted to direct. He started writing too because he only wants to work with his own stories. Then a friend introduced him to teenage-obsessed cult art photographer Larry Clark, who really liked his stuff, and Harmony wrote *Kids*, which was directed by Clark and produced by Gus Van Sant (*Drugstore Cowboy*, *My Own Private Idaho*). I've seen a short film of his that he did in the tenth grade, and it was kind of surreal and rambling and often perverse. He and Larry also codirected the video for Soul Asylum's cover of Marvin Gaye's "Sexual Healing." Harmony does not seem fazed by his instant success, and even wanted to tell you guys, "Watch out, 'cause I'm gonna change the world."

What's the Matter with *Kids* Today?

Lynn Hirschberg / 1995

From *New York* magazine, June 5, 1995. Reprinted by permission.

It's Wednesday at midnight, late January, cold as can be in Sundance, Utah, and there's a crush of snow-booted, parka-clad film obsessives pushing their way into the Egyptian theater to see *Kids*. Half social, half urgent, this crowd has the feel of a party with a mission. Everyone's shouting greetings and kissing one another hello-how-*are*-yous, but they're definitely here for a reason: At Sundance this year, *Kids* is the movie to see. Except for some documentaries like *Crumb* and *Unzipped*, film-wise, it's been a dullish couple of weeks. Not much to get enthralled by until a few days ago, when the *Kids* buzz began. No one has yet seen the movie—tonight will be the only screening for months—but the combination of *Kids*'s subject (New York City teenagers), its first-time director (the photographer Larry Clark), and its distributor, Miramax, adds up to surefire interest and inevitable controversy. "I hear it will never get an R," says a development executive who works for Disney, Miramax's parent company. "I mean, I haven't seen it, but. . . ."

Inside the charmingly dilapidated Egyptian, Clark and *Kids* screenwriter Harmony Korine are standing off to the side, near the back rows of the theater. They are an unusual couple: Clark is tall, and even though he is fifty-two, he has the affect of a college student—highly emotional and passionately committed to his worldview. It's all in his eyes. When he looks at someone, he bores in, which is both engaging and unnerving. Korine, meanwhile, is constantly bouncing. He's tiny and cute, like an updated urchin from *Oliver Twist*, and he hates admitting to his age, which is twenty-one. Until recently, Korine referred to himself as "the Famous Writer Harmony Korine," a boast that was true to his nature—both bratty and oddly hilarious. They're a set, these two—while Clark is serious, Korine is in a constant state of self-amusement—and they play off each other like some cross between siblings and a married couple.

"Are you nervous, Larry?" Korine is saying now, looking at the Sundance crowd filing past. "No," Clark says flatly. "It's a good movie, and it will speak for itself." He seems remarkably unaware of all the hubbub that surrounds *Kids*, the talk of sex and drugs and underage teenagers and ratings problems and all, but then again, Clark's photography has always been controversial. He's used to this sort of reaction. "Wait until they see the movie," he says. "Then we'll have something to talk about."

As people begin to find seats, Harvey Weinstein, co-chairman of Miramax, lights up his millionth cigarette of the evening and paces up and down the Egyptian's center aisle. Weinstein, who is something of a controversy magnet and maestro, passed on *Kids* when he and his brother, Bob, first read the script two years ago. "It was the first time in my company life I ever felt old," he recalls, looking anxious. "I said, 'This is a great script, but Jesus Christ, I don't know if I should be responsible for producing this.' Bob and I agonized over it, but ultimately we said it's early in our years with Disney"—they had sold the company only two years before—"and we decided to be conservative for the first time in the history of our lives." Weinstein takes a drag on his cigarette and scans the crowd. "But when we saw the finished film, it was so stunning that there was no question that not only should we acquire it—we are the only company who should distribute *Kids*."

But we're getting ahead of ourselves. First, the film. "This is like old Miramax," says Weinstein. "I used to be nervous at screenings. But what's scary is also exhilarating." Weinstein looks around for Clark. He wants the director to announce that the movie is fiction, that it's not a documentary. This is important—*Kids* stars only nonfactors, and although it is a nearly word-perfect rendition of Korine's screenplay, the movie appears to be improvised. The rough documentary look adds to *Kids*'s impact, but the movie also feels a little too close to the bone.

"That's something that's always been in my work," Clark explains before addressing the eager Sundance-ites. "This is a scripted movie, but my work has always looked so real that it makes people uncomfortable. They forget they're watching a movie; they think they're watching the real thing. But that's what you're *supposed* to do. I did what I wanted to do."

Kids takes place on one day, the hottest day of the summer in Manhattan, and tells the story of seventeen-year-old Telly, a so-called virgin surgeon. As the movie begins, Telly is smoothly seducing his latest prey, a sweet-faced girl who appears to be just out of puberty. After a lot of kissing and a lot of convincing ("Of course I care about you," he tells her, with great sensitivity), they have sex. Afterward, Telly bounds down the posh brownstone's three flights, meets his friend Casper, who's waiting on the stoop, and describes his conquest in intimate detail. For the rest of the movie, he and his buddies goof around, ride the subways, talk about sex, skateboard, talk about sex some more, go swimming, drink beer, smoke pot, and suck nitrous oxide until they are only half conscious. They're casually brutal. At one point, one of the kids gets into a scrap with a man in Washington Square Park; the group sets upon him, punching and stomping and swinging skateboards. When a house cat gets in Telly's way, he gives it a sharp, vicious kick.

The plot is the precise opposite of uplifting. While Telly is working on deflowering another young beauty, a former conquest, Jennie, finds out that she's HIV-positive. Since Telly is the only guy she's been with, she spends the entire twenty-four hours trying to find him to tell him what he's given her. Jennie finally locates him at a party. Kids are sprawled all over, dead drunk, in various states of undress. She finds him in a bedroom, having sex with his latest virgin.

The movie is relentless and brilliant and extremely disturbing. Because of its cinema-vérité feel and its loosely structured narrative, the movie presents itself as a document, a microcosmic look at New York youth in the nineties. It's powerful—both steel-eyed and sexy; horrifying and captivating. Just as a director like Martin Scorsese identifies with the lives of wiseguys, Clark sees himself in the world of teenagers. Their obsessions are his obsessions. And whether you see the movie as a masterpiece or as sensationalism (and it may well be both), Clark's artistic vision is remarkable. There's barely a moment when it doesn't *feel* true. The question one leaves with is whether Clark and Korine have put these children on the screen as they are, or as they imagine them to be.

After the lights come up, the Sundance audience staggers shell-shocked out into the snow. No one knows what to say. Even Clark and Korine seem surprised by the reaction. The first concerns are for the actors. "Were the kids underage?" (No, they insist.) "Where those real drugs?" (No.) "What were they drinking?" (Apple seltzer.) Through it all, Harvey Weinstein is standing to the side, looking content. "It went well," he says happily. "But the fun is just beginning.'

In certain circles, Larry Clark is renowned ("notorious," he says half mockingly. "I am notorious") for three things: his photography, which is simultaneously autobiographical and wildly provocative, journalistic, and stylized; his life story, which inspired the film *Drugstore Cowboy*;

and now *Kids*. "I rehabilitated my whole image," he says, sitting at the kitchen table in his Tribeca loft, "and now I'm going to be notorious again."

Clark laughs and takes a sip of water. The loft serves as a home, a studio, and a gym. There is no sofa or armchair in the all-white living room area. Instead, there's a punching bag hanging from the ceiling and a lot of art. A Mike Kelley series lines one wall, and throughout the large space there are works by, among others, Richard Prince and Cady Noland. Clark also likes tableaux—he has, consciously or not, set up still lifes throughout. On the windowsill are a dozen rainbow-hued candles; tacked to the kitchen wall are three newspaper obits (Sam Kinison, River Phoenix, and boxing legend Ray Arcel); in the office area is a small display of Roger Maris memorabilia ("He was before his time," Clark says admiringly); and on the door to the guest bedroom, where his kids (a son, who is eleven, and a daughter, who is nine) stay, is an assemblage of *New Yorker* covers, all depicting children. The loft, mirroring much of Clark's work, is one big collage. Within the parts, there is maybe jumbly chaos, but there is an overarching order to this universe. Clark's world has been carefully orchestrated.

Which is, perhaps, why he always wanted to make films. "There are things that I need to see," he explains. "I've always said that if someone else made the photographs—and now this movie—then I wouldn't have to make these images, and if I could see them someplace else, I wouldn't have to make them."

Clark began taking photographs as a kid growing up in Tulsa. His mother was a baby photographer, and she would take her son along as she went door-to-door. Growing up, Clark had a stammer (he's since lost it) and was a late bloomer—he was thin and underdeveloped, which plagued his youth. "I was the kid who didn't go through puberty until he was sixteen fuckin' years old," Clark has often said. "And everybody else is going through puberty in the sixth or seventh grade, right? By the time I got to the point to experience that, everybody is already three years past me. And I've spent three years looking at myself saying, 'Am I going to get some hair on my dick? If I'm not, I'm going to kill myself.'"

Estranged from his father, a troubled traveling salesman who spent most of his time in his room eating ice cream, Clark retreated into a secret life. When he was sixteen, he started injecting amphetamines with kids in his neighborhood. During the day, he'd take baby pictures for his mom; at night, he'd get high with his friends. For Clark, this period of his life seems to have been both vastly rich and hugely disappointing.

"I'm a case of arrested development," he says. "It's always been a fantasy of mine to go back to high school and do it again."

Instead, he's trying to capture that world. Around 1963, after attending the Layton School of Art in Wisconsin, Clark returned to Tulsa and started photographing his friends. Originally, he wanted to do a film, but he didn't have the equipment or the stamina. He did, however, have the story. There it all was: his buddies and their girlfriends, shooting up, having sex, messing around, playing tough guys. The resulting book, *Tulsa*, which Clark published in 1971, is admiring, romantic, and tragic—as Clark writes, "Once the needle goes in it never comes out," and many of his friends died before the book was printed.

And yet it's that messed-up, aimless, doomed world that Clark seeks to idealize through his work. What he calls "a perfect childhood" is violent and confused. There's no nirvana here—just bitterness, restlessness, and rage. But then, that's his obsession—strangely, that's what seems "perfect" to Clark—and he longs to live vicariously through these kids. In some sense, he wants to be one of them.

When *Tulsa* came out, Clark was a serious drug user. He received an NEA grant to do *Teenage Lust*, his next book (which took him twelve years to finish), and crisscrossed the country, getting into one jam after another. "By the mid-seventies, my life really derailed," he has said. "I was totally out of control and doing lots of drugs. Basically, I took on the combined persona of a lot of the people in the book and had begun acting out the sorts of scenarios I hoped to photograph. I was conscious of what was happening to me, but it was such a crazy time that I couldn't control it."

In 1976, Clark was thrown in jail for "assault and battery with a deadly weapon with intent to kill" (his criminal record is included in *Teenage Lust*), and he went to prison for nineteen months. By 1979, he was living in New York City, had met his wife, and was preparing to publish *Teenage Lust*.

A companion piece to *Tulsa*, *Teenage Lust* (neither book is currently in print, and copies of either, when found, can go for upwards of $700) is arguably a more disturbing collection of images. It's a scrapbook: There are many self-portraits (some naked, some with babes, some with friends) and more confessions, including a long first-person bio/rant that closes the book.

The imagery is terribly unsettling. A naked boy with an erection holding a gun on the naked figure of a tied-up girl (the title: *Brother and Sister*); a street kid named Booby, fondling himself as if he were showing off the merchandise; a guy on top of a girl, who looks to be whacked out of her brain (the caption reads, "They met a girl on acid in Bryant Park at 6 a.m. and took her home . . ."). And so on.

It's hard to imagine how or why Clark found his way into these rooms with his Leica, but the resulting images are nightmarish. They're stark, and Clark is unwilling to draw any conclusions about the worlds he gravitates toward. "I'm not trying to make some grand statement on human nature," he says. "I'm just trying to show things the way they are."

In 1985, Clark and his family moved to a leafy, preppy exurb of New York, and by 1990, Clark was working on large-scale collages. Again (and always), his theme was teenage boys. One collage combines, among other images, pictures of the early Rolling Stones; a picture of Roberto Duran; a clipping about Martin Tankleff, a Long Island teenager who killed his parents; an Annie Sprinkle postcard; and a picture of Jesus Christ. Around this same time, Clark became obsessed with the Pamela Smart case, in which New Hampshire teenager Billy Flynn was induced to kill his teacher/lover's husband. "I knew that situation," Clark says now, still intrigued by the case, which he made the subject of another collage. "I knew why he killed the guy. It was very simple: The kid didn't have a father. He was distant from his mother, and here's this teacher at school. Twenty-two years old and she starts fucking him. What could be better? You're fourteen, and you're in love with the teacher. That was the most important thing in his world. And then she said, 'Kill my husband or no more pussy.'" Clark pauses. "At that age, sure. Poor kid."

Clark wanted to photograph Billy Flynn and even attended the trial. "There was a rash of teenage killers," he says rather scientifically, "and they all looked kind of like nerd kids. But Billy Flynn—I saw a picture of him coming out of the police car, and I said, 'That's the way a kid killer should look.' That's the way I would have him look. He looked like I wanted him to look."

The collages were, for Clark, a stepping stone to movies. And his next project, Larry Clark 1992, pushed him further in that direction. Clark met a kid in a punk club, got permission from his parents to photograph him, and shot the kid for an entire day, in sequence. The photos in the second half of the book are all of one boy, who looks to be sixteen, in a white undershirt, white athletic socks, and baggy white boxers, playing with a gun. In nearly all of the stills, the gun is in his mouth and he is angled so that the viewer can see his penis curled against his thigh. The pictures, seen over and over and over again (the image stays the same), are both depressing and perv-y: This kid is about to blow his brains out, and you're distracted by his crotch. "I decided to print every picture I'd taken in sequence," Clark recalls. "I was just telling a story in a different form. I was getting ready to make a film."

When Larry Clark saw *Drugstore Cowboy* in 1989, at the Angelika on Houston Street, it really got to him. Director Gus Van Sant had been inspired by *Tulsa* and *Teenage Lust* and thanked Clark in the production notes. "I was a little bored by it," Clark recalls over lunch at Jerry's in SoHo. "And a little pissed off. It was my territory, right? And I thought I could have done better. I like the movie now, but then I said, 'Fuck—he's getting inspired by my work, and I should really show 'em how it's done.' Thank God for Gus making that movie, because it made me mad enough to say, 'I'm gonna make a movie.' I knew what I had to do." Clark pauses. "You know, *Drugstore Cowboy* was very good. I just would have gone a little farther, that's all." Clark chuckles.

Around the same time, Clark became fascinated with yet another segment of youth culture: skateboarders. "I thought there was this freedom there," he explains. So he bought himself and his son skateboards ("kind of a bonding thing") and, at forty-nine, learned to skate. "The whole thing about skating is, there's no parents," he says. "And I'm hanging with the kids and I'm thinking, 'I want to do something with these kids.' They're really special—they have this freedom and they're outlaws. They're like the Hell's Angels! I mean, everybody hates skaters. They get kicked out of every place. They can't skate anywhere. Everyone's afraid of them. And the cops would much rather these kids were shooting dope and burglarizing places and being criminals, because then they could understand it. But these kids are just stalking around. They have this freedom."

He even designed his own customized skateboard. The image on the board is a naked young girl bent at the waist, her rear in the air and her vagina exposed. She appears to be winking at the camera. "I became one of the guys," he says proudly. And it became clear that these kids would be the subject of his ultimate work dream—the true-to-life teenage film. "I always wanted to make the teenage movie that I felt America never made," he says again and again. "The Great Teenage Movie, like the Great American Novel. . . . In American films, it's always the generic fucking same old, same old teenage kid, and I hate all those kids. I wanted to go against all that Hollywood bullshit."

Around this time—early 1993—Clark met Gus Van Sant for lunch in San Francisco. Clark was in town for a show of his work, and Van Sant had flown specially to meet him. "I must say it was no big deal," Clark recalls. "I didn't really care." But Van Sant turned out to be extremely helpful. "He said, 'Do it!'" Clark says. "He told me to make a film. He gave me a lot of confidence."

Clark had an idea—a skateboarder whose passion is to seduce virgins—and he knew a kid who might be able to write it. "I thought, *Nobody knows the scene but me*, but I don't write—that's not what I do," Clark remembers. "And then I thought of Harmony."

Korine had been a skater for years, and he also knew Clark's work. "One day, Larry was photographing people in Washington Square Park and I was skating and I sat on a fountain and he started talking to me," Korine recalls. "I didn't really approach that many strangers, but he was there and he said, 'I'm writing a movie.' And I said, 'I wrote a short screenplay about a thirteen-year-old boy who on his birthday his father takes him to a prostitute.' And Larry was, like, 'Oh, wow, can I read that?' I said okay. And then he read it and called and asked me if I wanted to make a movie with him. I said, 'Sure. Why not?'"

Korine wrote *Kids* in three weeks, delivering pages to Clark every other day. "He told me, 'I've been waiting all my life to write this,'" says Clark. "He was only nineteen." This cracks Clark up. For him, in many ways, *Kids* has truly been his whole life. Over and over, again and again, that song has been playing.

It's around two on a Tuesday, and Harmony Korine is in his apartment on Prince Street, putting on his wig. He's off to lunch and says he doesn't want to be recognized. This is silly: Barely anyone knows who he is, and if someone did, this wig, which is only a slightly shaggier version of his own brown hair, wouldn't cut it as a disguise. It's a goof, the wig—it's some private chuckle that's completely ungetable, except, of course, to Harmony.

So anyway, he's got the wig adjusted and he grabs a handful of Chinese poppers—little white firecrackers—from a paper bag on his desk. These are harmless, but when one is thrown in, say, a restaurant, the explosion will make people jump. Another goof. "Okay," Harmony says, slipping on a jacket. "I'm ready."

He bops down the streets of SoHo, throwing a popper here (at a vendor), a popper there (at a pretty girl). His shoes are untied, laces flapping, and when you suggest that maybe he'll trip, that he should tie them, Harmony replies, "I don't know how to tie my shoes. A kid at school tried to teach me once, but that same day I almost drowned in quicksand." Harmony throws a popper at a man selling incense. "It was an omen."

There's a lot of stuff like that with Harmony. He's his own work in progress; he's making himself up—a bit of truth, a bit of fiction—as he goes along. He is, however, sweet; his type of self-invention is not about superiority or hipster cool. Instead, he's just larking about, coming up with stories and games that will amuse him.

At the restaurant (again, Jerry's on Prince Street—Harmony goes where Larry leads), Harmony orders pecan pie and decides that the waitress hates him. At the next booth is a woman with her seven-week-old baby. Harmony is fascinated and turns around to address the infant. "Have you taken her to the circus yet?" he asks the baby's mom. "That's one of my best memories."

In his official Miramax bio, Harmony maintains that he was in a traveling carnival and that he is the grandson of Huntz Hall, one of the original Bowery Boys. Although this could be true, it's somewhat improbable. The more likely scenario is that Harmony was born in Northern California, spent his early years in Nashville, then moved to New York, where he lived in his grandmother's basement. He did some normal things, like getting bar mitzvahed ("I looked pretty handsome," he recalls. "I was really small too. I was thirteen, and I looked around eight"), and he did go to high school, where, he says, he got nearly perfect (1,580 total) scores on his SATs. He's vague about his parents, who now seem to collect furniture from the fifties. "In the beginning," he allows, "my parents were what you would call hippies, but they became, like, Marxists. And then my dad became a Trotskyite. And now I think they're right wing. I'm not sure, though. You'd have to ask them."

When Harmony met Larry Clark, his life changed. He was now a prankster with a purpose. He always had projects—he makes videos in his apartment, and he and a friend put out a fanzine—but he was all over the map. Now he's focused. He has already completed two more screenplays, *Ken Park*, about teenage suicide, which Clark will direct next, and *Gummo*, which Harmony intends to direct himself. He is also working on a screenplay based on *Tulsa*, which Clark will direct. "That will complete the trilogy," Harmony explains, sounding authoritative. "And then I will never write a movie for anybody else again."

His goofiness camouflages his smarts—Korine is like an adult disguised as a kid. For all his brat behavior, he's quite sophisticated about filmmaking. This kid knows movies, he knows careers, he's studied what works and what doesn't, and he has the confidence of someone whose first screenplay is being heralded as brilliant. "I always wanted to make my own films," Harmony says, smushing whipped cream all over his pecan pie. "I was never interested in telling other people's stories. I'm going to make movies like no one's ever seen before. It's just gonna be a new movie. I think I have a total understanding of cinema. . . ." He takes a bite. "I have so many cavities," he says, interrupting himself. "You know, I never got along too well with adults until I wrote this screenplay. And now it seems like they like me. Before it seemed like they belittled me or talked down to me."

Not in Hollywood. After he finished the screenplay and before financing for *Kids* had been secured, Harmony's script started floating around L.A. It was an instant sensation. The first agent to see the script, Josh Lesher at United Talent Agency, suggested a trip out West, and by the time Harmony arrived last spring, he was done. "L.A. was kinda strange for me," he recalls. "I felt like people were trying to get me, kind of. Everyone was super-nice. I met so many agents, I couldn't remember who I was talking to."

As ever, CAA was especially aggressive. The agency set him up with director Martin Brest (*Beverly Hills Cop*, *Scent of a Woman*), and Brest drove him around, acting as a lure for the agency. "We picked his kids up at school, and he said, 'Everyone in Hollywood has an agent,' and I said, 'Well, I'm not in Hollywood.'" Being Harmony, he did have some fun, though. At one agency, he told the assembled aspirants that the last agent he met with "said I could fuck his sister if I signed with him." They fumbled for a moment, trying to think of a topper, until they realized Harmony was just goofing around. "It was funny," Harmony recalls. "I wanted to see what they could come up with."

Ironically, they all wanted Harmony, but they did not have much hope for *Kids* getting produced. It was too raw, too extreme. "They would say, 'This is the greatest script I've ever read,'" remembers Clark. "'This is amazing. It's the best script in the whole world. But is this the final draft?' I finally said to this one guy, 'Listen, motherfucker, if this is the best fucking thing you ever read, why do you want to change it? Go fuck yourself."

Luckily, the script was read by Cathy Konrad, who took it to her boss, Cary Woods, a producer who had just signed deals with Disney and Miramax. Previously, Woods had been known for more mainstream movies ("We want to put FROM THE PRODUCER OF *RUDY* across the top of the

Kids poster," says Mark Tusk, vice-president of acquisitions at Miramax),
but he was intrigued by Korine's script. "I just wanted to meet the young
genius," Woods says. "And maybe we'd do something in the future."
When Harmony walked into the office, the producer asked to see his ID.
"Harmony looked fifteen," he says. "I thought, *You gotta be kidding me.*"

Yet within a few weeks, the deal for *Kids* was in place. Woods knew
of two men, Michael Chambers and Patrick Panzarella, who wanted to
finance a small-budget film. He called them, and they immediately put
up the funds. Then he flew to New York and met Clark. "Cary had confidence in me," Clark says. "Confidence in the script. And the investors
knew me and liked my work, and they said, 'It's your vision. We back you
100 percent. You make it the way you want to make it.'"

They had six weeks of preproduction and six weeks to shoot. Korine
and Clark decided to go with all nonfactors, mostly friends of Harmony's. The script was not, however, precisely autobiographical. "Jim Carroll called me after the film and asked if I was Telly," Harmony says, "I
told him that it wasn't me, but it was based on a friend of mine, minus
the HIV.

"But I did know almost everyone we cast in the movie," he continues.
Chloe Sevigny, who plays Jennie and was the subject of Jay McInerney's
"It"-girl piece in the fashion issue of the *New Yorker* last year, is now Korine's live-in girlfriend. And even though he no longer skates, Harmony
has stayed in touch with his skateboard pals, many of whom appear in
the film.

There were some problems with this—after the first week of shooting, the kids took the clothes from the wardrobe trailer and wore them
home—but basically, it was the only way to achieve Clark's vision. "Actors stuck out like sore thumbs next to those kids," he explains. "You
have to have all one or all the other."

Now Clark, Korine, and Woods are a permanent troika. Neither Clark
nor Korine signed with an agent—they just have Woods. "Cary wants to
keep me pure," Harmony says, playing with his food. "He knows I don't
want to know. I don't want to hear about the business or the politics of
people telling me to tie my shoes. Just, like, whatever. Why can't I stay
the way I am?" He looks up and throws a popper at a passing busboy. "It
gets me angry," he says. "It just does."

At Miramax, they don't like to talk about the controversy surrounding
Kids. Instead, they concentrate on Larry Clark's artistry, Harmony's per-
fect-pitch dialogue, the faces of the actors, and so forth. "The sideshow

obscures the movie," says Harvey Weinstein, sitting in the Miramax conference room a couple of weeks before *Kids* is to screen in competition at the Cannes Film Festival. "Everyone keeps forgetting that there's this terrific movie. They've called this movie a masterpiece. Now, I'd much rather see a masterpiece than the most controversial movie of the year. At the end of the day, a controversy only works for a week or two."

The *Kids* controversy, though, will probably last for a good long while. The battle over whether to *Kids* or not to *Kids* will likely center on a potential war between Miramax and its parent company, Disney. Meaning it's impossible to imagine Disney will choose to distribute this movie. According to Miramax's deal with Disney, the parent company will finance and distribute any movie Miramax acquires as long as the film is under a certain price (Miramax paid $3.5 million for *Kids*) and receives no worse than an R rating. In the past, this ratings restriction has created problems. When Martin Lawrence's concert film *You So Crazy* received an NC-17 for language, Miramax knuckled under to Disney and the film was distributed by Samuel Goldwyn, where it went on to gross $10 million. "That will not happen again," says Weinstein, who thinks he made a huge error with *You So Crazy*. "I had a great relationship with Martin Lawrence, and now he's making movies for someone else."

There are industry rumblings that the Weinsteins brought *Kids* to deliberately provoke Disney; that since Jeffrey Katzenberg, who was their friend and champion, left to co-found DreamWorks SKG, Miramax has been looking for a way to get out of its contract. "Absolutely not," Weinstein says emphatically. "If I had wanted out, I would never use this movie as a wedge."

And then there is the matter of *Priest*, Miramax's most recent in a long line of controversies. *Priest*, a good and sensitive movie about a gay clergyman coping with the limitations of the church, was originally set to open nationwide on Good Friday. After intense, understandable protests, that date was moved, but the movie continued to be the favorite target of not just Catholics but a wide range of conservatives including Bob Dole. The *Priest* controversy obscured the quality of the film and did not attract moviegoers, and it got ugly—Disney and Miramax executives received threatening phone calls and bomb threats. "After *Priest*," says a Disney executive, "no one wants to even think about *Kids*."

Even if *Kids* should somehow manage to get an R from the MPAA ("It's an R," maintains Clark. "There's no nudity! There's no nothing. If I wanted to make an NC-17 movie, I would have really done it"), Disney still may not want to put its name on it. It's too soon after *Priest* and, besides, this isn't exactly *Pocahontas*. "Will Disney be involved?" Weinstein asks. "That's anybody's guess. They are a billion-dollar company with a worldwide image, and this is tough stuff. But they will allow us to buy *Kids* back and distribute the movie ourselves."

Toward this seemingly inevitable end, Miramax is prepared to create Excalibur, a new wing of the company. There's a slight Disney jab in that name. Excalibur, the sword in the stone, could be removed only by Arthur, proving that he was the true king. And, of course, there's a Disney animated film of the story. (Disney has refused numerous requests to comment on *Kids*.)

Kids is set to open in July, and Miramax has put in place a strategy designed to foster the buzz without letting it get out of hand—a controlled burn. The first step was the Cannes Film Festival, where Miramax has always had great success. Last year, it won the Palme D'Or with *Pulp Fiction*. "We screened it for Gilles Jacob [czar of Cannes]," Weinstein says. "And there was a reticence to play this movie in competition. But every year I have my moment with Gilles, and basically I had my moment over this film. And to his credit, he knew this was extremely important."

Jacob, saying he was concerned about content, arranged only one 5 p.m. screening of the movie last Monday the twenty-second, complete with a warning. Weinstein would have preferred a different, later hour, but he knows this movie will be seen whenever it's screened. "I'm not worried about interest," he says. "Since that one screening at Sundance, everyone has been curious about seeing *Kids*."

He is more interested in perception—how the movie will be *sold* to paying American audiences. Genius marketers ("My wife says, 'Lousy husband/good marketer,'" Weinstein jokes), Harvey and his brother, Bob, have come up with one winning campaign after another, from the "Don't reveal the secret" of *The Crying Game* to the packaging of *Pulp Fiction*. Not surprisingly, with *Kids*, Weinstein wants to stay away from selling the movie with sex. He imagines a poster with strips of stills from the movie, constructed like shots from a photo booth. Interspersed among the stills will be critics' quotes, raving about the film. "I've never seen faces like these," Weinstein says. "And that will be intriguing. Rather than putting a sex scene on the poster."

As for the trailer, Weinstein is concerned that *Kids*'s documentary-like effect will get in the way of its being perceived as a drama. Miramax's first trailer for the movie is image upon image, synced to a hard-rock beat (Lou Barlow of the band Sebadoh did the *Kids* soundtrack), and the plot of the film is not clearly summarized. "We need to have a narrative of the trailer," Weinstein says. "An audience has to know this movie has a script."

Although he is often lighthearted in his marketing, Weinstein is very serious about *Kids*. The idea is to stay as far away as possible from anything exploitative. "This one's complicated," he says. "We have to make conscientious decisions about which way to go. The idea is not to bring *Kids* to a small audience. We want to bring this to as many people as possible." Weinstein pauses and lights a cigarette. He may have the whole world (including Disney) yelling at him, but he credibly professes not to care. "I had to have this movie," he says. "That's all that matters."

"You know," Larry Clark is saying, "it is about sex. That's what it's about: Sex. Sex. *Sex*." He laughs. He is doing a final sound mix on *Kids* for Cannes, and he's feeling cheerful. "Miramax is nervous about sex, but that's what the movie is about," Clark says. "We sent some stills of the movie over to *Artforum*, and when the package arrived, Miramax had taken one photo out. They thought it was too provocative." Miramax denies the story, and the still—of a rape scene—made it into the magazine anyway.

Clark is mystified by Miramax's concern. "He's like Chaucey Gardener when it comes to his own work," Cary Woods says. "Larry truly doesn't understand that his work can be shocking." When *Details* commissioned him to do a fashion shoot with the kids from *Kids* last year, he was amazed when the magazine didn't run all the shots. "There were two girls kissing and they wouldn't print that," he recalls. "And another, with a girl with her hand down a guy's pants. They chickened out. They said they were worried about car advertisers."

At this moment, Korine bursts into the room. He's come to check on the movie and on Clark, not necessarily in that order. "I helped with the translation for Cannes," he says. "They were making it even *more* perverse." Clark and Korine laugh. Despite the thirty-one-year gap, they have that close-friend telepathy born out of spending days and days in each other's company. Harmony has just come from buying a gray suit at Brooks Brothers to wear at Cannes. "You're not going to wear a tux?" Clark asks. Clark is planning to wear an Armani dinner jacket. "Nah," says Harmony, who is fiddling with his tennis shoe, which has the word SCUM inked on the side. "Cary said I could wear a suit."

Clark has to go back to work, and Harmony is maybe going to go see a movie. They're both eager for Cannes, although they have no real idea what to expect. "I can't believe there's really going to be all this controversy," Clark says. He leans back in his chair, exhausted by the notion. "But I do want to fuck with people," he says finally. Harmony nods. Mission accomplished, he seems to say. Mission accomplished.

Interview with Harmony Korine

Roger Ebert / 1995

From *Chicago Sun-Times*, June 4, 1995. Interview conducted in Cannes, France.
Reprinted by permission of the author.

Harmony Korine has seen the future of the cinema, and it is him. Nobody else is as young, as bright, as original, as inspired. Certainly not Quentin Tarantino, who is ancient at thirty-five.

"I mean, he's fifteen years older than me. That's a totally different generation. Someone wrote, 'We don't need another Boy Wonder at Cannes.' And I was, like—well, I don't think he's a boy, and it's like, he's not MY generation. There's no one making movies that's my generation, you know; no one's as young as me."

Well, the Hughes Brothers.

"They're older than me."

They're about 23.

"That's still older than me. 'Cause no one's a teen-ager in art movies."

That's true. You're not, either.

"But I was. I wrote my screenplay when I was eighteen or nineteen. I was the youngest in history; I looked it up."

Harmony Korine is the writer of *Kids*, which, in a year when Cannes drowsed and twitched in the midday sun, at least provided life and controversy. The movie, directed by Larry Clark, follows a group of Manhattan teen-agers through one long day of sex, booze, drugs, rock 'n' roll, skateboards, aimless violence, and despair. Take your choice: It is either (1) a searing and accurate cry for help from a generation without hope, or (2) a cynical exploitation film that skirts the edges of kiddie porn. Both views had their defenders at Cannes; I tend toward the first choice.

The film has not yet been rated. It cost $70,000, and was bought for $3.5 million by Miramax after its sensational reception at the Sundance festival in January. If it gets an NC-17 rating, which is likely, Miramax will not be allowed to release it by its parent company, Disney. It may be sold

32

to another distributor, or, one hears, Miramax partners Harvey and Bob Weinstein may form a separate company to release it.

The supporters of the film say it SHOULD be seen by those under seventeen, because it sounds an alarm about the dangers of promiscuous sex in the age of AIDS. The attackers quote François Truffaut, who said there is no such thing as an anti-war film because all movies make war look exciting. The film is so unrelenting in its dark, savage attitudes that even skilled apologists for sex and violence are struck dumb; for many of the movie critics at Cannes, *Kids* may at last have been the film that made them wonder if they were getting too old for their jobs.

What is certain is that no other film at Cannes this year had a defender quite like Harmony Korine. He is now, I think, twenty-one years old, although for Korine even that age seems so advanced that he is not quick to claim it.

Clark, a celebrated photographer who wanted to direct a feature, found Korine in Washington Square Park, hanging out with a loosely knit crowd of skateboarders. He discovered that, at sixteen, Korine had talked himself into a job as a production assistant on Paul Schrader's *Light Sleeper*, a Susan Sarandon film, and had written screenplays in high school—before dropping out of high school, as he has dropped out of every other institution that tries to define him, including his family and his own generation.

The day after *Kids* premiered at Cannes, we talked about it on the Miramax yacht, out in the harbor behind the Palais des Festival. Korine had his legs doubled under him and was kneeling on a couch, sipping ginger ale, talking fast, like one of those kids who wants to explain a *Star Trek* movie to you after you've seen it.

I wouldn't ask this of somebody who had written a different kind of film, I said, but . . . what kind of a family background do you have?

"I have a pretty good family. But ever since I was little I just felt like I wanted to be on my own. It was the same thing about school. I was sitting in my classrooms, and I would feel the teachers were never telling me anything I didn't know, or they were always trying to dictate to me how I should think, or . . .

"I mean, I love my parents, but it's always been the same thing; it's always been people telling me what to do and I JUST CAN'T STAND THAT. So I wanted to be on my own. I moved to my grandmother's house and she was pretty much—she's kinda—not senile, but she really can't speak very well and she falls down sometimes and I could like, do whatever I wanted to, you know. I was out there and I was learning things on my own. I tried college and I hated that. I seem to quit everything I do. I just like finding things out on my own."

Your parents. What do they do?

"They do different stuff. Now they live in Nashville, and they like, sell children's clothing. But they do different things."

Was Harmony the name you started out with?

"I was born Harmony and it was weird because when I was a little kid, I was picked on so much that when I was thirteen I changed my name to Harmful. I thought it was a tougher name, so I had it legally changed. And then, I don't know, it just didn't seem to catch on, so . . . legally, my name is still Harmful, but I just said I'll go back to Harmony. My parents were Marxists when I was little and then they became Trotskyites. I really haven't kept in touch with them. I spoke to my mom before I came here; she like tried to give me a pep talk or something. Once I saw my dad on Canal Street; he was selling like turtles."

He was selling turtles?

"Like sea turtles, those little turtles? It was pretty funny."

And you, like, sort of lived the life that you portray in *Kids*?

"Yeah, I've pretty much been witness to most of the stuff. I mean, all the characters in the movie were based on kids I knew. I wrote it specifically for the people that are in the movie. I mean, it's fictionalized obviously, I made it up, but it's all based on stuff."

It's pretty frightening.

"I don't think this is representative of like, all teen-agers. I just think like, this is a small segment. But at the same time it's like I think this is taking place everywhere. I do think that kids are living like this wherever you go, even in rural areas across America, middle America, anywhere. Like even here in France, we invited some fifteen-year-old skateboard kids from the beach to see the movie, and afterwards they went, like, 'Dis ees my favorite movie. Dis ees my life.'"

What Harmony was basically saying, I guess, was, don't shoot the messenger. *Kids* is a docudrama about how real kids really live in a street society without rules or boundaries or parental presence. And Harmony has traveled among them and returned to write the story. His next screenplay, he said, is named *Ken Park*, will also be directed by Clark, and will take place inside the homes of the same kinds of characters who are in *Kids*.

But before that movie is made, he will direct his own first film, *Gummo*. It starts shooting this summer, maybe. The name comes from the fifth

Marx brother, the one who wanted to sell women's lingerie instead of being a comedian. But it's not about the Marxes: "It's about middle America. It's about this small town where this tornado hit in Ohio and it's not really one main character; it's just totally random."

Korine's terror of being included in any group extends to his fellow filmmakers. He recoils at being compared with Tarantino, Roger Avary, Kevin Smith, and other video brats who grew up in video stores and with camcorders in their hands.

"I'm not a video brat. I don't derive all my inspiration through movies. I get it from a lot of other places too. Quentin Tarantino seems to be too concerned with other films. I mean, about appropriating other movies, like in a blender. I think it's like really funny at the time I'm seeing it, but then, I don't know, there's a void there. Some of the references are flat; just pop culture.

"You can be inspired by other movies but not be derivative. I think that's a problem with a lot of the video kids. I don't even like video. I think you should see movies on the big screen. Because if you look at their movies, all these video brats, their movies to me look like . . . television, you know what I'm saying?"

Kids, it must be said, does not look like television. It plays and feels like a seamless window on life. After the screening, I talked with many sophisticated viewers who reacted personally to the irresponsible sex life of Tully, the central character. They "knew" he was an actor, in a scripted part, and yet they reacted to the film as if it was a documentary. This would have been high praise for the film, if it hadn't made them so angry.

"I didn't think about shocking people when I wrote it," Korine said. "I didn't even think about a message, you know. I wanted to make a movie and I wanted it to be like you're just looking at a picture; like there's no judgment. Because what I hate is all the crap that comes out of Hollywood right now. It's belittling to the audience. They tell you exactly what to think. They pound you over the head with these messages and then there's nothing left. There's no margin of the undefined; it's all there for you. In all my favorite films there's always something missing. Something to make me curious. I wanted to do that with *Kids*. I think one of the reasons why everyone's so angry is because it doesn't give you a definitive YES or NO—this is bad, this is good. If you have any kind of sense you'll take away some kind of message, but if you can't see past the shock, you're not going to get anything."

As Korine kept talking, I began to get the idea: Like another of the Marx brothers, he did not want to belong to any club that would have him as a member.

"I just don't want to be a part of any of those 'generations,' you know. What I'm gonna do is like stuff that people have never seen before."

He includes the so-called Digerati, the computer generation: "I don't know anything about that. That's like Plato's cave or something—the synthetic existence. I think that if I got into computers, I'd maybe get addicted or something. I have so much trouble with just like the real life, you know. Waking up, I feel so sad in the morning or something; I get so depressed just being alive sometimes. That'll just give me a whole 'nother world to get depressed about."

Nor does he plan to get an agent: "I couldn't stand it. I just feel like everyone tries to steal your soul, and corrupt you. I'd rather quit than be corrupted or anything. I'd just rather not do it, you know. I'd just rather sit in my room and sing or something."

Toronto International Film
Festival Webcast

Ray Pride / 1997

From Sundance Channel Toronto International Film Festival Webcast, September 1997.
Printed by permission of the author.

Ray Pride: You have expressed disappointment that more journalists have not been rude to you when they don't like your work.
Harmony Korine: I would like that instead of these polite questions like, "Do you feel like you're exploiting people?" Exploiting people, I don't know what they mean.

RP: How do you react to critics who drag out the dreaded "self-indulgent" label to describe *Gummo*?
HK: How can an artist be expected not to be self-indulgent? That's the whole thing that's wrong with filmmaking today. Ninety-nine percent of the films you see do not qualify as works of art. To me, art is one man's voice, one idea, one point-of-view, coming from one person. Self-indulgent to me means it's one man's obsession. That's what great artists bring to the table. When fucking critics or whatever say, "he's self-indulgent," I don't know what that means. The reason I stopped watching films is because so many people lack any kind of self-indulgence. But I don't believe in being boring.

RP: So "boring" is a scarier word?
HK: Oh, much more. Entertaining, to me, is what it's all about. We can talk about aesthetics and influence but in the end when I go to see anything all I want is to be entertained in a different way. It could be informative or shocking but I want to be entertained. I don't want to be bored by the bland and generic. Film is like a dead art because of people not taking chances.

RP: What kind of film is *Gummo*?
HP: Oh, it's completely southern. It's totally, 100 percent southern. I'm a southern boy so how would it not be? I'd say *Gummo* is an American film; it's southern, but it's strange. But it fucks with it, it's a genre-fuck. I love the South, love it, love it. I didn't leave until I was eighteen. I had to move out to understand it. I couldn't have made that film if I hadn't left Tennessee for those four or five years.

RP: *Gummo* is overtly an experimental narrative, and under the Time Warner name as the Fine Line logo unfurls, a child chants the film's first words, "Peanut butter, peanut butter, motherfucker."
HK: I love it, I love it. To me that's the most exciting thing. That to me is the future. The most subversive thing you can do with this kind of work, the most radical kind of work, is to place it in the most commercial venue. I have a novel coming out in April called *A Crackup at the Race Riots*, from Doubleday, and that's Michael Crichton's label. It's the most fucked-up book, but to me that's exciting. When Godard did *Breathless*, the reason it became influential and changed the cinematic vernacular is that it came out in a commercial context. I only think things change when they're put out to the masses, regardless if somebody dislikes them. The Velvet Underground put out their first album, and almost nobody bought it, but everyone who did started a band that sounded just like them. For me to put it out to as many people as I can get it to is much more subversive than if you're giving it to the same three theatres with the same crowd that always goes to see this kind of film.

Mike Kelly Interviews Harmony Korine

Mike Kelly / 1997

From *Filmmaker*, Spring 1997. Reprinted by permission of the publication.

With a poetic, impressionistic take on film narrative, a visual style incorporating everything from elegantly framed 35mm to the scuzziest of home camcorder footage, and a startling mixture of teen tragedy, vaudeville humor, and sensationalist imagery, Harmony Korine's first feature *Gummo* is perhaps the only recent film whose artistic strategies draw as much from the visual art world as the film world. (A gallery installation of work from *Gummo* opens at L.A.'s Patrick Painter Gallery in late September.) We were thus very happy when Mike Kelley—one of today's most essential and subversive artists—agreed to interview Korine on the eve of a major gallery installation in Copenhagen.

Like Korine, Kelley blithely shreds conservative notions of high and low art as he mounts major gallery shows, designs album covers for bands like Sonic Youth, and plays in Destroy All Monsters with Thurston Moore. In fact, one of the band's songs, "Mom and Dad's Pussy," opens Korine's film.

Harmony Korine: So how did you like your song? It starts the movie with those shots of the little girls.
Mike Kelley: They were little boys, actually.
HK: Oh, the boys are singing about pussy, but that image in Super 8 we kept repeating of the girl in front of the trailer—I just knew that that song would fit that image.

MK: I guess I couldn't tell the gender of the kids.
HK: I think they were little girls. We were just driving around—that's how I got a lot of that footage, the Super-8 and video stuff. Just walking around neighborhoods, walking up to people.

MK: How much footage did you have of that?

HK: I could probably make another two movies with the excess footage. Some of this material I'm going to use in this art work. In a strange way, I want to get to a point where the next movies are even more random and more incidental without them being overly arty. I just want things to become a succession of scenes, images, and sounds. I was thinking about the gallery show . . . the problem you run into doing multimedia projection is that a lot of the time, the style takes over. It threatens and reduces the content. It becomes almost like a music video—mixing all these forms for no reason.

MK: A post-modern pastiche?

HK: Exactly. And it's so boring. It's like a Sprite commercial. With *Gummo*, I wanted to invent a new film. I know that there isn't any true invention that hasn't been done before, but I feel that this hasn't been seen in a real commercial context. We tried really hard to have images come from all directions. If I had to give this style a name, I'd call it a "mistake-ist" art form—like science projects, things blowing up in my face, what comes of that.

MK: Something alchemical?

HK: Exactly. When we switched forms, when the film went to video, Hi-8, or Polaroids—I wanted everything to feel that it was done for a reason. Like they shot it on video because they couldn't get it onto 35mm or they shot it on Polaroids because that was the only camera that was there.

MK: Did you do many effects in post-production? That shot of a cat eating—that was phasing.

HK: That's what I mean by mistake-ist. There was a script, but as a screenwriter, I'm so bored with the idea of following a script. I felt like I had the movie in the script so we'll shoot the script but then shoot everything else and make sense of it in the editing process. That cat tape was a tape that a friend of mine had given me, of him doing acid with his sister. They were in a garage band and there was a shot of their kitten. That [phasing] was an in-camera mistake. The editor, Chris Tellefsen, caught it and said, "That's kind of interesting."

MK: You were splicing footage together after the fact. Kind of indexing it.

HK: Exactly.

MK: How did you decide the structure of the film? I know that there is a script but you can see that a certain amount of improvisation is going on. How did you make decisions about how things flow from one to another?

HK: I have so little understanding of how other filmmakers make their movies. I wanted to set up a process of making a movie that would best suit me. We went down to Tennessee—I grew up in that area—and I hired all these kids, family, and friends—people I went to school with. Everything in this movie is about access, the trust that they give me. If an actor is a crack smoker, let him go out between takes, smoke crack, and then come back and throw his refrigerator out the window! Let people feel they can do whatever they want with no consequence.

MK: A lot of the movie is about framing things that are basically performative. Here's a kind of action and let's let people go with it. The tap dancing scene, the kids shooting the boy with the bunny ears. . . .

HK: Or the scene where the brothers beat each other up.

MK: But other scenes are more pictorial.

HK: We go from scenes that are completely thought out, almost formal, scenes that resonate in this classical film sense, and then we go to other scenes where it's like, total mistakes, stuff shot on video where the kids forget there's a camera there and talk about how much they hate niggers. I felt like shooting each scene on its own terms and then making sense of it afterwards. And I felt that the styles would blend, that there would be a cohesiveness.

MK: There's a cohesiveness there for a number of reasons. One is that, okay, despite the surreal element, it's a milieu that would allow for that. It's not unusual for people to do odd things in reality so you can have a realist film and have strange things happening and it doesn't seem surreal. In traditional narrative film, where there's a shift in style, like when the image gets fuzzy, you see it as a shift of point-of-view, like a dream sequence.

HK: I hate that shit! That's why I hate Fellini, because it's all like a cartoon to me. It's not based in any kind of realism. I don't care about it if it's not real.

MK: That's funny. If I had to compare you to anybody, I'd compare you to Fellini.

HK: And he's someone whose films I couldn't stand. The films of his I like are the more realist early films like *Il Bedoni*.

MK: But he uses non-actors, it's biographical, there's stylization. It's just that the stylization is really overt.
HK: But it's surrealism, and I was never so interested in surrealism. This odd thing that I do—it's like surrealistic realism. Everything seems like it's normal, everything is presented as if it's 100 percent true, but at the same time, a lot of the stuff that goes on is kind of outrageous, made up.

MK: How do you think the realist element comes through with all your playing with style? I think people could mistake this as being like MTV. What would you say to someone who says, "This isn't realist. This doesn't follow traditional realist tropes."
HK: I'd go after their ass!

MK: It seems to me that you could only have a feature film like this post-MTV. Otherwise it would be seen as an avant-garde film.
HK: I don't know. Look at Griffith, what he was doing. The commercial movies now, I see so little progress in the narrative form unless you're talking about Oliver Stone, who to me is making films that are completely empty and all about style. I was talking to my friend Christopher Woole about the difference between style and substance. He said, "You should never worry about that because substance is style." Most art makes me sick because everything has become like solving math problems. Everyone is working from the wrong direction, from the outside in. Approaching *Gummo* like a piece of art that entertains, I wanted it to be more from the inside out, less about solving problems and more about going with my obsessions. I wanted to create a cinema of obsession, a cinema of passion. No one does that anymore.

MK: The night before I saw your movie, I saw *Sling Blade*.
HK: Oh, I hate that film.

MK: But there's a whole bunch of white trash movies in the last ten years. There are ones like *Sling Blade*, the pathos ones, and then there are the freak show ones. It's even found its way into fashion photography. And I saw this new Wendy's commercial with people who live in a trailer. So I say, okay, this is a genre. If I'm looking at *Gummo* and I'm looking at this

other stuff, structural questions are important because otherwise your film becomes about "white trash, our new outsiders."
HK: I felt that *Sling Blade* was this kind of failed, romanticized Flannery O'Conner. I didn't understand any of that film.

MK: Well, unlike yours, it was extremely script-oriented. Which is strange because you don't see so many films now that are so much about scriptwriting. That was the only thing I liked about it . . . it was well written, in terms of dialogue.
HK: I didn't like the dialogue either. Those scenes in the forest—I was waiting for him to molest the little kid. I wasn't interested in any kind of white trash chic. It was about going back to where I grew up, casting kids I grew up with, like the black dwarf—I went to high school with him.

MK: When I saw that black dwarf, I thought it was the guy from *Penitentiary Three*.
HK: I haven't seen it.

MK: Oh, you must see it. It's fantastic. It's by this guy named Jamaa Fanaka, a black independent filmmaker from the seventies.
HK: I've seen parts one and two.

MK: Those aren't good.
HK: Going back to that whole thing—I just wanted to show these kids beating each other's brains in. I wanted to show what it was like to sniff glue. I didn't want to judge anybody. This is why I have very little interest in working with actors. [Non-actors] can give you what an actor can never give you: pieces of themselves.

MK: I really like that about the film. When they were acting in a way that was completely unnatural, they were real people acting unnatural. That reminded me of the best aspects of the Warhol Factory system.
HK: You know who I love and who no one really knows about? Alan Clarke, the British director. He's a real influence. He did *Scum, Made In Britain*, this film *Christine*, about this girl growing up in council flats with size 14 feet. She walks around with a cookie tin under her arm and hooks her friends up with dope. She'll go into houses and kids will be lying there with a box of Ritz crackers on the television. You'd have these really long tracking shots of her walking. And he used real people or

people who seemed right. He did this other film I like, *Elephant*, which is just sixteen separate executions, one after the other. There'll be all these Steadicam shots. You see a hit man walking through a gymnasium, walking up stairs and corridors.

MK: Are these first-person POV shots?

HK: Exactly. And then he'd shoot the janitor and he'd fall on a pile of jockstraps. But the intention wasn't comedy. After he died in 1988 of cancer, there was a retrospective of Clarke's work at MoMA and there were only about ten people in the audience. I was watching this film, *Elephant*, and in the beginning it was a little bit disturbing. And then I started to find this humor in the repetition—watching some Indian car washer get his head blown out on a squeegee. I start cracking up, and this British bastard in front of me turns and says, "Don't you know what this represents? This is the IRA, you son of a bitch!" He wanted to kill me. I liked that idea. He thought it was about the IRA and I thought it was about Ritz crackers.

MK: You're talking about inebriation a lot. Are you trying to make a movie that's a kind of visual inebriant? I wasn't bored watching the movie, even though you couldn't say there was a plot. But, afterwards, I didn't know how much time had passed. I was in a half nod looking at people whose lives are in a half nod.

HK: I wanted it be more of a tapestry, so if that was the effect of watching this kind of tapestry of people. . . . I was as concerned as you looking at the dolls strung up when the kid gets his hair washed.

MK: I loved the art direction.

HK: It was very minimal.

MK: A lot of it was found but in certain cases, you must have had to play with it some. I couldn't believe some of those houses.

HK: Oh my God, in that house where you see piles of shit everywhere and the bugs run out the painting—not only was all that stuff there but we had to take out stuff to be able to put the camera in the room. I found a piece of a guy's shoulder in a pillowcase.

MK: There are certain motifs that run throughout the movie, sort of structural loops that hold it together. One of them is the recurring figure of this Bunny Boy, the other is the cat hunting. Were those elements planned from the beginning?

HK: Oh yeah, that was in the script. I have a feeling the movie is much more scripted than you would think. It's about 75 percent scripted.

MK: So the script would have a scene that would be imagistic, and another section would say, "Now there's going to be a party."

HK: No, this is what would happen. I wrote out the script perfectly. We would ask the actors to do the scenes without me imposing my ideas of how it should be blocked. Most of the time, it was a different way than I dreamt it. In some cases, it was worse, and we'd go with my blocking. In other cases, it would be really exciting and I'd change the scene spontaneously.

MK: There's a certain milieu that's pictured, but [the film's] not really of it. You're using black metal [music] but the kids are wearing Dio t-shirts and are cutting "Slayer" into their arms.

HK: It goes further than that. There's a whole vaudeville subtext. Kids in Dio t-shirts doing Jimmy Durante routines. That standup Tummler does on the glass table after he goes with the whore—that's like a Henny Youngman monologue.

MK: Calling the cat Foot Foot, like the Shags song. That's a funny inside joke.

HK: Oh, there's millions of those.

MK: That's one thing I wanted to ask. Are Dot and her sister modeled after Cherie Curie?

HK: Oh completely, that was a total theft. I wanted that in there but I didn't want it to not make sense. I wanted [the girls] to adapt to their environment. [The film] is a total mix of history and pop, a making sense of pop. To me, that is what is always lacking in film—there's never a relationship to pop culture. America—and I'm not talking about New York and L.A.—is all about this recycling, this interpretation of pop. I want you to see these kids wearing Bone Thugs & Harmony t-shirts and Metallica hats—this almost schizophrenic identification with popular imagery. If you think about, that's how people relate to each other these days, through these images.

MK: That's the thing I liked best about the film. How it showed how all these Hollywood clichés about middle America are just completely wrong structurally. When you see Hollywood movies that show these white trash milieus, they make them too uniform, not as weird as they are. That's why I hate all this neo-pop art. It makes too much sense.
HK: You said it. It lacks this kind of cohesive schizophrenia.

MK: It becomes about "hip-dom" rather than some idiosyncratic person mixing multiple genres.
HK: Yeah, I don't give a shit about that whole hip thing. I like the idea of seeing kids who still have Ratt tails and a tattoo of Janet Jackson on their forearm.

MK: Wearing a shag hairdo. It makes no sense.
HK: Yeah, but it makes sense to them. It goes to this homeschool kind of aesthetic I wanted to run through the film. For me, Dot and Helen—I wanted them to seem like homeschool kids. You know, those kids who never had any true interaction with large groups. I love that—kids within their own home sort of guessing and coming up with these hipster things. They almost make a homeschool hip language. I wanted this inbred vernacular. I want to avoid any of the easy answers. And that's why I think your artwork—I always felt it was successful because it went against that kind of thing. I wanted to make a movie where nothing was done for any purpose other than that I wanted to see it. I wanted to make the first film that would hopefully play in malls that you would see these images with very little justification other than that these were things that I wanted to see. That's why everyone gets upset with the girl shaving her eyebrows.

MK: People don't like it when you use retarded people.
HK: Even though I had met her months before, played Donkey Kong with her, and she had no eyebrows then. That was her style.

Harmony Korine with Antek Walczak

Antek Walczak / 1997

From *Index* magazine, 1997. Reprinted by permission of the publication.

In the short time since he moved out of his grandmother's house in Queens and lost twenty pounds, Harmony Korine has been hard at work. He is, first and foremost, a storyteller, and at nineteen, he wrote the script for the film *Kids*, directed by Larry Clark. At twenty-three, he is behind the camera, directing his first film, *Gummo*. And although it's not so easily pinned down—either by story or style—*Gummo* does what films are supposed to do: it keeps your eyes glued to the characters on the screen, and keeps you wondering what they're going to say or do next all the way through to the end. *Gummo* is such an original film that it's bound to be copied, and although we'll probably have to suffer through all the movies it "inspires," we can't really complain. After all, Harmony managed to coax Linda Manz out of retirement—she hadn't appeared in a film since 1978's *Out of the Blue*—and her performance here is sure to attract more than a little attention. Of course, most importantly, and even regardless of whether you love *Gummo* or not, Harmony has reminded us that a film is only truly independent when it does exactly what it wants to do.

Antek Walczak: Now the purpose of what we are about to do, Harmony, is to get down to the facts, for you are notoriously loose with the facts. What do you think would be a good question to start with?
Harmony Korine: Oh, I don't know. . . . We should just talk about the fact that I prefer butter on toast more than the wine that . . . that you're not drinking.

AW: Here's a toast, then . . .
HK: There you go. A toast to the woman on my left and to the woman on my right. Jesus, that ass is boomin'.

AW: Tell me, this is your first interview ever, isn't it?
HK: No, no, I've done a few hundred. [laughs] But this is one of the first ones for this movie.

AW: So you don't know what the pattern of questions will be? Can you anticipate that?
HK: I'm not exactly sure what people will take with them, and I'm not really trying to prepare anything. But . . . you know what you were saying before, after Versace was shot? I was really just worried about things of that nature. Today, when I walked downstairs with my assistant—we were going to the bar next door—and my doorman told me that a forty-year-old Hispanic man had been looking for me. He wanted to know if I was home. He said that he was a bookseller and he wanted to sell me books. My doorman told me that the guy was saying that I played basketball with his godson, or something like that. And he was saying my name in a way that would kind of infer a friendship. But it couldn't be true because I haven't played basketball since I was eleven.
[Dinner comes to the table]
    Wow, this food looks good, but I've gotta take out my gold teeth. You should ask me about my gold teeth.

AW: What motivated you to start wearing gold teeth?
HK: I decided to get them when I met Old Dirty Bastard. I just admired him. I admired his fronts, his gold teeth. He had them on the top and the bottom. I liked his style. I thought I'd mimic it.

AW: Where did you get them?
HK: I went to Fulton Street in Brooklyn. The guy that sold me them was this guy wearing a black cape with a T-shirt underneath that said "Hugs Not Drugs."

AW: Are you a little worried now, with your work, that some people are going to accept you unconditionally? And how do you account for the mainstream?
HK: You mean, how will I want to infiltrate a pop culture scenario? That's the goal, I think. Not the goal, but the challenge. I want to put my movies out in the malls for people to see, for kids to see. I think that's much more important than anything else. I don't know how I'm gonna do it. . . .

AW: Did you ever believe in the underground? There are still a lot of people out there who really appear to believe in integrity and staying underground.

HK: I don't really know if there's such a thing anymore—if the underground exists. It exists for someone like Dostoyevsky. But at the same time I can see it in the eyes of Janet Jackson. I can see it in the . . . in the palm of Michael J. Fox. So it exists, but exists in a gray spot only to be found between the pages of *Celebrity Sleuth*. I think that's where it's at right now. But I'm not really concerned with any idea of underground or credibility, just the gray spots of celebrities.

AW: The gray spots?

HK: You know, that vague area, that hidden notion of fame and the undertow of its trappings.

AW: Do you get motivated by things that disgust you?

HK: Definitely.

AW: Negativity?

HK: That's a key.

AW: Is it hatred or love that wins in the end?

HK: If I have to pick, I will definitely be on the side of love, but for me, at least in my work, hatred is much more plentiful, much more driving. Maybe anger leads the way.

AW: What specifically do you . . .

HK: Things that I hate?

AW: Yeah, or even something that just drives you. . . .

HK: Gosh, it's so vast. I'm trying to think what I've really been disliking lately. I've been disliking things that are kind of complicated. I've not been liking things that appear mathematical. It's hard to explain. I'm digging the ditch of a simpler time. I don't know. . . . It was interesting when Robert Mitchum died, and the very next day Jimmy Stewart died, and then Charles Kuralt died. And with each day, each man died, and the death of each man was somehow a symbolic force for me, an influence for me. Those three men represented some kind of fantasy that I thrive off of.

AW: You're digging the ditch of simplicity. . . .

HK: Do you want some more wine? What about some bump? Want a bump? What about this waitress?

AW: I'd like to talk a bit about *Gummo*, which to me doesn't draw so much on styles from other films or filmmaking. And the closest thing, if I wanted to cite a reference to it, and I don't know if you'll agree with me or not, is vaudeville.

HK: Oh, totally. I'm a huge fan of vaudeville—like Fanny Brice, Eddie Cantor, and Al Jolson. And actually, one of the main characters in *Gummo* is named Tummler, and the name Tummler was given to the kind of lower level comics, Catskill comics from back in the day. The guys that would check you into a hotel room, take your coat, and at the same time throw a few one-liners out. They're like the warm-up, the lowest level comedian. The tummler. I'm a big fan of vaudeville. That type of entertainment, I love, that real showmanship. That's been a big influence on me.

AW: What's interesting with vaudeville was that the skills of the acts would vary wildly. You would have someone who was just there for their physical presence, and they'd be stuck right alongside real performers. There seems to be some of that going on in *Gummo*.

HK: Yeah, exactly. There's this random tragedy associated with the decline of the vaudeville entertainer, which is a theme in *Gummo*, that I completely stole from vaudeville. I love that. I love the idea of Jolson stealing jokes and Milton Berle having a thirteen-inch flaccid member. Those are all parts of the vaudeville repertoire.

AW: And you consciously avoided the narrative . . . like with vaudeville, you could always pick and choose. If you got bored with the boxing cats, you could get off on the next act.

HK: I know that people say that there's no narrative in vaudeville, but I think there is a narrative and there's a definite narrative in *Gummo*. It's just maybe more hidden, it's more the idea that the narrative comes through the idea of association, just by virtue of the scenes being kind of run along, put next to each other, that a narrative forms. It's like looking at a book of private photos. There's a picture of you in front of a castle or maybe a monument. And next to that is a picture of your grandfather on the toilet. And next to that is a picture you took of Michael Jackson. If you looked at them on their own without knowing the context, then they would seem singular or random. But just because one is next to the other, a kind of narrative comes through. That goes along with *Gummo*. That's how *Gummo* was written.

AW: You cast Linda Manz in *Gummo,* and she hadn't appeared in a film in a long time, although people certainly remember her for *Days of Heaven* and *Out of the Blue.*
HK: I had always admired her. There was this sense about her that I liked—it wasn't even acting. It was like the way I felt about Buster Keaton when I first saw him. There was a kind of poetry about her, a glow. They both burnt off the screen. She had married an orchard farmer in Northern California, and had three boys. She had to return my calls from a Texaco station.

AW: And what was it like working with her?
HK: It was what I knew it would be. She was very elf-like. Always dancing around. She would spin on her belly.

AW: Is there anyone else you especially want to write parts for and work with?
HK: Paul Reubens. I would love to work with him, but not as Pee Wee, as whatever his next incarnation is, as something more sincere. He's this emblem of tragic comedy. An American original.

AW: In *Gummo,* you show people of varying degrees of handicap, be it mental, physical, or socioeconomic. What do you have to say to someone who would accuse you of creating a "pornography of disability?"
HK: I would say that I feel no need to justify what I'm putting out there. Maybe it's unusual because in most movies everything you're seeing, you're seeing for some kind of reason, there's some kind of explanation. And what's done in *Gummo* is that you're seeing these images and I'm not necessarily justifying them. The reason you're seeing these things is because these are all images I wanted to see, these are people I wanted to see, these are all obsessions, maybe personal obsessions—which I think is lacking in cinema today, and even in cinema past. But I think it should be this way, I'd like to create a cinema of passion and obsession. And that's what this is. I mean, justify Julia Roberts, justify Mel Gibson's tight ass . . . I don't give a fuck. I just want to do whatever I want to do. I don't care about any of it. I don't feel like anyone's being made fun of. I just wanted to see this.

AW: You're pretty much standing alone in American cinema.

HK: I have no bond or any kind of relationship to any other filmmakers working, not just in America, but anywhere. I personally don't feel a part of any movement. I don't feel a part of anything. I feel totally removed. In fact, I almost feel that what I'm doing is completely separate. If what I go to the movies for now are movies, I almost feel like *Gummo* is not a movie—if that makes any kind of sense at all. I don't know what it is. I mean, it's definitely a movie. But I just feel like there's no relationship between what I'm doing and what others are doing, and the way my movies are made and the way others are made. When I watch the E! channel, and I hear actors or directors talking about the kind of experiences they have in the way their films are made and what goes on, raising money and their creative process, I'm sitting there not understanding anything they're talking about. It seems like I have no idea what's going on. It's like I have a completely separate job. And I enjoy that. I am curious as to what those guys are up to, but I have no idea what it is.

AW: There is this vague notion of an independent film movement in America these days. You consider it to be pretty much a red herring?

HK: Yeah, I don't understand that at all. I don't think there's such a thing. Independent movies—when I hear that term I think all an independent film is a mainstream movie that looks ugly. I don't even know what it is. I think it's all fallacy. It's all shit. I'd like to shit on it. I'll open its mouth and piss in it, in its lips, in the lips of an indie. I'm totally not independent at all. I'm a patriot.

AW: Do you ever imagine that there could be a movement which you could at least say you're a part of?

HK: Never.

AW: What's your opinion on other, more credible, film movements?

HK: I don't think there's any history of an American "New Wave." The only history of radical cinema in America is of individual filmmakers. Even the French New Wave to me is just a load of crap. Rohmer, Truffaut, Chabrol—in my opinion, those guys were just bores. The French New Wave was only Godard and continues to be to this day. I think it's always just one significant director and a bunch of people that latch onto that person.

AW: Now you're an industry-supported filmmaker, backed by a pretty nice-sized studio—I mean, behind Fine Line there's New Line, and then there's Ted Turner, I think. Are you getting the kind of freedom that you actually need?

HK: I have it rigged in a secretive way. I am 100 percent commercial, patriot, auteurist, new waver, and I'll die with my secrets of independence and righteousness.

AW: Brad Pitt was getting photographed in my building today. Pitch me a movie starring Brad Pitt.

HK: Brad Pitt gets his arms amputated. I will call the film "Brad Arm Pitt." It will flop for sure—a stupid movie, a dumb idea.

Harm's Way

Rachelle Unreich / 1997

From Movieline, 1997. Reprinted by permission of Movieline, LLC.
www.movieline.com.

If Hollywood types haven't knocked down Harmony Korine's door—so far the anarchic screenwriter of the 1995 insider cult favorite *Kids* has been studio-free—that's probably because they're terrified to do so. With a diamond-encrusted bridge plastered to his teeth ("I also wanted to get 'Harmful' etched on, which is what I changed my name to when I was eleven"), and his generally subversive attitudes, the twenty-three-year-old Korine has deliberately styled himself as someone the industry is unlikely to schmooze. "I don't fraternize with the enemy or associate with what I consider might be damaging to my innards," he explains. And he's managed to direct as well as write a second film, *Gummo*, without the benefit of major studio backing, thank you.

Gummo is, from a certain perspective, an advance on Korine's first effort. The casual sex, drugs, and racial slurs of *Kids* remain, but now there's some animal torture and abuse of mentally disadvantaged girls thrown in for good measure. Korine claims that in telling his stories about bored-shitless-white-trash teens, God is his copilot. "I was born with a purpose," he says. "I just think that my reasons are divine." Hence, he's not worried about the possibility that the non-actors who engage in destructive behavior for the sake of his movie might continue doing so when the cameras stops rolling. On the contrary, "I would encourage it," he insists. "I'm not saying I want people to die—most people's films aren't worth that—but what I'm doing is holy." If this movie thing fails, might Korine have a second career in cult religion? "I have trouble waking up in the morning and tying my shoes," he demurs. "To lead other people, I wouldn't know how to begin."

Korine comes by his oddness honestly: he considers his parents to be not merely Communists, but somewhat violent Communists. "They like to firebomb houses," he claims (word has it, the houses were empty; this was in the seventies). How will he ever top his current status as the anti-prince of extremely indie filmmaking? "One day I'll walk away and do something else. I'll move to the Gaza Strip and I'll wear a rebel flag yarmulke." What if Hollywood comes a-callin' before then? Korine isn't worried. "I don't think Hollywood has my phone number," he says.

Moonshine Maverick

Geoffrey Macnab / 1998

From *Sight & Sound*, April 1998. Reprinted by permission of the British Film Institute.

In *Hearts of Darkness,* Fax Bahr and George Hickenlooper's 1991 documentary about the making of *Apocalypse Now,* Francis Ford Coppola came up with an unlikely prediction. Exhausted by the stress of making a multi-million-dollar *folie du grandeur* deep in the jungles of the Philippines, he speculated about where cinema could go. The future, he suggested half-ironically, would probably lie with a teenage girl in the Midwest making home movies with a camcorder.

Twenty-three-year-old Harmony Korine may not quite fit Coppola's description, but his debut feature *Gummo,* shot on location in Nashville with a mainly non-professional cast, has a humor and originality that mainstream Hollywood cinema misses by a mile. On the surface, Korine's subject matter seems familiar enough. From *Back to the Future* to *American Graffiti,* from *The Last Picture Show* to *Pretty in Pink,* countless other filmmakers have attempted to capture the agonies and ecstasies of small-town American adolescence. Korine's characters, however, are a long way removed from the prom queens, leather-clad rebels, and high-school football jocks we are used to seeing. His inspiration comes as much from Buñuel's *Los Olvidados* and Hector Babenco's *Fixate* as from Hollywood teen pics.

There is something picaresque and cruel about the two scrawny protagonists—Solomon (Jacob Reynolds) and Tummler (Nick Sutton) who ride around town on their bikes killing stray cats. It is enough to see them as victims of poverty and broken homes, but in their own irrepressible way, they might equally be described as nineties counterparts to Tom Sawyer and Huckleberry Finn. (With his curly hair and oversized head, Reynolds even looks as if he might have stumbled out of a Victorian children's fantasy.) Korine insists he has no polemical axe to grind. Despite all the *vérité-style* camerawork, he is not making a neorealist drama-documentary about the plight of the urban poor in the Midwest. The title itself suggests that the writer-director is not entirely in earnest: *Gummo* was the little-known Marx brother.

Korine dispenses with the niceties of plot (a word he loathes) and instead offers a series of snapshots of young adolescents running amok in a small Ohio town. Imagery ranges from the sublimely poetic—a kid with enormous pink rabbit ears walking across a grey, rain-strewn cityscape—to the bizarre: Solomon and Tummler with airguns firing off pellet after pellet at the carcass of a dead cat. Certain sequences—for instance, the drunken arm-wrestling contest between a disabled dwarf and a beer-swilling redneck—seem like blue-collar realism given a surreal twist. Others—the ritual shooting of Bunny Boy by two eight-year-old cowboys—could be straight out of Lewis Carroll.

At times the film has the directness and naiveté of a home movie. Whether Dot (Chloe Sevigny) and Helen (Carisa Glucksman) putting masking tape over their nipples or the two skinhead brothers beating lumps out of each other in the family kitchen, the camera captures moments that seem private and spontaneous. *Gummo* is also often highly stylized. Korine wrote the film as a series of self-contained scenes: "A mother washes her son's hair, twisting it into a fluffy shampoo peak on top of his head"; "a boy and two girls goof off in an above-ground swimming pool during a summer storm. Raindrops bounce off the surface of the water as they splash around, kissing and playing." The cinematography has a studied informality about it, as if director of photography Jean-Yves Escoffier was under instruction to make everything look as if it was shot on the hoof, even as he went to elaborate lengths to stage and light each sequence.

Like *Kids*, which Korine wrote for director Larry Clark when he was eighteen, *Gummo* has been given a rough ride by the censors. And US critics have already labeled the film "one of the most repellent cinematic efforts in recent history" and "the worst film of the year." The *Hollywood Reporter* suggested that, "whatever small audiences *Gummo* attracts—they will be drawn mostly by the prospect of watching something 'shocking'—will wind up leaving the theater in a state of disgust."

As usual, the negative hype seems wildly misplaced. The inhabitants of Korine's world may all be oddballs, but he treats them with tenderness and humor. Just as critics and audiences in 1932 were so repelled by Tod Browning's *Freaks* that they failed to realize what a human film it was, many of *Gummo*'s detractors seem blind to the warmth and humor in Korine's small-town fable. Korine knows his cinema. His conversation is liberally laced with references to Bresson, Fassbinder, Godard, and Cassavetes. He is tiny, politely spoken, and highly articulate. *Gummo* is his third script, after *Kids* and *Ken Park*, also written for Clark but shelved after bickering between the director and his collaborators. "I was fed up with the whole thing," Korine says now of the aborted project. "I wanted to make another film, but I didn't want to write for other people. *Kids* was a success, so I knew it was my time."

At the press conference for *Kids* in Cannes in 1995, Korine loftily proclaimed that he was "going to make movies like nobody has ever seen before." With *Gummo*, he has been as good as his word.

GM: Tell me about the gestation of Gummo.
HK: I wrote *Gummo* in two or three months. I didn't write straight through—it was more like I was thinking of the film as individual scenes, almost like photographs, things I wanted to see. Then after I'd written about two hundred scenes I started to play with the order, trying to find, if not a narrative, a story that went through the film. Then Fine Line gave me the money and I went away to where I grew up—Tennessee— and made the film with the people I grew up with.

GM: There are only four or five professional actors in the film.
HK: I have almost no interest in actors. If I write a script about someone who fights alligators, I'd rather find the person who would fight the alligators for real than ask Tom Hanks to play the part.

GM: What was your approach to filming?
HK: I was mostly concerned with setting up a chaotic environment, giving my sister a camera, handing everyone Polaroids, 16mm and 35mm cameras, whatever was to hand, letting situations happen and not concerning myself with story or anything like that. I wanted to set up situations so I could turn my camera one way and film and then turn it the other way and there would be something going on. Then from the chaos I would work out everything at the editing stage. As long as what I was filming was compelling and what I wanted to see, then I knew it would make perfect sense. I think film ought to be like collage.

GM: You use a lot of videotape.
HK: I think video is beginning to change the way people make films and watch cinema. Hopefully it will change cinema not only aesthetically, but will make it a less elitist art form.

GM: Were you ever worried about patronizing your characters or about falling into the trap of "white trash chic"?
HK: No. I don't patronize anyone. I spent months before the production just photographing these people, going inside their homes and spending time with them. I knew almost everyone who appeared in the film from hanging out with them beforehand. For me as a filmmaker or an artist, to go in and make fun of someone—I don't even understand the concept. As long as I'm not forcing anyone to do what they don't want to do, I don't see how there could be any question of exploitation.

GM: How would you place *Gummo* alongside other teen movies?
HK: I think I've seen every youth picture ever made. But I don't think *Gummo* is a teen film. It goes beyond that.

GM: I was intrigued by the casting of Linda Manz. She seemed to have disappeared after *Out of the Blue.*
HK: I'd always been a fan of her work, so I tracked her down. It turned out she had married an orchard-picker in northern California. He was the guy who threw a wet rag over Michael Jackson's head when his hair caught fire during that Pepsi commercial. Linda was working at a hospital at the time, so when Michael was rushed into hospital Linda must have fallen in love with the guy who saved him.

GM: I heard you had difficulty getting the film past the censors.
HK: What is really hard in the States is the ratings board. They were kicking me with an NC-17, and my only requirement was that I had to turn in an R film. They were giving me an NC-17 for "nihilism." How absurd can you get? I had to recut the film seven times. They really tried to destroy the movie. You can't hold them to any kind of rules—there are no guidelines to follow and everything is subjective. They were offended by the film in a hundred different ways. They'd tell me to cut fifteen seconds. I'd cut the fifteen seconds begrudgingly and then they'd say it wasn't enough. At one stage I wanted to scrap the whole fucking movie.

GM: Which scenes caused problems?
HK: The scenes that bothered them most were the ones that dealt with little kids using drugs. Remember the scene where the little boy moves the picture and the bugs run out across the wall? The camera shows the kids sitting on the couch, huffing aerosol cans. When I was little, that's what we used to do—take socks and put them over aerosol cans to breathe

in the fumes. The little boy was sitting on his sister's lap. The camera pans up, showing all the bug bites on his legs. There's a Bach cello piece playing in the background. Anyway, without any direction from me, the kid grabbed the can out of his sister's hand. He was a four-year-old kid and it looked as if he was getting high. In fact, the cans were empty. But it became something almost holy to see this kid, who looked like he was a baby nursing a bottle. To me, that meant everything. It was the whole film. It showed the repeating process, the dysfunction. But the ratings board flipped when they saw that. They said it was the most disgusting thing they'd ever seen. I didn't give a fuck what they thought—it's just that they have the power to say that if I don't cut that shot out, nobody would see my film.

GM: Roaming around town, Solomon and Tummler remind me of Huckle-berry Finn and Tom Sawyer. Would you agree there's innocence there, despite the mischief?
HK: Definitely. Even when they murder the grandmother, when they kill the cat, I don't think any of it is done out of any kind of evil. I know from growing up, the way I lived, the things I've seen, that all that kind of dysfunction and messed-up living comes out of boredom. When you have nothing, and nothing to do, you make do by experimenting.

GM: What was your budget? And did you have final cut?
HK: The budget was around $3 million. I would never make movies if I didn't have final cut. If anybody told me what to do, I would quit. I can't understand people who collaborate like that. If there comes a point in my life where I have to listen to studio people, if there is a chance someone can take the film away from me, I won't make the film. The movie should be one person's vision, and that's it. The reason most movies are the way they are is that there are too many voices. I wouldn't allow that. Anyway, *Gummo* is the kind of film that baffles studios, and that's fine by me. I liked the idea of them just giving me the money and leaving me alone.

GM: I heard it said that Alan Clarke was a major influence on *Gummo*. Is that true?
HK: Alan Clarke is maybe my favorite filmmaker, the best of the British New Wave. *Christine* is a masterpiece and I like *The Firm* and *Made in Britain*. What I like is that he approaches drama in a different way. There is

never a beginning, middle, and end—the films just exist, the drama just seems to happen.

GK: How did you come to see his films?

HK: A few years ago they screened about twenty of his films at MoMA. That's when I saw them all. I've seen so many movies. There was a time from when I was about fifteen until I was twenty when my life seemed to consist mainly of seeing movies. I had difficulty sleeping so I would see about four or five a day. I rapidly ate up movies. I thought I'd already found all the masters—and then I saw Alan Clarke. I couldn't believe that here was somebody who made movies in this way and I'd never heard of him.

GM: What is it about his films that you like?

HK: He was doing something dramatically that I'd never seen before. And his films are so honest—the way the characters speak, as if they just exist, as if they're organic. Plus, of course, his use of violence is very interesting to me. It's more than real. And there's such an energy to his camera, such a fluidity to his movies. The steadicam shots can last for five minutes at a time. Clarke had a real style. And there is no one less pretentious. With a lot of British filmmakers politics tends to get in the way of the storytelling, but Clarke seemed to be more interested in telling stories than in solving problems. There are shots in *Gummo* that I took straight from his work, like the scene where the two girls are walking and talking right after they've watched the boy playing the tennis match. The use of the steadicam shot there is pure Alan Clarke—stylistically at least.

GM: Could you say something about your family background?

HK: My father was a documentary filmmaker. I didn't go to school much because I was following him around where he was working. He was very much into circus clowns and children who rode bulls. He had these obsessions that would require the family to follow him. At one stage he tried to do a movie about the last great moonshiners. So I spent a lot of time in rural communities when I was growing up.

I started to drink moonshine when I was young. That was a big influence on me, both aesthetically and otherwise. Then, at a certain point, he became a Trotskyite. He really got into Marxist propaganda and started firebombing empty houses across the South. That was when I broke away from him. When I was growing up he didn't speak to me so much. He'd throw shoes at me or hit me, but he did it out of a sense of love. One way he communicated with me was through film. We would watch a lot of movies together. When I went back to Nashville, where he had a house, there was a theatre near the university that would play double features every day. That was where I saw a lot of the films that influenced me early on—*Night of the Hunter*, Dreyer's work, early Bresson.

GM: You were chucked out of high school when you were a kid for assaulting a librarian.
HK: No. What happened was that when I was about thirteen, I was reading a book which quoted Kierkegaard so I went to the library, found a book by Kierkegaard and tried to check it out. I looked young for my age—I was thirteen but I probably seemed about eight. The librarian verbally assaulted me and told me I wasn't old enough to check the book out. And the same thing happened when I tried to check out Walter Benjamin's *Illuminations*. I wanted her to die and I said so to her face, "Die, bitch!" I told her. I threw a chair at her. I was thrown out of school. One week later, she went skydiving. Her parachute didn't open and she died. I went to the funeral and I tried to dance on her grave. Then the police came. It was a fucked up situation.

GM: The film's little corner of small-town America is very distinct. Are you going to be tackling the same sort of locale and subjects in your future films?
HK: Well, Middle America is where I came from. To me, it's the most interesting and left-out part of the US. America is not New York and Los Angeles.

GM: Do you see yourself as following in any sort of tradition?
HK: There's no tradition of an American New Wave, but there is a tradition of American mavericks. There were certain directors—Peckinpah or Cassavetes, for instance—who told stories that dealt with sections of America that for the most part have been ignored. In my next movie I want to go even further with the kind of fracture I was exploring in *Gummo*. I want it to be completely random. I'm aiming for completely objective filmmaking, where it's all about the images—about something you can't verbalize.

Here's Looking at You, Kid

Sean O'Hagan / 1999

From the *Guardian*, March 13, 1999. Reprinted by permission of Guardian News & Media Ltd.

Harmony Korine is telling me how he cast the female lead for his new film, *The Julian Chronicles*, currently shooting on location in New York. "I was watching *Hard Copy* [a tabloid-style TV show], and I saw this vision: a beautiful, totally blind figure-skater whose dream was to be an Olympic Gold. Her performance had a strange beauty, all skewered and distorted, her legs getting tangled up.

"I mean, if I'd written that sort of thing, I'd have gotten so much flak for being gratuitous, but here it is for real, on TV. So, I searched her out. Took me three months, but I found her. The thing is," he adds ruefully, "I thought she was fourteen, but it turns out she's only ten, so I've had to cut out the anal intercourse scene between her and Ewen Bremner, who plays her hard-core schizophrenic teacher."

In the few hours since we met, in the bar of the Gramercy Park Hotel, Korine has regaled me, and other open-mouthed patrons, with a succession of similarly surreal anecdotes. I've heard, for instance, how he once had a sexual predilection for teenage amputees, and how, during an adolescent LSD trip, his two companions, both practicing Jehovah's Witnesses, performed a mutual circumcision ceremony. It is difficult to do justice to Korine in print, not least because of his singular speaking voice—an enervated, slightly high-pitched, adolescent whine—that rises in pitch and volume when he grows animated, which is often. He is prone to strange, spasm-like gesticulations when emphasizing a point, and has a tendency to order two drinks at once and gulp from each of them in turn.

None of the above traits endeared him to the wary-to-point-of-jittery bar staff, one of whom hovered around our table obviously convinced that we were about to do a runner at any minute.

(I learn later that the hotel had only recently re-admitted Korine, following an incident last year when he overturned a table and chased a persistent German fan into the street, brandishing a broken beer bottle and shouting, "Leave me alone! I'm only a kid and I'm insane!")

By the time we repair to his nearby apartment, he is in full, unstoppable flow. A treatise on "the lost art of vaudeville," which began back in the hotel bar, continued in its wildly lateral way as we ambled half a block along Lexington, and seemed to have fizzled out in the elevator, is suddenly, inexplicably reignited when he reappears from his bedroom wearing a pair of implausibly tiny patent-leather tap-shoes. There follows an impromptu display of tap-dancing, Harmony Korine–style. Arms splayed, brow corrugated in concentration, he skids and clatters across the wooden floor like Groucho Marx on amphetamines, scrunching underfoot the unanswered faxes that litter the room. Then, just when I am convinced it can't get any weirder, on cue, the apartment intercom buzzes and a dislocated voice calls out his name from four floors below. "Oh shit," wails Korine, pacing the floor, scratching his newly-shorn head. "I can't let this guy in. What's he doin' here? He's just escaped from Bellevue prison."

By now, I am convinced that there are two often conflicting personas fighting for space in the young director's overcrowded, hyperactive head. The first is an eccentric intellectual, who can hold forth on the failure of French nouvelle vague cinema, quote whole chunks from Walter Benjamin's *Illuminations*, then segue into a spiel on "the essential cruelty of comedy," with particular reference to Buster Keaton and Samuel Beckett. This Harmony Korine will often make grandiose statements, such as, "At an early age, I became obsessed with the transcendentalist cinema of Ozu and Bresson, with the idea of poetic beauty as the one key truth of filmmaking." The other Harmony Korine is, if anything, even more complex: a postmodern street punk, obsessed by the more extreme detritus of American popular culture—tabloid TV, gangsta rap, deviant sex—and high on his own particular brand of male machismo. Legend has it that, when a Hollywood agent boasted, "I'll match any offer you've been made," Korine replied, "The last guy told me I could fuck his sister. Can you match that?"

The two personas often overlap in surreal fashion: one moment, he is dazzling me with his erudition, the next threatening to break my legs if I misquote him. Even more problematic, in terms of the interview contract, is his seeming inability, or perhaps unwillingness, to differentiate between fact and fiction, particularly when it comes to the details of his own life. "What you have to understand about Harmony," a mutual friend had told me, "is that he constantly blurs the lines between truth and fantasy. Most of the time, it's a smokescreen to keep you guessing, like the young Dylan, but, sometimes, he just gets carried away and doesn't seem to know he's doing it. The odd thing is, the stories that are the most unbelievable are often the ones that turn out to be true."

As far as I could ascertain, the only time Korine can be trusted to be utterly truthful is when he is talking about his work. In his apartment, where, intriguingly, a tacked-up copy of Bob Dylan's anti-novel, *Tarantula*, shares wall-space with a pre-pubescent Brooke Shields from Louis Malle's film *Pretty Baby*, and a triptych of homoerotic photographs by Raymond Pettibone, he explains his still-embryonic assault on mainstream cinematic values thus: "I want to change people's expectations of what cinema can do every single time I make a film. Cinema, as Herzog says, is still a form in its infancy, like a baby where the first leg is sticking out of the uterus. It's like we're only just plopping out of the womb, and, already, our sensibilities are jaded almost beyond repair. In a sense, my whole approach is fuelled by anger at the mediocrity of American film, at the peddling of lies and falsity and formula, at the denigration of this century's most powerful art form."

Because of the iconoclasm, and often extreme nature, of his vision, this twenty-five-year-old self-styled artist, photographer, novelist, and reigning enfant terrible of US cinema has managed, in his short but incendiary career, to offend more people than he has enthralled. Chances are that, if you have heard of him at all, it was in relation to the controversy engendered by the two feature films that have borne his name: 1996's *Kids*, a Larry Clark film, the screenplay for which Korine had written when he was just nineteen, and 1997's *Gummo*, his startling directorial debut, released in the UK last year. Both have garnered as much condemnation as critical acclaim for their supposedly amoral vision of a dysfunctional teenage America. One influential critic, Janet Maslin of the *New York Times*, succumbed to the sort of moral panic that attends every generation's attempt to define itself in extremis—whether through music, fiction, or film—calling Korine a "nihilist" and dubbing *Gummo* "the worst film of the year." ("She obviously hadn't seen *Three Heads in a Duffel Bag*," quipped a rival critic.)

Elsewhere, he has been hailed as a true original whose skewered vision of the US owes more, paradoxically, to the auteurist tradition of European cinema. *Gummo* landed the Critic's Prize at both the Venice and Rotterdam film festivals, and he has impressed an influential handful of his cinematic peers, most notably Gus Van Sant and the esteemed German director Werner Herzog, who has called Korine "the future of American cinema." His next two feature films will be made under the aegis of Dogme 95, the Danish filmmaking collective formed by Lars von Trier and Thomas Vinterberg, directors of *Breaking the Waves* and *Festen*, respectively. In the pages of style magazines such as *Dazed & Confused* and *The Face*, the young director has been virtually canonized, albeit against his will, as the voice of the post-slacker generation—"I'm just the voice of Harmony," he says wearily.

This month, critical opinion will, no doubt, be divided once more with the British publication of *A Crackup at the Race Riots*, Korine's first novel—though, in this instance, the term applies more as an adjective than a noun. For a start, the book eschews linear narrative in favor of an assortment of seemingly unrelated ideas, one-liners, suicide notes, borrowed quotes, lists, and cod-aphorisms. An anti-novel, if you like, that wilfully defies literal meaning. Korine, who cites the designer Charles Eames's ethos of "the unified aesthetic" when describing his overall vision, sees himself as "a contemporary collage-ist," but the term "chancer" could just as easily apply in this instance.

One chapter, Rumors, simply lists sixty-one semi-scurrilous one-liners: Placido Domingo likes sherbet; Roberta Flack is scared of going to the dentist; Flavor Flav is a classically-trained pianist; Jerry Garcia tongue-kissed his older sister on her deathbed. Elsewhere, T. S. Eliot's last words—"I'm so unlucky the mirror I broke was a black cat"—sit side by side with the late Tupac Shakur's *Ten Favorite Novels*, which include works by Freud, Goethe, and Schopenhauer. Except that Eliot never said any such thing, and Shakur's name has been substituted for that of one of Harmony's heroes, the German film director Rainer Werner Fassbinder. Funny and infuriating by turns, the book, according to Korine, "does possess an underlying narrative of sorts, but it's more of a swervy, thin line than a story." Which is, perhaps, why Doubleday, its US publisher, tied itself in knots trying to market the book, describing it as "*Slacker* meets James Thurber" and, even more pointlessly, as "the ultimate postmodern video novel." In its fragmented and encoded way, the book may well reflect the culture that spawned it, though, as one US reviewer noted, "Korine seems too much inside his own head to speak for anyone outside it."

"In many ways, the term 'writer' or, indeed, 'filmmaker' is too constraining for what Harmony does," says Walter Donahue, his publisher at Faber. "If anything, he's an artist in the truest, most all-embracing sense. In *Gummo*, there's both an instinctive vision at work and a rigorous, formal intelligence applied to the subject matter. He's young and still excited by the possibilities of filmmaking, and he's not burdened by the past, although he knows it inside out. He's free to invent a new language, which is what he's in the process of doing."

Thus far, that new language has found its most powerful expression on the screen rather than on the page. Korine didn't go to film school, and his interest in filmmaking seems to have been engendered, at least in part, by his somewhat unorthodox upbringing. Though the book blurb claims that "Harmony was raised in the carnival," the truth is more prosaic. His father, an Iranian-Jewish emigre, seems to have travelled extensively around America, first as a hippy, then as a boutique owner. Korine Jr. was born in Bolinas, California, and soon after the family moved to Nashville, Tennessee, where he attended "a progressive school that catered to people who were a little out of the ordinary."

He describes his childhood as "solitary," and says he was "a very slow developer," claiming not to have hit puberty till he was sixteen. "My dad didn't really talk to me when I was growing up. If he was angry, he'd whop me with a bat or throw a shoe. The other side to that was, 'Let's go see a movie.' He preferred a form of communication where he didn't have to actually say anything."

When the family relocated to New York, the teenage Korine, now convinced of what he calls his "otherness," spent an inordinate amount of time alone in one of the city's then plentiful repertory cinemas, absorbing the work of the European and American avant-garde, including films by Cassavetes, Herzog, Godard, and, most important in terms of his development, Fassbinder and Alan Clarke. "I'd see a Fassbinder film, then go and get a book about him out of the library, and find out that he was into melodrama and Douglas Sirk. Then I'd go and seek out all of Sirk's work. That's how I figured out there was a continuum in cinema and directing that, hopefully, I'm part of today."

The sense of wonder he felt during those solitary evenings has stayed with him, and, to a degree, underpins his old-fashioned belief in cinema's enduring power to convey wonder and astonishment. In one of his more poetic moments, he tells me, "There is something mysterious, almost inexplicable, about the idea of strangers coming together to sit in the dark, in silence or in laughter, responding to a filmmaker's work. It's a sensual and a cerebral experience, which is why video, nor any of this interactive crap, will never replace it.

"I knew from a very early age—from the moment I saw the poetry of Buster Keaton—that there is no other art form that compares to film."

His otherness notwithstanding, the by then eighteen-year-old Korine had managed to become a teenage skateboard phenomenon, complete with corporate sponsorship, when the photographer Larry Clark met him in New York's Washington Square Park. Korine showed Clark a short script he had written about a thirteen-year-old boy who is taken to a prostitute by his father as a coming-of-age present. A couple of years later, Clark—who was now so in thrall to teenage skate culture that, at fifty-two, he was togged out in hip-hugging baggy pants and skateboarding himself—asked Korine to write a screenplay about his everyday life. The result was *Kids*, a film described by one reeling critic—Janet Maslin again—as "a wake-up call to America," and by others as an extended, and vacuous, essay in amoralism. The truth lies somewhere in between.

Three years on, *Kids* stands as an ambitious but strangely soulless attempt to capture the enervated and, yes, amoral, gestalt of a certain kind of adolescent American inner-city reality. It follows a group of New York kids around the city, dispassionately recording them as they take drugs, fight, and screw—lovelessly, ruthlessly, aimlessly. Underlying the often disturbing imagery—everyone in the film looks under-age, yet their demeanor and dialogue suggests that, though barely into adolescence, they are hardened survivors—is a moral tale about unsafe sex and the spread of HIV.

It was the film's deadpan tone, detached point of view, and provocative style more than its subject matter that seemed to upset many critics, who accused Clark—and, by proxy, Korine—of exploitation rather than documentation. In the US, Republican Bob Dole described it as "a nightmare of depravity," while here, Social Democrat MP, Emma Nicholson, called it "disgusting material that panders to pedophile fantasies."

Kids, as Korine is quick to point out, is essentially a Larry Clark film, and loaded with the latter's usual preoccupations-cum-obsessions—casual violence, drug-taking, and warped adolescent sexuality. "For me, it was just a job for hire, y'know?" shrugs Korine, still an adolescent himself when he "banged out" the screenplay in just three weeks. He now seems less than interested in rekindling an old controversy. "I would have made a very different film from Larry's. In fact, I'd have made it more non-judgmental and detached. But there is a morality there. I was reading a lot of Greek tragedy at the time, and I was obsessed with the idea of the sins of the fathers, of everything coming round. It's just not the usual kind of black-and-white Hollywood moral tale, where good triumphs and everyone learns a life lesson. Where I grew up, those rules did not apply."

If *Kids* showed that Korine had an ear for dialogue, a natural aptitude for casting unknowns—the much-acclaimed Chloe Sevigny, his erstwhile girlfriend and ongoing muse, made her debut in the film before going on to star in *Trees Lounge* and *The Last Days of Disco*)—and an ability to write from the inside about the more transgressive elements of US youth culture, his directorial debut in 1997, *Gummo*, was nothing short of a revelation. Arguably the most original film of the nineties, it conjures up an at times nightmarish vision of a dysfunctional middle America that, outside of the sixties photography of Duane Michaels and, significantly, Larry Clark, had not been documented before. Blocked on bad drugs, in thrall to gangsta rap and death-metal, and drawn (through boredom rather than desire) to loveless sex, Korine's characters are the trailer-park, white-trash youth of middle America, whose dead-end lifestyle he records without judgment or idealization.

Shot near Nashville, which doubles for Xenia, Ohio, a small town devastated by a tornado back in 1970, it opens with footage of the aftermath of the storm, including one unforgettable image of a dog impaled on a satellite antenna. "The metaphor of the tornado freed me up, and I began to think in terms of pure images and scenarios. Anything but plot. Plot disgusts me. Real life doesn't have plots."

Using hand-held video and Super 8, as well as stop-action photography and Polaroids, Korine created an often wilfully jarring but utterly mesmerizing montage of a society where, as he puts it, "none of the normal rules apply." Employing non-actors alongside relative unknowns, he manages to pull up short all our preconceived notions of filmmaking, merging various older genres—home movies, fly on-the-wall documentaries, the German realist cinema of Fassbinder—into a new form that effortlessly transcends the sum of its parts. What is initially disturbing about *Gummo* is how the camera seems to be recording "real" people in unrehearsed situations: two skinhead brothers who, seemingly unable to converse, simply punch each other in turn in a ritual test of endurance; a retarded girl lovingly shaves her eyebrows in front of a mirror in order to "look more pretty."

"What I'm concerned with is the presentation of reality," says Korine. "I present my films as real and organic, while, simultaneously, I'm actually manipulating everything you see. *Gummo* might look in places like fly-on-the-wall documentary, but it was mapped out, scene by scene, though more as a montage than as a linear narrative. I want people to feel like the images fell out of the sky. Ultimately, I'm a trickster."

Gummo's narrative, what there is of it, follows two paint-sniffing protagonists as they eke out a living shooting cats to sell to a local butcher. *Forrest Gump* it is not. Perhaps because the film does not conform to any of the usual cinematic narrative genres—rites-of-passage, loss of innocence, redemption through action—or offer anything remotely resembling a moral subtext, it was difficult to finance. Harvey Weinstein, the influential head of Miramax, which had funded *Kids*, baulked at the idea of a youth-oriented film that included teenage prostitution, transvestism, and cat killing. In the end, Cary Woods, a Hollywood heavyweight who had produced a string of successful genre pics, including *Copland* and *Scream*, raised private funding to make the film through Ted Turner's FineLine, which had previously courted controversy with David Cronenberg's *Crash*. Woods has since said that he will back any film Korine wants to make, so great is his belief in the young director's ability to "create a new kind of cinema."

"I still feel sore that *Gummo* was dismissed by mainstream American critics for all the wrong reasons," says Woods. "There was certainly a generational and moral misunderstanding of what Harmony was trying to do. I got the feeling that many metropolitan critics shared a moral-cum-political consensus: they either didn't believe that the America he portrayed existed, or, more likely, they didn't want it shown. That said, anyone with even the slightest grasp of cinematic artistry should have seen that we were dealing with a fresh, new talent here. I've produced fourteen films and, to be honest, Harmony possesses the kind of ambition that could be dangerous in an artist with less talent. He sets out in each film to do something entirely new and visionary. Even when he doesn't pull it off, his boldness is breathtaking."

Yet, in pursuing his singular vision, Korine does, almost as part of his artistic raison d'etre, court moral outrage. His employment of non-actors in *Gummo*, particularly the casting of a Down's Syndrome sufferer in the role of a retarded teenage prostitute, led to inevitable accusations of exploitation. "I think that notion is, of itself, ridiculous," says Korine. "For a start, it suggests that people with handicaps are too stupid to know what a movie is. Is it exploitation to use someone with an illness to play someone with an illness? Or is it exploitation to get Dustin Hoffman or Tom Hanks to fake it? I mean, you won't see any slobber on Tom Hanks's face, no blood or shit on his underpants. What you will see is the lovable Hollywood-style eccentric schizophrenic, all exaggerated ticks and twists. That's real exploitation. That's real ego."

In one scene, one of the central characters, Solomon (played by the strangely captivating Jacob Reynolds), bonds with the girl in a moment of non-sexual intimacy and, in the process, Korine turns a potentially gratuitous interlude into the film's most tender moment. "It would have been so easy to be sleazy," he grins, "but it's much more challenging to set that up and then go off in the opposite direction. People never credit me for that, because they're too busy complying with the ongoing Gumpification of cinema and of life. America simply isn't ready for realism. It wants the simple message spelled out in big letters. When I read the critics' line that there is no morality in my films, I think, 'Where do these people live?' Where I come from, people do not pay for their sins in an obvious way, and people do get away with doing bad stuff. Plus, morality is relative, anyway. What's bad to you and me might not be bad to a kid trapped in a violent family in a dead-end town. If your father beats up on your mother every night and you witness that from a very early age, you can get inured to the pain and suffering, and then start to think, 'This is how things are.' If that's how you're raised, what's the first thing you're gonna do when you get married at eighteen?"

Latent violence crackles like static through the film's disconnected narrative, but its most explosive moment occurs when an enraged redneck batters a steel-framed chair out of shape in a confined, and crowded, room. Though no one is hurt, the scene has a visceral power that jolts the viewer in a way that the choreographed violence of a Tarantino or Scorsese film no longer can.

"The main thing I learned in making *Gummo* was never to say, 'Cut!'" says Korine, giving some insight into his unorthodox methodology. "If you tell the actors what to do up to a point, then just keep shooting after the scene is supposedly finished, there's often a chemistry that occurs that can make a scene explode and burn. I love that. You see it all the time in Alan Clarke's films; the notion that a scene could begin or end anywhere. His films are like life. They just go on. They don't really start and end like other films. He understood the randomness of life. That's where I want to go. The totally scripted film is over as a format as far as I'm concerned. The screenplay format hasn't changed in essence since day one, and it's become an anachronism in many ways."

For his new film, *The Julian Chronicles*, he has dispensed with a screenplay altogether, in favor of an extended treatment; scenes are blocked out and briefly discussed with the actors, then shot with as much energy and chemistry as possible. Featuring Sevigny, again, Werner Herzog, Ewen Bremner, and Chrissie Kobylak, the aforementioned blind figure-skater, it is the first Korine film to be made under the Dogme 95 manifesto, which insists that members adhere to ten creative tenets to ensure a new kind of honesty and purity in filmmaking—these include filming in natural light, shooting scenes only in chronological sequence, and using hand-held cameras.

"I've signed the Dogme vow of chastity," says Korine, clearly proud to be directing the collective's first US film, "because it makes perfect sense to me. One of the things that's killing films—apart from the idiots who make them—is that it's an elitist medium. New digital video technology challenges all that. That's why the big studios hate it. Video is a new psychology as much as anything—it's cheap; you don't have to have a big, obtrusive, and impersonal crew; and you have the freedom to shoot for as long as you like on as many cameras as you like. It's liberating—it takes the so-called mystery out of directing."

The onus, though, is on the actors. Bremner, best known for his role as Spud in *Trainspotting*, worked in a New York psychiatric rehabilitation center for the criminally insane for six weeks in preparation for his role as a man going through the first stages of schizophrenia, a part based on Korine's uncle. "It's been a challenge all right," says Bremner, "mainly because, at Harmony's insistence, it's all coming together at the last minute. I mean, there's no scripted dialogue, just blocked-out scenes where we can improvise and get to the heart of the thing. You hardly know from day to day what's going to be shot or how. It's scary and exhilarating, and I'd probably be shitting myself if it wasn't a Harmony Korine movie."

I ask him if the volatile Korine is easy to work with. "Well, I guess some people mightn't think so. He's totally uninhibited and totally rigorous. Every scene is mapped out in his head. It took me a while to figure out how he can be so spontaneous and so disciplined, but I guess it's just down to self-belief and purity of vision. It's a rare gift, but he has it."

Korine is also engaged on a more protracted, and potentially problematic, Dogme project, entitled *Fight*: "The premise of the film is that I go up to the biggest men I can find and taunt them until they beat up on me. Basically, I have to say whatever it takes to make the guy throw the first punch. My cameraman, who's usually across the street, has got to keep filming unless it looks like I'm gonna die." Ignoring my look of disbelief, he grows more animated as he describes the fights that have already been recorded. "The one I had with two Arab taxi drivers was brutal, man. Then, there was the one with the bouncer at Stringfellows, who jumped on my legs and broke my ankle." He pulls down his sock to show an ugly protrusion where a bone has not set properly. "The video footage of that one is exceptional."

Wondering if, perhaps, this is one of his moments of slippage from fact into fantasy, I later ask his fellow filmmaker and friend, Oran, if *Fight* is for real. "Oh, he told you about that, did he? Yeah, it's for real all right. I saw him after one fight and he was badly bashed up. He'd been to hospital for concussion, his ribs were cracked, and his face was a mess. It's disturbing but, y'now, that's Harmony. He's a, how shall I put it, very complex guy."

Indeed. Thus far, it turns out, Korine has been beaten up four times and arrested twice for his art, but, to his dismay, he has only about thirteen minutes of footage in the can for his troubles. "I kinda overlooked the fact that fights don't last very long, and how damaging it is when someone really beats you up. My hospital bills are soaring, plus I can't get arrested a third time or I'll go to jail." His intention, though, is to fight "every demographic in New York—Italians, Puerto Ricans . . . and I've got to find an aggressive Jew like myself. Jews don't like to fight, they just curse you out in Yiddish. I want to find a big, butch motorcycle dyke, too."

When I ask Korine to explain the reasoning behind this extreme, even by his standards, piece of cinematic performance art, he goes off on another wildly lateral monologue about "the essential cruelty of comedy," and how he wants "to make the funniest film ever made, like Buster Keaton makes a snuff movie." Perhaps sensing that I am genuinely disturbed by both his masochism and his sick sense of humor, he grows serious: "Look, I've always gotten in fights. It's because I'm a runt. I'm so little, I'd always get smashed. Then, I started to like fighting. I started to get off on being punched. I like the pain. I identify it with some kind of love. Ultimately, I think violence is really necessary. It's one of the ways I keep myself from not killing myself, because I have so much anger inside me."

And, there, perhaps, is the rub. Right now, Korine is the most intriguing prospect in US cinema because of the extremity of his artistic vision.

He is also a total refusenik, breaking virtually every formulaic rule of Hollywood filmmaking, storytelling, and moralizing. In the process, he is creating a new sense of the possibilities of cinema. Young and ambitious, he possesses the self-belief, and arrogance, of his years—and, God knows, cinema needs his kind of iconoclasm now more than ever. He is, as the critic Kurt Andersen noted in the *New Yorker*, "a malcontent as young artists were once supposed to be malcontents—not in the disengaged, everything-sucks, nothing-matters fashion, but fired up with specific and impolitic impatience at mediocrity and wall-to-wall conformity."

And yet . . . and yet, there are some strange and disturbing demons lurking beneath his angry young punk exterior that neither film, nor indeed fiction-making of any kind, may be capable of containing or, indeed, exorcising. Korine is a contemporary enfant terrible in every sense of the term; a product of, and a reaction to, a culture where dysfunctionalism has come to be embraced as an aesthetic. Maybe the question is not can Harmony Korine save cinema's tarnished soul, but can cinema save his?

Pure Vision

Jefferson Hack / 1999

From *Dazed and Confused*, May 1999. Reprinted by permission of Jefferson Hack.

Acclaimed screenwriter, award-winning first-time director, neophyte artist, pending author, comedic bit part actor . . . a twenty-three-year-old instigator of controversial ideas. Harmony Korine is attempting the almost impossible, to infiltrate his uncommercial, and uncompromising agenda—a pure vision—into the mainstream. For as soon as an artist takes notice of what other people want he ceases to be an artist, and becomes a dull and amusing craftsman, an honest or dishonest tradesman. As the saying goes: "He chooses you, you cannot choose Him."

EXT: MERCER STREET. LOWER EAST SIDE—MIDDAY

Outside some shops, a young girl is standing alone. She is dressed like a gypsy princess. She has the body of a thirteen-year-old, but the face of a beautiful woman. Korine spots her from a distance and immediately begins asking her name, age, and where she's from. Her mother exits the shop holding a violin. She looks nervous that a strange man is talking to her young daughter. The girl's father follows and, recognizing Korine, begins saying, "I shoot for *Screw* magazine, I shoot real hardcore. You want to see real New York, I'll show you real New York. None of that fucking *Kids* stuff, I'll show you hookers, the youngest girls, and rent boys. I do real reportage." His daughter stands next to him, looking unfazed. Korine asks her for her telephone number and she asks him why he wants it, "So I can call you, I'd like you to be in a film," he explains. She looks at him up and down, and with a completely straight face says, "No, gimme your number. I'll call you."

Gummo, Korine's debut film has been championed by directors Gus Van Sant, Jean Luc Godard, and Larry Clark, and has earned the congratulations of Werner Herzog, Lars von Trier, and Abel Ferrara. They are all far older than Korine, yet all unconventional directors in their own right. Perhaps what they see in *Gummo* is a pure and daring singular vision, something that is almost impossible to achieve let alone maintain in the commodified world of popular culture. With so many careerists, crowd pleasers, recyclers, fame for the sake of fame seekers, insurrection, especially in an original and powerful voice, is not only to be celebrated, but practically revered.

Gummo has won both an International Critics' Prize at the Venice Film Festival and, more recently, the Grand Jury prize at the Rotterdam Film Festival, yet it also has its detractors and has been denounced in some parts of the US media as "boring, redundant, and sick," as well as "the worst film of the year." "When it comes to boy wonders exploring the cutting edge of independent cinema," wrote Janet Maslin in the *New York Times*, "the buck stops cold right here." Two-dimensional media analysis paints Korine as a genius wunderkind on the one hand and a cause-celebre opportunist on the other. Perhaps he is both, but more likely he is neither. Real original voices are rarely understood and nearly always marginalized by those who control the status quo. The laws of our media landscape are there to either mock or scapegoat those who attempt to do new things. Korine's a three-dimensional rebel, the real thing, that's why the mainstream media in America have done their best to try and discourage him.

The portrait of an artist as a slightly younger man shows "Harmful" Korine, the teenage skateboarder, and the Mohican-sporting photographer meeting in Central Park. Korine told Clark about a short script he had written. It was the story of a boy who is taken by his estranged father on his thirteenth birthday to a prostitute for his first sexual experience. It wasn't until almost a year later that Clark, remembering Korine's script, talked him through a brief outline for a film. Three weeks later, the nineteen-year-old Korine finished the first draft of *Kids*. With the help of executive producer Gus Van Sant, the film began shooting in the summer of 1994. Although he is an avid cinephile, Korine never studied film or scriptwriting, yet *Kids* showed a natural ear for dialogue and cinematic structure. Korine teamed up with Cary Woods, the producer of *Kids* and subsequently *Scream* and *Cop Land* to make *Gummo*. Woods's protective style suited Korine's creative independence and although *Gummo* was eventually made with Fine Line, a mini-major, for approximately $1 million, it was virtually uninfluenced by corporate strategy. In fact, given the increasingly commercial climate in the US film industry, it's incredible that *Gummo* was even funded.

EXT: A SIDEWALK IN FRONT OF A MUSIC SHOP—AFTERNOON
"You've dropped your pocket." Korine walks past a couple shopping and taps the man on the shoulder repeating the line, "You've dropped your pocket." The man looks down at the ground, confused, searching for nothing he has lost. "Watch this, he'll be there for half an hour. We'll get to the end of the street and he'll still be there." We walk further, into the distance and I turn around as we reach the end of the street. The man and wife are now both on their hands and knees, arguing with each other, and looking for the nothing they've lost. "You see, it works every time," says Korine.

Welcome to the world of *Gummo*; a film where you are never quite sure what is going to happen next; a cinema of unpredictability, where conventional structure and plot are discarded in favor of a non-linear approach to storytelling. Welcome to Xenia, a tornado-devastated town in Ohio. Where *Kids* exposed us to a compelling portrayal of twenty-four hours in the life of a group of New York teenagers—their attitudes to underage sex, drugs, street fashion, and AIDS—*Gummo* transports us to small town, run down, rural America, where handicapped sex, breast cancer, teenage transvestitism, pedophilia, and racism are subtexts. Korine takes no moral stance, leaving it up to us to work out whether we should laugh or cry, feel embarrassed or afraid at this mirage of truth, closeness, and access. This is what more cinema should be about—not a fast food, pop cult-fiction package, where we all consensually laugh and cry in syncopated rhythm. It's imagery that keeps popping back into your mind weeks after you've seen it, and a film whose unresolved dilemmas are left scratching away under the surface of the skin: a Down's Syndrome girl shaves her eyebrows because she thinks it makes her look more beautiful; a midget arm wrestles a big bear of a man and wins; a deaf couple argue through intense hand gesticulation; teenage boys kill cats so they can buy glue to get high; an albino waitress in a car park describes what she finds attractive about men; three extremely young white trash sisters get touched up by a middle-aged man. It's a vortex of original ideas; part poetry, part nonsense, part youth culture rhetoric, and in Korine's own words a "complete genre-fuck." There's no cynicism here, no irony or postmodern mask. Korine's observed sense of realism almost verges on social anthropology. Shot mainly in Nashville, Tennessee, Korine's hometown, *Gummo* features only four actors; Chloe Sevigny (*Kids*), Linda Manz (*Days of Heaven*), Max Perlich (*Beautiful Girls, Drugstore Cowboy*), and Jacob Reynolds (*The Road to Wellville*) in an ensemble cast of over forty speaking parts. The lives of the local people, old schoolfriends, and acquaintances are seen through the hypnotic and beautifully inventive cinematography of Jean Yves Escoffier, who has also worked with Leos Carax on such classic films as *Les Amants du Pont Neuf* and *Trois Hommes et un Coffin*, as well as Martin Scorsese's short film *100 Years of American Cinema*.

INT: KORINE'S APARTMENT—LATE AFTERNOON
Korine puts on a video cassette to show me a scene from *Gummo* cut by the censors.

INT: APARTMENT IN XENIA, OHIO—AFTERNOON
The sound of a Bach cello concerto. A small child begins by removing pictures from the living room wall. Behind the framed prints, spiders, cockroaches, and woodlice crawl. He squashes them with the edge of the picture frame and gets off his stool to return to the couch where a couple are inhaling aerosol fumes. The TV is on, but the sound is switched off. The house is a mess. The young child climbs into his mother's lap and in a framing reminiscent of the Madonna child, she holds his head and offers him the aerosol. He cups its flute with both hands as if it were a baby bottle and takes a deep breath.

Korine's precise mixed-media approach to collaging *Gummo* sees Polaroids, home movie footage (shot by many of the kids) as well as sampled TV clips cut up Escoffier's fluid filming. There is a rhythm and layering that isn't far removed from the looping and sampling process of drum 'n' bass. Korine brings to cinema a contemporary vernacular and streetsuss; a new beauty, a new way of seeing and thinking, and in the process a big fuck you to everyone else. As well as *Gummo*, Korine's debut novel *A Crackup at the Race Riots* will be published in America in April. He is also represented as an artist by two prestigious galleries: the Andrea Rosen Gallery in New York where he recently exhibited a collection of fake suicide notes, and the Patrick Painter Gallery in Los Angeles (which also reps Mike Kelley, Richard Prince, Larry Clark, and Douglas Gordon) where he exhibited video installation pieces. (The installations sold to the San Francisco Museum of Modern Art.) This month Korine tears up the big screen in a hilarious but very brief part as a convict in Gus Van Sant's *Good Will Hunting*. Korine looks like a schoolboy; a blur of unkempt and undone K-Mart shoes, hip-hop stances, and heavy metal T-shirts, but he's really fifty-three years old. He's just got one of those rare anti-aging diseases that makes him look permanently eighteen. He was an authoritative documentarian in the sixties and now he is busy reinventing himself as a renaissance man, thinly disguised as a cheeky adolescent filmmaker with the concentration span of an art star on coke. The urban mythology of Korine: He pretends to be drunk on the *David Letterman Show*, his on-off relationship with long-term partner and prominent actress Chloe Sevigny is peppered with alleged supermodel affairs; he has been banned from a New York hotel bar after starting a fight, and has slagged off big films like *Boogie Nights*. Although it seems to have calmed down a lot in recent months, his reputation as both auteur and raconteur precedes him. In a medium where everything is autobiographical and everything is fictional at the same time, Korine's fiction is ultimately a branch of his truth, and being one stage removed, it's hard for me not to see him as the main character in the movie adaptation of the story of his life.

EXT: SOHO. BUSY STREET CORNER BY A BAR—EARLY EVENING
Leonardo DiCaprio and Korine are walking together. They approach a group of bikers who are busy drinking outside a bar. Korine accidentally knocks into the biggest biker as he walks past. He is enormous; his hair hangs in a ponytail, his fists bandaged in leather, fingerless gloves. He partially spills his drink and begins screaming at Korine, "Come here you little punk, you fucker." DiCaprio stands behind Korine, taunting the biker with a highly animated gorilla impression. DiCaprio's arms are swinging from side to side as Korine walks towards the biker and instinctively pulls a switchblade from his back pocket, the street lights reflecting off the steel blade. The biker backs off, and Korine, avoiding a prolonged stand-off, starts walking down the road. With the sound of the cursing biker fading in the distance, Korine turns to DiCaprio, they put their arms around each other, and laugh at the ridiculousness of the situation.

Jefferson Hack: Did you ever have an attention deficit disorder when you were younger?
Harmony Korine: I'm sure I had it. When I was a kid, my parents didn't take me to the type of people that would know what that was . . . I should have been on Ritalin. I was a total Ritalin kid. But I guess my parents weren't into that. You know, instead, I would like, light my yard on fire.

JH: You lit the yard on fire?

HK: Yeah, I remember my parents went to see *The Outsiders* at the shopping mall a hundred miles away from our house and I stayed home and lit the yard on fire. The fire trucks came and there I was trying to put it out with a wet towel. The fire trucks were there for hours but my parents were at the shopping mall. When they came back, the yard was all burnt and there was still smoke. So knowing my father's penchant for violence, I took a chair and I pulled my pants down, exposing my ass and I said, "I lit the yard on fire; you can beat me," and he didn't say anything. He went outside and got a yellow bat and he smashed me without saying anything. That's what I remember most, that he wasn't saying anything. He wasn't even out of breath. It was amazing.

JH: Most kids would just try to run away from what was going to happen. But you just decided to face the music.

HK: I guess I never thought about it like that.

JH: Are you interested in making documentaries?

HK: I feel documentary always falls short. I think cinema verite is a fallacy, that the documentary is manipulated, there's no such thing as truth in film. The idea that Godard said about twenty-four frames of truth, was always for me the ultimate lie. It's just twenty-four frames of lies. But the best cinema to me works on a kind of theoretical level where it's twenty-four frames of sort of truth. For me, being a writer and an artist and a viewer, the only thing I'm interested in is realism. If it's not presented to me in a way that's real, with real consequences, real characters, I have no desire to see it, because then it's fake. It's a cartoon, and I just don't care about that stuff. But at the same time, in this ultimate search for truth, for realism, I know it's impossible to attain, so what do you do? It's like *Gummo*, people say, "Oh my god, it's got no script." And there's a total script. But that's what it is, a trick. Everything is presented as if it's real. I'm manipulating everything.

JH: I liked the philosophizing. There were simple one-liners of the "I'm going to kill myself and will anyone care when I'm gone" variety. The "life is great, without it we'd be dead" rhetoric.

HK: "Life is great, without it we'd be dead," was an old Vaudeville joke.

JH: Or "America would be nothing without wood!" I assume what you're doing is just punching people with ideas, images, sequences, and then hopefully they will extract their own truth from it.

HK: I am also interested in the whole kind of beauty of nonsense and in fully trying to make all the connections a lot of times come up short and I'm saying things that aren't really the intention.

JH: What would you say to someone who said "Well, it's not realism, it's just as stylized as MTV"?

HK: I wouldn't understand that. I never feel the need to defend my work at all. I sometimes will, but it's either gotten or it's forgotten and that's fine.

JH: I remember talking to you when you were very worried that the film might not get a rating. And that was the time that you were probably at your lowest point after the film had been made. What happened?

HK: I'm a 100 percent commercial filmmaker. I have nothing to do with independent directors, alternative cinema. I make Harmony movies. It's a cinema of obsession and passion. But at the same time, I can't differentiate between notions of underground. Underground film, underground music, alternative culture, to me it doesn't exist. To me the future is either good or bad and it's kind of making sense of both those things. Like the film—I involve scenes and situations that are the scenes that I love. It's only scenes and images that I wanted to see, with no real explanation. Nothing coming before it. So getting back to the question, I was basically free to make this movie this way, which is a miracle. Because what's on screen is a pure vision. The way things are structured is that people leave me alone. I have nothing to do with anyone. I have no idea about how other people make their movies. I don't make very much money. I don't concern myself with others. I don't fraternize with the enemy. I just work, and I love and I fight and I just do my own thing. So I am making this film and I finish editing and it has to go before the ratings board. The only stipulation in my contract with the studio Fine Line is that I had to turn in an R rated film. Basically, in America, few studios will distribute NC-17. NC-17, in the States, is a kind of word for X. Basically, that's because 75 percent of the theaters in America won't accept the film. Ninety-five percent of the video chains where you make half your money won't accept it, like Blockbuster. You can't advertise on MTV. You can't advertise in 90 percent of magazines or newspapers. So right there you're limited to a percent of the funds.

JH: So there was this point where you were being told it was going to be given an NC-17.

HK: We gave it to the NPA, who are these people who have these really vague guidelines. There is nothing really to follow. It's more like "How do you feel. . . ."

JH: What did they find particularly outrageous or shocking about *Gummo*?

HK: They would say "You're lingering on these boys huffing glue out of their sacks. You're lingering on it for too long." So we'd cut it, but it wouldn't be enough. And then basically after the seventh time and I was going to cut no more and I'd cut a few more minutes out of the film. . . .

JH: You probably could have cut those sequences shorter. . . . Instead of lingering on the kids taking drugs the image would have been less exploratory and far more punchy and perhaps even more destructive.

HK: That was the whole point. They were saying that if it were more MTV. If I cut it, if it was really rapid. . . . If I stripped the film of any type of content, if I made it totally void of any kind of meaning, if I made what *Trainspotting* was, if I made it heightened and I made it cartoonish, and something that was much more over the top and much more satirical that you could laugh off then you would realize that it was a movie, it would be OK.

JH: So you must have wanted to punch their heads in. . . .

HK: I went nuts.

JH: Did you go in front of the board? Did they summon you or did you ask for the meeting?

HK: After the seventh time, you're allowed to—it's kind of like going to court—you're allowed to call the jury. And then you're allowed to make a speech and there's supposed to be a certain number of representatives from the ratings board and I swear to you every single person was over sixty-five years old; they looked like Bush. There's only one woman; they're all men. I made my speech. I said, "If you look at the film, you're seeing almost no nudity; there's no violence except violence toward animals." I went into this whole speech that I hated myself for having to explain to these fuckers but I knew I had to do it, and then it took them forty-five seconds to vote me down. Forty-five seconds to say NC-17. They didn't care. So the next day I called. I told them what they were doing was illegal, I'm calling all the newspapers, I am going to expose you. . . .

JH: Who?
HK: Someone on the board. And I meant it. It was someone who was a liaison between the ratings board and the studio who I felt was lying to me. I told him without hesitation that I'll take the next fight over and I'll stab him in the fucking throat. I said, "I'll cut your fucking head off 'cause I didn't grow up as a rich kid playing that whole game. I'm not a part of that and the work means so much more and if I can't show it, it's not only a betrayal to me, it's a betrayal to all those people in the film because these are people that gave themselves to the film." The next morning I got a call from my agent and he's freaked out that I threatened someone's life but the rating was reversed.

JH: That's amazing. Absolutely amazing. Do you think it took them forty-five seconds to reverse it?
HK: I wish we could have timed it.

JH: Do you think all films should be R rated or can you see some reasons for a ratings system?
HK: I think it's fine . . . I think ratings systems are fine. Some Disney films should be PG.

JH: Did you ever apply to film school? Were you ever interested in learning the art of cinematography or studying the art of filmmaking on that level?
HK: I feel strongly about that because I'm not making movies for the same reasons that most people make films. I grew up in the cinema. Buster Keaton changed my life. I realized that there was something so pure, there was a kind of tragic beauty that I had never seen before, and it was so moving and so big, what could be more amazing than what I was seeing . . . ? So for me there was almost something holy about the cinema. My life is always 50 percent watching movies and 50 percent living life. Living life is always more interesting than films. I find life is more exciting, because it's limitless. Films can only imitate life. They can only go to a certain point and then life begins. Watching films, I started to realize that they are all starting to seem the same. That they all have the same kind of humor, the same kind of actors, the same kind of

characteristics. Why is that? And I started to realize that everybody is going to these film schools and these are all people, who, fifteen years ago would have gone to doctor's school and now they want to make movies. None of them have any kind of stories to tell. All of their films are about this kind of process, about this generic kind of storytelling. More than anything, the great films are about life. There was once a day when cinema had glory. When John Ford was making movies, and Fassbinder was making movies, and Cassavetes, when there was glory 'cause films once had the essence of life to them. And then something happened. I felt that film school was this place that was only teaching people to be technicians, and to think the same, have the same sense of humor and the same stories. And I realized that all you ever need to be a filmmaker is to watch films. I understood this at a young age.

JH: Would you have made *Gummo* if you only had $20,000 and only one camera or would you have waited until you got $1 million?
HK: Yeah, I would have waited.

JH: And what if it never came?
HK: I would have walked away.

JH: You wouldn't have made the film?
HK: No. . . .

JH: Isn't that bullshit? If you're that passionate about it, if it meant that much to you to tell that story and not be a technician . . .
HK: I might have made another film. The thing is this, it's like the reason I never did music videos and all these other things that came along, is because I only wanted to make *Gummo*. I only wanted it to be this way. It either had to be perfectly this vision or it fell short.

JH: *Gummo* does not obviously reference any other film, and if it does, it's very hidden. And what's interesting is that right now, everyone is being ironic; everyone is using parody or heavily quoting their influences. All the young and maybe middle generation filmmakers seem more interested in the past than the future.
HK: I only was interested in inventing a new film like the way I wanted to watch movies with images coming from all the right places. A "mistakist" art form.

JH: Explain that term to me.

HK: I think it's important to give a kind of aesthetic or form a name just because it's easier for people to reference. What I mean by mistakist is almost like anti-Hitchcock. When Hitchcock would make a film, before he made it, it was finished. When I make a film, the script is the script and that's the bare bones and it's dead. All the accidents, all the life that's come to it, that's the film.

JH: There are moments you could never direct. They are undirectable, like the chair smashing scene.

HK: Jean Escoffier, the cinematographer, and I talked before we shot about what films we might reference and we both decided to reference nothing. We decided to let the situation dictate the way it's filmed. And so what we did is. I set up chaos. Everything around me was chaos.

JH: You mean behind the scenes there was chaos?

HK: Both behind the scenes and in front of the camera, a lot of the time mixed. And I was setting up situations where a chaotic event would happen and I knew it would happen. And I would give everybody a camera. I would give my little sister a camera. I would give Escoffier a camera. I would give someone a video camera, or a Super-8 camera and everyone would be filming.

JH: So there's a large element of collaboration with the subjects of the film, the actors, the non-actors. They were collaborating in a way that they were helping you make the film. This is what negates any sense of exploitation for me.

HK: It's all about life. That is what's interesting to me.

JH: In a sense you are working from the inside out.

HK: Because art for too long has been from a distance. . . . It's been coming from the wrong directions. It's about artists trying to solve problems and then go inside.

JH: Like math problems . . .

HK: Exactly. That's what it's become. Postmodern art to me is like math problems.

JH: So your book, the film, the scripts you have written, are a random collection of your obsessions and thoughts. What's the spirit of what you're trying to say through all of it?

HK: I would never answer you as far as what I am trying to say. Because for one I don't even really know, and for another, I do the work and I would never take on the responsibility of answering. The one connection would be what Charles Eames talked about "a unified aesthetic." I could design a chair; I could do a tap dance, or I could write an opera, or hang glide. . . .

JH: You don't feel precious about any particular medium. . . .
HK: . . . Or I could go in my bathroom and hang myself and die but it would all be part of the same person and the ideas. There would be this unified thought. This unified aesthetic.

JH: There was a thing that you mentioned last night, you said that "There are people that want to hurt me. They really want to hurt me and I won't let them," and that was a reaction to the people that want to maintain the status quo.
HK: You mean the people complaining about my nihilism? Like the guy in *Vogue* magazine who was screaming that I was a nihilist and I was the reason that the world was bad.

JH: People need scapegoats for the reason that things are the way they are. You are a twenty-three-year-old director working to bring new images and new ideas into the mass arena where they don't already exist. In a sense you are a flag carrier. These people want to maintain the status quo, that power. Are you worried about that or does that excite you?
HK: What excites me is that these people are old and I want to destroy these dinosaurs. I feel that they are ruining the air that we breathe, killing the films that I watch and the way that I live. I want to get them out of the way. In another ten or fifteen years, the people that understand and appreciate *Gummo* or my work will be in positions of power, but for right now the bourgeois fuckers, they must die. Vive La France.

JH: That's exactly what I was hoping you were going to say.
HK: But it is. It's time for youth culture to take over, I know it sounds silly, but it's true and I am not even saying that I have this great belief in the youth, because I don't. I have a great belief in certain individuals. Certain talented individuals. I don't have a great belief in a group of

people, but at the same time many of them aren't getting the attention that they deserve and maybe it's time for them to step up.

JH: Tell me about the final days of filming.
HK: We shot the entire film in twenty days. There's a scene in the movie where the girls are in a swimming pool, in the rain. I had this picture, this image and we could never get it to coincide with the rain and at the same time I wanted it raining at the finale. Every day it was supposed to rain, it wouldn't rain. And these were the really important shots and I kept putting it back and putting it back. And people kept saying, "You're nuts, there's no way we'll ever finish this movie." I knew not to worry. I always have. So on the final day, we had a storm. That day, out of twenty days of sunshine, we had a storm. We shot the swimming pool scene and we shot the finale with the rabbit. We shot the entire arm-wrestling scene and we shot my scene, last of all, with the black dwarf.

JH: All in one day?
HK: All in one day.

JH: Were you drunk when you shot the scene with you and the dwarf?
HK: I never work when intoxicated or under the influence, but I knew for the scene I wanted something special, so I got very drunk. I did that scene and I was totally out of it and it was two in the morning and that was the end of the film. It was dead quiet and everyone was shaking because here I am trying to make love to a black dwarf and I'm being rejected. And the dwarf was in his tight white underwear and I'm whispering in his ear that I'll give him $100 if he takes off his underwear and he won't do it for me. So I stand up, it's two in the morning, and I stand up and I scream: "We made a movie. We finished the film. We made an original movie." I am screaming and I'm totally out of my mind. And everyone starts clapping and is happy but I don't really know what's going on. My younger sister who's nineteen, who worked on the film, runs up to give me a hug and I threw her through the door. Then I take a painting that's lying in the house and I start running and smashing the windows through the house. And Chloe and a few people start crying. Everyone starts flipping out and my sister's bleeding and I'm just smashing up the windows. Then this huge grip, this bald guy that looks like Mr. Clean, takes me by the neck and just throws me in a car. He drove me back to my apartment and then we all kind of had a party afterward. I tried to

walk home and somebody gave me a cigar on the street and I took some scissors and I started cutting my pubic hair, with my pants down, and I just fainted into a plastic bucket.

JH: Let's talk about all these other directors. There's this whole list that's generously prefixed before you in articles. Godard, Cassavetes, Fellini . . . etc. Which of these are really your favorites and which are just critics sticking them in to make themselves sound important?

HK: The idea of being a pragmatist or being a worker doesn't appeal to me. It's only about great artists. For me, it's certain directors, or maybe certain films that have influenced me. Of course, the most interesting career is Fassbinder's career because he was working at such a rate, such an intense level. One year he made nine feature films. He was famous for saying that his films were like a house: Some were wood floors, some were walls, some were the chimney. At the end of his life, the whole idea was that he could he live in this house of his work and I love that idea. The two things I remember about films: It's characters and certain scenes. I never remember plots; I never remember the whole thing—I only remember specifics—and Fassbinder was so great because there are certain scenes that he would show you that no one else would give you.

JH: How did you come across Alan Clarke, because he's quite obscure in America?

HK: If someone said to me who is the greatest director or my favorite, I would say Alan Clarke without hesitation. His stories, without ever being derivative, and without ever having a simple ABC narrative, are totally organic, precious and amazing. It was nothing but him. In a strange way I don't even like talking about him in the press or to people because he is the last filmmaker or artist that is really sacred. But especially in America no one knows who he is. Even in England there is very little attention.

JH: How did it feel to win the Critics' Award in Venice?

HK: It's good that people liked the movie. There is someone who likes it and someone who hates it and I just got to keep truckin' baby.

JH: You are getting your ass licked by the whole of young, avant-garde New York. It must be quite strange. Do you feel how temporal all of that is?

HK: Because my ass is all slippery? To be honest with you, I'm working so I don't deal with it, but I guess now, that the film is over and I am doing all this promotional stuff . . . I just deal with it. I was a little bit more prepared for it because of *Kids*. When *Kids* came out I had just turned nineteen and all that stuff happened and that was traumatic. I was almost having nervous breakdowns. I was going from living in my grandmother's house with no money to . . .

JH: . . . Being around supermodels and film stars. . . .
HK: Right, which to me was really unfulfilling.

JH: Is that the kind of world you feel quite comfortable in now?
HK: Obviously not. The only time I have anything to do with them is when they approach me. I have the same friends I've always had. And it doesn't really matter to me. You know, I have nothing to do with any of them, except when they bother me.

JH: Do you think you would work again with Chloe in a film?
HK: In the future the more she works with other directors, the less interested in her I become.

JH: Do you really mean that?
HK: I totally mean that, and that's not to say that she shouldn't be working with other directors. If she likes the script, she should do what she wants to do. I mean that for almost anyone.

JH: Do you think she's one of the best actresses of her generation?
HK: Definitely. I don't even think she has any competition. Because I don't think she's scared of taking on characters. I don't think of Chloe as a leading woman. I think of her more as a character actor, which is the only kind of actor I would ever be interested in.

JH: The final question is that everyone must think that you are absolutely loaded, that you must be a very wealthy young man.
HK: It's a lie!! It's a fucking lie!

Nashville. Harmony's House. Present Day. Part II.

Eric Kohn / 2013

Previously unpublished.

Eric Kohn: You wrote *Gummo* in 1995 and shot it that year.
Harmony Korine: It wasn't written in a linear fashion. It was put together in pieces. Then I tried to get money for that. Bob Shea at New Line Cinema gave me like a million dollars or something. He said, "You can make this movie as long as it's not art."

EK: He used those words?
HK: Yeah. (laughs) That's what he said to me. I said, "Art? I hate art!" I remember a couple of years later bumping into him. They had shown *Gummo* at the Whitney Biennial. He was pissed off about it. He was like, "I *told* you I didn't want to make art!"

EK: But he still gave you around a million dollars to do what you wanted.
HK: Yeah, it could've even been more. I don't remember exactly. He said, "I tried to read your script and quit after page six. I have no idea what this is about but if you say it's going to be good and not just an artwork then I think we can fund it." So I was like, "Of course."

EK: This was the first instance when you showed a real disinterest in plot. Thinking back on it, how do you feel about this early manifestation of your creative process?
HK: Thinking about it now, you have to imagine, I felt like I was just on fire. In a way, I could say that I was interested in breaking down all these narrative devices, but it was something simpler than that—something within me. I needed to tell a story that way. I don't even know where it came from, but it felt like this movie was making itself. I'd lived all these

ideas and I really wanted to throw down the gauntlet with that film. I wanted to make a movie that caused the birds to chirp a different way. Obviously that doesn't always happen. It's like listening to music all the time and then when you decide to make it, it comes out a different way. I don't even know where it came from.

EK: But did the result meet the standards you set up for yourself?

HK: It's hard to explain. I didn't even envision it like a movie. I wasn't even referencing other films. I came back to Nashville and handed everyone cameras, telling them, "This is what I want to see." I'd say, "I want to shoot on Polaroid, video, Super 8mm." I would go into these areas, people's houses, and cast kids I'd grown up with. I was with [Jean-Yves] Escoffier [*Gummo*'s cinematographer], and we'd just walk around and it was all fair game. I wanted to make something that was completely new and entertaining, that would entertain me in some way. I think it was then, naively, that I had no doubt it would work. I just felt like there was some greatness to it. Not a conceit but just a purpose.

EK: Did you feel egotistical?

HK: I don't know. I definitely had an ego. I was just focused on greatness. I was thinking that if I never made another film, this movie should be able to stand alone with some type of significance. I wanted to destroy it all, pissing on it and rebuilding it.

EK: This was the root of what you called "mistakist" art.

HK: I started saying "mistakist" because generally the mistakes were what interested me—the awkwardness of things, the randomness. That's what I found transcendent, you know what I mean? It was never about perfection. It was always going to be perfect to me because I was doing it, but I felt like the answers and the poetry were in the mistakes, the accidents. I used to say it was like chemicals—putting all these elements together and shaking them up until they explode.

EK: Do you still feel that way?

HK: Yeah. I definitely feel like what I do now is more refined. I understand that power more and how to use it better. I can play with it, but in essence, it's still very close to what I used to do. It's very much about the specific movie you're making, the characters, and the environment. It's still a chemical cocktail. Remember, I was never trying to make a complete circle. I was always more concerned with missing pages. A lot of it,

with *Gummo* and other stuff, was about the stuff that wasn't included—
leaving the margins that were undefined.

EK: So you felt like you had really hit on something big.
HK: Something within myself. I was very much sure it was great regardless of what anyone said or felt. I knew even the people that came after
me were wrong.

EK: Do you still feel that way?
HK: Yeah. I watched *Gummo* five or six years ago. I think there's probably greatness in it.

EK: At that point, you entered into a whole new stage of interviews, including your appearances on *Late Night with David Letterman*. Did you
bring the same agenda to the cultivation of your public persona that you
brought to your filmmaking?
HK: I was having fun with it. It was a circus in which I enjoyed the mayhem. It was exciting for me. I was aware of what I was doing. Maybe I
was partially an idiot, but I also knew what was happening. A lot of the
things that people thought I was making up were true and the things
that were true were made up. So it just was a strange thing. I was just
always inventing things. Nothing began or ended. It all seemed like the
same to me. I wanted it to seem like everything was feeding everything
else. I didn't want anyone to know where things began or ended. Life
didn't feel like that to me. It was more abstract. Characters just existed.
Some things were true and others were not true but in the end it was all
true. Even the things that were made up were true.

EK: How much of your rebellious act was a reflection of genuine con-
victions? In an interview with Jefferson Hack in 1999, you complained
about people who disliked *Gummo* by saying, "the bourgeois fuckers . . .
must die."
HK: That kind of thing actually makes me cringe. A lot of it was probably
heavily narco-cized—do you know what I mean?

EK: Do you regret it?
HK: I don't regret anything. But when I was saying things like that, in
that way, a lot of it was just narco dreams, narco philosophies, hallucinatory rantings. I don't think you can take that too seriously.

EK: You weren't actually trying to change the world outside your own work.

HK: No, but also, remember, I was a kid. I was maybe delusional. There is this feeling that you can shift consciousness of the world. At that age there was so much desire and so much energy that nothing seemed impossible to me. You dream of blowing it all up. All I wanted was to be great.

EK: What was it like to take *Gummo* to Telluride and see people walk out within the first fifteen minutes?

HK: I was surprised. I remember that it was mostly older white people. I remember introducing the film and then I was outside. Herzog had also premiered *Little Dieter Needs to Fly*. I was in the parking lot with him and Dieter. I'd met Herzog six months earlier when [Telluride founder] Tom Luddy had shown him a copy of *Gummo*. Herzog called me out of the blue and said, "I've just seen your film, you're a foot soldier in the army, please come to San Francisco to meet me." In the parking lot at Telluride, people started walking out, and I thought maybe they didn't like the title credits. Then, after twenty or thirty minutes, more people were walking out. At least half the audience walked out in the first half hour, then they started yelling, "How could you make something so disgusting?" And I said, "I thought it was beautiful." I think I threw a rock at somebody. There was this writer from *Vogue* who tried to come after me. I pulled out a fork and tried to stab him. That was it. That was the first time I was like, "Wow, people don't like this stuff." (laughs) I realized that old white people *really* don't like it. It's a miracle that movie even exists.

EK: Still, even then, *Gummo* had its champions.

HK: With *Kids*, even the negative aspects were more expected. With this one, I was just figuring it all out, and had an extreme amount of love and accolades from people I really admired—and then there were a lot of people who just didn't get it or viewed it as some type of a bratty provocation. Mostly, at that point, the things that disturbed me were to hear grownups be dismissive. I had thought even the people who hated it would still see the merit in it. When people just come after you, when you're a kid, you don't know how to register that. I think I was pissed off, too. I didn't really care before; it was disturbing all of a sudden to find out that I cared. I would wake up every morning and find a fax machine filled with things. I don't get caught up in all that. I don't get bogged down in anything good or bad. I don't think about it too much. You always want people to enjoy the films. You never set out to make people hate or come after you. I know what I'm here to do. I'm not going to think about it too much—the compliments *or* the criticisms. It's all good. I honestly never felt there was a right or wrong way to do it. I would get frustrated that people would talk about the movies like they were riddles. I never wanted them to qualify themselves. It was the experience that was the movie.

EK: You weren't in favor of analysis of your work.

HK: I never really cared about truth, or some kind of idea of ultimate truth. It was transcendent, a more emotional truth, something more inexplicable. The films mostly deal with a tangible energy. I wanted to make films you could live through. I remember seeing Cassavetes' *Husbands* at Anthology Film Archives and felt like I had lived a life, gone through a heavy experience. It was amazing. But I was also entertained.

EK: At what point did your personal life start to complicate matters?

HK: After *Gummo*, all of a sudden, living in New York at that time was crazy. There was a lot of energy around—girls, narcotics, and stuff like that. I was getting into trouble. Later was when it got really bad, but at this point I was really experimenting.

EK: How did that scene impact what you wanted to do next?

HK: At a certain point, I remember becoming something of a shut-in. I didn't want to hang out so much. I started doing dope to make it easier, to make things quiet.

EK: What drugs did you do the most?

HK: Well, heroin. It was a lot of places. I was never a super-social drug user.

EK: Did that impact your creativity?

HK: I never worked high. I tried it. But I realized I had to set some parameters. I would make artwork high. I just wouldn't make movies high. I had always felt movies were sacred so I tried to keep myself awake as much as possible.

EK: So you didn't really think drugs had a positive effect even when you were doing them a lot.

HK: It was positive in that I enjoyed them a lot. I had a lot of fun on them. I liked being out of my mind. It was nice to medicate myself and make things quiet. But with the writing and directing, I didn't like it, because I knew enough to know that it could sway things. I always wanted to work in an emotional way. With drugs, it was anti-emotional, it was cutting emotions off. I would be trying to approximate emotions rather than conveying things in a true way.

Complete Harmony

Daniel Kraus / 2000

From *Gadfly*, January/February 2000. Reprinted with permission of *Gadfly* magazine, www.gadflyonline.com.

MOVIES:

1. A newspaper reporter realizes that his wife has been lying about her age. This makes him wonder what else she has been lying about.

4. A former prostitute with a low IQ poisons her priest.

16. A gay man gets hit by a car and no one cares.

The above excerpt is taken from Harmony Korine's 1998 "novel," *A Crackup at the Race Riots*, a collection of one-page vignettes, sketches, snatches of dialogue, celebrity rumors, really bad jokes, suicide notes, and imaginary letters from Tupac Shakur. Occasionally disarming in its lack of any distinct design or purpose, *Crack-Up* is, by its chaotically episodic nature, unsatisfying. But it does illuminate the inner workings of this twenty-five-year-old artist who is responsible for writing the brilliant, controversial *Kids* (1995), directing the misunderstood, but potentially life-changing *Gummo* (1997), and directing the immediate and disturbing new movie, *Julien Donkey-Boy*.

Also found in *Crack-Up* are lists labeled "Titles of Books I Will Write," "Rumors," and "Her Two Favorite Cigarette Jokes." As with all things in Korine's art, they are instantaneous thoughts, caught on the cusp of being cultivated, stopped short and thrown immediately into the artistic mix. And, like most ideas before they're ruined via committee, they are sole and streamlined and, therefore, fascinating.

Korine's first film, *Gummo*, was a surreal, yet extremely authentic, nonlinear nightmare mash of improvisation, documentary footage, and fictional scenes detailing the scattered, ruptured community of children in the tornado-ravaged town of Xenia, Ohio. The only nod at continuity involved two recurring characters, Solomon and Tummler, as they wandered through the town of albinos, deaf-mutes, and black dwarves, killing cats and selling them to a Chinese restaurant. After *Gummo*'s 1997 release, Korine became the stuff of nihilist legend. His film was so loathed by mainstream media (the *New York Times* called *Gummo* "the worst movie of the year") that critics like CNN's Paul Tatara joined the thrashing of the uppity youngster, cracking that the film was "the cinematic equivalent of Korine making fart noises and eating boogers." The *New Yorker*'s David Denby called it "beyond redemption." Meanwhile, the unfazed Korine made a legendary, quietly aggressive appearance on *Late Night with David Letterman* and gave repeated interviews trashing such current Generation X film heroes as Kevin Smith (*Clerks*, *Chasing Amy*). If this is the future of film, preached Korine, then I want to be dead.

Aside from the endorsement of high-status fellow provocateurs like Bernardo Bertolucci, Abel Ferrara, and Gus Van Sant (who aptly called Korine's shiftless, watchful characters "heavy-metal Holden Caulfields"), no one wanted to be near the kid, lest they catch his fatal media disease. Then, as Korine prepared his new film *Julien Donkey-Boy*, the notorious Danish filmmaker and rule-breaker Lars von Trier (*Breaking the Waves*, *The Idiots*) rang Korine and asked if he would like *Julien* to be an official "Dogme 95" release (more on Dogme 95 later). Korine, whose ideals of realism were already heading in a Dogme direction (Korine was planning to shoot most of *Julien* with hidden, spy, and surveillance cameras), said yes.

I hung out with Korine on the eve of his U.S. premiere at the New York Film Festival.

Daniel Kraus: I want to read you this quote: "To me, the great hope is that now these little 8mm video recorders and stuff will come out and some people who normally wouldn't make movies will be making them and suddenly one day . . ."

Harmony Korine: The Coppola quote?

DK: Yeah, " . . . and suddenly one day, some little fat girl in Ohio is going to be the next Mozart and make a beautiful film with her father's little camera, and for once the so-called professionalism of movies will be destroyed forever and it will become an art form."

HK: That's a good quote. It's like he's making better quotes than movies.

DK: That's what I was thinking.

HK: For me, just speculating, it's like [Coppola] wishes one thing but he can't do what he really wants to do, because he's got like one hundred wine cellars and four thousand people to feed and has to live in some kind of mansion and can't be the Fat Girl that he really wants to be.

DK: I know, and it's hard to feel sorry for him. He used to be so good. It makes me wonder: Is film dead?

HK: It's a weird thing, all these sixties critics that decided on "auteur-ism" in film and what cinema is in a very narrow definition. A lot of them have declared the death of cinema. But for me, in a historical context, you have to look at it next to something like the novel, where the written word has been around for so long and come full circle so many times, with something like James Joyce's *Ulysses* and all these novels that have done so much. Film to me, after one hundred years, is just in its infancy, it's just now being born, it's like a foot coming out of the birth canal. There's so much more room for it to progress and get more complicated and more interesting. That's not to say I have faith in a movement or group of filmmakers that are going to push it ahead. But there'll always be a few people who are concerned with this stagnation and want to prevent it in film.

DK: Would you say we're at such stagnation now?

HK: Definitely, for the past, you know, since the eighties, and there's a lot to that, what audiences want and what they're willing to accept and if they even want an "art film" to exist, if they even want to be challenged in a different way.

DK: I don't know if the "art film" does exist anymore. We just have a lot of these Sundance "indies" that follow a very rigid "indie" formula.

HK: Yeah, they're just like regular movies but look worse. The idea of independent cinema is like, to me, there's no such thing. It's like alternative music. What is it alternative to? I mean, I'm not an "independent" director; I make my movies through a studio system. It's just that I'm independent minded, maybe.

DK: What was the last movie you saw?

HK: I saw the new Woody Allen [*Sweet and Lowdown*]. I haven't really liked a lot of his later pictures; his new film was just kind of minor. The thing about Woody Allen is that even a bad Woody Allen movie is better than 99 percent of movies that come out.

DK: Did you see Spike Lee's *Summer of Sam*?
HK: I walked out of it. I was just bored.

DK: A movie I didn't like was Kubrick's *Eyes Wide Shut*.
HK: I didn't like it either. I mean, the whole thing was just depressing. It wasn't a great picture.

DK: But surely there's one popular filmmaker you like who is "independent minded"?
HK: Not really. There's nothing about everyday films or filmmakers that excites me.

Since Dogme 95's inception in 1995, the once-laughable declaration of apparent pomposity has turned into the most influential film movement of our time. The "Vow of Chastity" set out by von Trier and fellow Dane filmmaker Thomas Vinterberg (*The Celebration*), was an attempt to shake off the falsity and distance that the mechanizations of modern cinema impose on the art and to narrow the chasm between actor and filmmaker. Included among the rules: no sets, no lights, no props, no sound effects, no musical score, no tripod, no superficial actions (guns, murders, etc.), and no credited director.

It is perhaps fortuitous that Dogme 95 surfaces just as the so-called "Digital Revolution" is dawning. Although predicting the rise of a revolution before it happens is rather suspicious, the hoopla surrounding the cheap, high-quality digital cameras now available has some merit. It seems that we are heading into an age in which the practical occupation ceases to exist; we'll all be filmmakers with our own home computer editing systems, and the already saturated film market will reach a hurricane-status flood. However, despite this deluge, as Steven Soderbergh (herald of the original Sundance "revolution" with his 1989 film *sex, lies and videotape*) is credited as noting, there will still be only two or three good movies a year. It'll just take more work to find them.

Dogme 95 embraces and gives artistic credibility to the Digital Revolution and is very aware of the particular aesthetic properties that video carries with it—a "cheap" look and a sense of intimacy that until now have been used only for very personal home videos. Although seemingly exclusive in nature (an accepted film gets to put a big, official-looking certificate at its start), the supposed democratic beauty of Dogme 95 is that anyone with a video camera and a dream can join.

During Korine's first Q&A at the New York Film Festival, he used such lofty phrases as "the Dogme Brotherhood" and "a redemption in cinematic terms." The Danish filmmakers added, "Dogme 95 desires to purge film, so that once again the inner lives of characters justify the plot." "Purge," by the way, isn't a nice word. To purge is to rid of impurities, to empty the bowels. Take this pill, this magic vow of chastity, and rid yourself of the shit of your art.

It isn't hard to see why some regard Dogme with disdain.

DK: What were some of the problems that you ran into while making a Dogme film?

HK: There's no problems I had with Dogme. Dogme's just like this set plan, that if you follow these ten rules, you'll be forced to reckon with something, some kind of truth or some kind of substance that you couldn't get if you were making a film in a different way.

DK: Vinterberg, after he finished *The Celebration*, drew up a list of ways he had cheated the Vows. Give me some of your own examples.

HK: How I cheated? Or how I sinned?

DK: Is that what they call it?

HK: Yeah, a sin against the Vow of Chastity. Just really technical things. . . . I mean, Chloë [Sevigny, star of *Julien* and *Gummo* and occasional Korine flame] wasn't really pregnant, so we had to put a fake belly on her. [The actual "confession" states that Korine would have to impregnate Sevigny himself, but there wasn't enough time.]

DK: There's a scene in which Julien's father relates a story in voice-over while we watch his daughter cut his hair. I thought a voice-over was against the rules.

HK: Not how we did it. We used a microcassette recorder and taped him telling the story to live music. When we filmed that scene, we had Anthony [Dod Mantle, the cinematographer of both *Julien* and *Celebration*] holding a one-chip camera in his hand, and we played the song into the camera's speaker, and it was all done naturally on the spot.

DK: Cinema has always been predicated around a certain artificiality, though. Dogme 95 says that all Dogme filmmakers must declare "I am not an artist" and even reject screen credit. Yet you use overt narrative and editing techniques that really draw me out of the story and make me contend with you as a distinct artist. Isn't that at odds with Dogme?

HK: No, that's the irony of all of this; it's an anti-aesthetic approach to filmmaking, but if you look at every one of the Dogme films, there's a unique artistry involved. I think it's one of the things that attract certain directors to Dogme. Even though it's like an anti-auteurist, anti-bourgeois rescue action, you still end up with a very artful group of films.

DK: You seem to abhor plot.

HK: Well, I like stories, and I don't mind the narrative. I think there's a narrative to *Julien*. I just think that plots are so easy, and it's always one of the things in movies that in general kills it for me, because it's like this simple device that's thrown in arbitrarily to keep audiences happy. In life I never feel or see plot, I just see things as existing, and I just want my films to mimic that.

DK: To achieve that, you use "real" footage mixed in with your fictional stuff, like the little kids swearing and the handicapped girl who shaves her eyebrows off for the camera in *Gummo*. Those two scenes piss a lot of people off.

HK: I had heard those kids cursing around, "suck my cock," at the craft service table, and I was like "holy shit." I had never heard kids talk like that, you know, little babies, so I asked their parents if I could put them in the movie and they were like, "I don't give a fuck what they do." So, yeah, it's real as far as she was actually shaving her eyebrows, it's really happening, but it is doubly compounded by the fact that there's no history of realism in America, except for maybe John Cassavetes. It's like the history of American cinema is escapist cinema and in England all they have is realism.

DK: So, in *Gummo*, you're essentially saying that cats are tortured, kids piss off overpasses, and handicapped people have sex every damn day.

HK: Yeah, right, but as soon as you show it, these are things certain people don't want to see.

DK: I think it's because you're removing them from their context, their own hypothetical documentaries. For example, who is the eyebrow woman? What is her official medical condition? You just leave us with the condition itself.

HK: But I think documentary is fake as well. I'm manipulating all my characters, so in one way, my movies aren't that much different than *Star Wars*.

DK: And, along those lines, you'd say *Star Wars* is not that different from a . . .
HK: A documentary, right, surely, in the way that people go about getting what they want in order to make a dramatic feature. The whole thing for me is: What I remember from films are specific scenes and images, so in my movies I don't want to have to hear the story to justify the images, I just want to make a movie to see [those images], only.

DK: Every adult I encountered hated *Gummo*, but most kids love it.
HK: Yeah, yeah, yeah, yeah, it's weird, I just started to notice that, it's like an ageism, an ageist sort of thing. It's like my first memory growing up in Tennessee was Ozzy [Osborne]. When I was ten years old, I had never heard of Ozzy, but all the parents in the churches were getting upset because Ozzy was coming to town, and it was the first time I heard people with a passion saying something was horrible for kids, so I had to see it, I had to see Ozzy, because all the parents were against him.

DK: Marilyn Manson said about you, "I'm relieved that America has someone new to hate other than me."
HK: I don't know about that.

Julien Donkey-Boy, which has already garnered a surprise rave from *Entertainment Weekly* ("an astonishing leap forward . . . out of the [Dogme] limitations has come aesthetic brilliance") as well as a rather hesitant recommendation from old Korine nemesis the *New York Times* ("visually arresting"), seems poised to grant Korine what, to a certain extent, he deserves: credit as a harbinger of change and a potentially major influence in cinema. In fact, it's hard to imagine seeing his two films and not being influenced by them; their vivid images burn into your eyes.

The mainstream media seem to be waiting for Korine to "grow up" and step into the shoes of an adult narrative filmmaker. But what these critiques seem to miss is that Korine never looks down on his misfits—he's always hunkered right down among them, watching them to such a thorough extent that it begins to be a free-for-all of unprecedented honesty. What's so shocking to the younger generation of Korine viewers is not that elementary school kids smoke pot and kill cats, or that middle schoolers sniff glue and have sex, or that high schoolers dress up like girls for kiddie-porn Polaroids; it's that someone has put it accurately on film. This is the Truth, shows Korine to the older generations, and it is uglier than Hell.

But it is a Hell handled with startling tenderness and empathy. Having grown up in the carnival and educated himself, Korine finds pieces of humanity, if not of himself, in each of his miscreant characters. Among those miscreants are Julien, a wild-haired, gold-toothed schizophrenic, his pregnant ballerina sister, his athletically driven brother, his blind ice-skating girlfriend, and his calmly domineering father, played with an eerie tranquility by famed director Werner Herzog, who originally championed *Gummo* to the International Critics' Prize at the 1997 Venice Film Festival. Interestingly, Herzog's own films (most notably the 1982 film *Fitzcarraldo* where, to shoot the hauling of a boat over a mountain, Herzog actually hauled a boat over a mountain) epitomize the extreme ends of the kind of firsthand filmmaking that Dogme and Korine strive for.

DK: How did you feel that this first screening of *Julien* went?
HK: I wasn't there.

DK: I wasn't sure everyone was into it. Does that worry you?
HK: I don't really make movies for a massive audience or for a general audience, but an audience that's willing to take on a certain kind of film.

DK: So, I guess 20 percent of a grab-bag festival audience is sort of on track for you.
HK: Uh, yeah, I guess. (laughs)

DK: For the first twenty minutes of the movie, Julien, our protagonist, is really scary. Was this intentional?
HK: The thing is, the disease of mental illness, it is very scary. And at least with what I've witnessed with my uncle [the basis of the Julien character], it's extremely scary on the outside and it's so hard to get past that appearance. I wanted to show a dimension to Julien that you think he's going to be one way and he's not in fact at all that way.

DK: I like that, how he changes.
HK: Well, really he doesn't change appearance, physically. You just become more at ease with him as the movie goes.

DK: But it's a change on our part—
HK: Right, exactly.

DK: There are many issues of family in *Julien*, whereas in *Kids* and *Gummo* there was a distinct lack of family.
HK: Yeah, but in *Gummo* and even in *Kids*, it's like there is a sense of family, it's just more scattered, or it's just like these two sisters [in *Gummo*] are the only family they have. With *Julien*, I wanted to show a more complex unit and how they all deal with Julien's illness in a different way, like his father feels only shame and hatred and resentment and the brother is embarrassed and the grandmother is just oblivious and the sister is very affectionate.

DK: There's a scene where the brother, who is training to be a wrestler, beats up a garbage can. It's a lot like the chair beating in *Gummo*.
HK: (pause) I guess it's a motif. I like people wrestling with these kinds of objects. (laughs)

DK: I love that you found Nick Sutton [one of the stars of *Gummo*] on an episode of *Sally Jesse Raphael* entitled "My Child Died from Sniffing Paint." Any similar discoveries in *Julien*?
HK: I always keep a pen and pad on my bed and whenever I'm watching television late at night and there's something unique on, I jot it down. A few years ago I had seen this documentary made like twenty years ago on the Learning Channel at two in the morning, and there was this guy playing the drums with his toes and it was an amazing image. I'd written him into this movie, not knowing if he was still alive or if we'd ever find him. We had people track him down in Canada and it took three months or something.

DK: Julien hears lots of voices. I got the impression that one of them was God.
HK: Hmm. I mean, yeah, that could be right, that sounds as good as anything else I've heard.

DK: And another of the voices is obviously Hitler.
HK: A lot of it's just stuff I've seen my uncle do and it's just me basically regurgitating it. As far as how I see it or what my intent was, it really doesn't matter, 'cause it's just another opinion ultimately.

DK: Did your uncle hear Hitler?

HK: It was always, "Christ, trying to kill me, Christ, Christ," this, that and the other, and there were always religious figures and Hitler and, well, there'd be Frank Sinatra and Jesus Christ.

DK: I see a lot of similarities between your work and the films of John Waters. Waters uses so-called "freaks" as actors. You use so-called "freaks," too.

HK: Yeah, but he's using his characters to make fun of them, and that's something I try never to do. If I use a character that somebody considers grotesque, I'll try to go the opposite way with them.

DK: Maybe this is why people are so vehement in their dislike and mistrust of you. It's almost impossible to separate film and filmmaker, especially in "exploitation" film. Even Dogme 95 stated that they were willing to proceed "at the cost of any good taste." Since both you and Waters are obviously using real "freaks," then that must mean that you consort with these freaks and therefore that you are not to be trusted and it is not beyond you to pull some dangerous and illegal shit.

HK: Of course, yeah, sure. Definitely.

It seems to me that Harmony Korine has been mislabeled. He is not a bad-boy shockmeister or petulant demon-child; instead, he goes to great pains to explain that it is not and was never his intention to shock anyone. And though that seems slightly naive, I understand the intention behind these words—he wants to give screen time to those who've never been given it. "The media are in New York and L.A.," explained Korine. "And anything that happens in the middle they either don't want to see, or they're going to fabricate. So when they do see [an accurate portrayal] they're going to get angry, or deny it, or not want to like it."

Korine is not disrespectful, angry, or even, for that matter, possessed of genius—he himself has trouble explaining why he makes certain artistic choices. What Korine does possess, however, is an extraordinary ability to watch life move around him and to pluck out the moments which cry out the loudest. It is his luck—and our good fortune—that there are people who will take a chance on an instinct without convention, fear, or even a script (*Julien* was entirely improvised). Though his influences seem overtly European, he stoutly maintains that he is "an American boy," and his appetite for American pop-culture is, refreshingly, subordinate to his affection for an American subculture.

A random, untitled Q&A from his novel:

> Q: A person can characterize himself as a democrat, a tyrant, a Christian, a resistor, an anarchist, a liberal, a conservative. How do you describe yourself?
> A: I'm a romantic anarchist.

DK: I noticed folk singer Will Oldham in the credits of *Julien Donkey-Boy*. Why?
HK: He actually named it. (laughs) You're the first person I've told that to, but it's true. He just called me up one day and said [in a country accent], "You gotta call it *Julien Donkey-Boy*."(laughs) He's a good friend of mine.

DK: Would you say you know how to make a movie?
HK: Well, I've made movies, so, well, I know how to. . . . Yeah, I know how to make a movie.

DK: But if someone gave you $80 million to make a movie, what would you do?
HK: I'd probably make twenty little movies. Or maybe not, if I had a movie that was $80 million worth of story. But it's rare that I would think there are stories that require $80 million to tell.

DK: There's probably not. I can't think of any.
HK: I can't either. (laughs)

Conversations in World Cinema

Richard Peña / 2000

Originally broadcast on the Sundance Channel in June 2000. Published with acknowledgement of the network.

Richard Peña: Please welcome Harmony Korine. So what are your first memories of the movies? When did you first start going? When did they first seem like a special world to you?

Harmony Korine: The first time I really remember wanting to make movies was seeing Buster Keaton in *Steamboat Bill, Jr.* I loved Keaton. That's when I knew there was something in cinema that I'd never seen before, a kind of poetry.

RP: What about other early memories? Did you make a distinction between European and American art movies?

HK: I got really voracious with films later in adolescence when I started to watch a lot of movies. I'd be watching Douglas Sirk or something and then found out about Fassbinder and how he was influenced by Sirk to make melodramas. That's how I began to really find out about other directors.

RP: What about short films? Were you already making them when you wrote the screenplay for *Kids*?

HK: No, I mean, I'd made one short film in high school—but for me, I didn't really see that much purpose in short films. This idea of short films—it was fun to maybe experiment, but I never saw short movies so I was never really interested in short films. I was more interested in writing. I always knew I was going to make movies, that I was going to make features. For me, I was never interested in telling other people's stories, so I just figured that was the reason I had to write my own stories.

RP: What does a screenplay need for you? As a professor at a film school,

I know there are a lot of techniques that are taught about acts. What's most important for you? Is it character? Situation?

HK: For me, I think it's basically . . . it's different. I'm not so concerned with this idea of plot in films, this device that drives the story. It just seems like a really old idea. What I remember about the great films—what I remember about films in general—is usually specific scenes and characters. So for me, right from the beginning, I was always interested in writing scripts that basically consisted of that: just scenes and characters without really having to explain things. We've had one hundred years of cinema and we're at a point now where films are becoming more and more redundant. They have been for a while. The screenplay format—this idea of a screenplay—is pretty much indicative of the final product. I don't really believe in the traditional screenplay. I think it falls flat. I think it's pretty much useless.

RP: What did you give to Larry Clark for *Kids*? Was that a more "traditional" kind of screenplay?

HK: Yeah, I mean, that was the first script I'd ever written. I'd just graduated high school and he was really eager to make that film. At the time, I was also watching a lot of these transcendentalist films. I was really into, like, Ozu, Bresson, Dreyer. These movies where the story would just evolve. That was really the most traditional script I'd written. But at the same time, when I was writing that—it seems so long ago now—I'd never really worked with outlines. I didn't even know how it was going to end until I got to page seventy of the script. I was just sitting in my bed thinking about it.

RP: Did more formal scripts exist for *Gummo* and *Julien Donkey-Boy* or were those outlines that evolved in the process?

HK: I was starting to deconstruct more with each movie. With *Gummo*, it was basically scripted up to a point. The scenes that worked best were those where the actors would leave my ideas or take my dialogue somewhere else. I started to think about that when I was writing my next movie, how bored I am with writing dialogue and imposing these dead words on something that's real and in front of me. So I wanted to improvise a movie around different random scenarios and ideas. That was *Julien Donkey-Boy*. That would allow me, as a director, to concoct things—like chemicals. For me, it's more exciting to set things up in a chaotic environment and then document this chaos.

[Clip of Herzog in *Julien Donkey-Boy* plays: "Tell him to slap his face!"]

RP: Was it harder finding people willing to go with you? Because I think usually people want more safety nets.

HK: It wasn't really hard for me to find the actors. I approached the people that I felt were perfect for the roles. I said that once you're in character, once you're *in* character, that anything you choose to say or not to say is really right. There's really no wrong. Once you are that person, once you become that character, then anything that happens within the context of that scenario is real life. That took some of the pressure off. It made things better.

RP: There's this magic word, "dogme." It's certainly on the minds and lips of so many critics when they talk about your work or just new cinema in general. What was your first contact with the people from the Dogme group and your reaction to their films—*The Celebration, The Idiots*—when you saw them?

HK: I like both of those movies. And I liked Lars Von Trier's films from before that. For me, it was interesting, because Dogme approaches cinema as if it were a rescue mission. A lot of it is also a reaction to the failure of this sixties new wave—the bourgeois romanticism of this auteurist filmmaking and how it failed, pretty much, except for Godard. So I liked the idea, and I liked the Vow of Chastity, which was like a ten-step technical guide to filmmaking. I think that by following these rules, it's important, it forces you to reckon with something that's not an ultimate truth but that's perhaps more truthful and intimate in filmic terms than doing a different kind of film.

RP: Did working digitally open up things for you? I read somewhere that you shot something like eighty hours or so for *Julien Donkey-Boy*. What's it like in the thirtieth take?

HK: Well, the hours weren't really spent shooting multiple takes. It was more that I really wanted to use up to twenty-five cameras at once.

RP: How were you using all those cameras at once?

HK: Before Dogme, pretty much right after *Gummo*, I started to think about why I was attracted to video. It wasn't because of the aesthetic of video. It was more that I liked the idea that it allowed me to work as quickly as my mind worked. I didn't have to wait for crews to set up. I could improvise in cameras as quickly as I could improvise with the

actors in the scene. I wanted to be able to make a film where I could improvise almost like you improvise with music. The only way I could do
that was to shoot it digitally. This movie was much more cerebral than
anything I'd done previously because a lot it was like geometry. I'd have
to question myself, because I'd have to think to myself, "Why am I using
twenty-five cameras? Why do I need that?" And also, "Where am I going
to put twenty-five cameras so that they're not revealing one another?" It
was difficult but it was good.

RP: After you had the twenty-five cameras and the footage, what's the
editing process like?
HK: For me, each stage—the writing, the production, the editing—are
equally important. I want to make each stage equally unique. I wanted
to approach it in a really kinetic, improvised way. I worked with a Danish
editor, this woman who wore like four scarves and mittens and smoked a
pipe. She was really good. I didn't let her watch any of the footage until
the shooting was finished.

RP: Had she read a script?
HK: Yeah, she did read the script. But the movie was entirely different
from the script. By the time it was finished, it was a different movie. So
when she got to each scene, we were editing it much in the same way we
were shooting it, in this improvised, very natural, excited way. She also
didn't know what was coming next. She was really attacking each scene
on its own merit. So it was fun.

RP: In terms of Dogme, there are ideas about music. One of the things
you see so much in films these days is wall-to-wall music. Did that limit
you or how do you like to work with music?
HK: Well, I love music in movies. I think film is ultimately the most
complex art form. You have everything: sight, sound, text if you want
it. I always think of the sound and the image not necessarily having to
be connected or related. So with music—a lot of times I take the sound
from something different. It's kind of like a collage. With this picture I
wanted a lot of music, but because it was Dogme, it had to be done live.
We always had bands running around playing music behind the scenes.
(laughs)

RP: Was that distracting?
HK: No, it was great. It was fun.

RP: Let's take a few questions from people we have in the studio.

Audience Member: In *Kids*, the colloquialisms that your characters use were really believable, very urban, even a lot of the situations that went on—like that whole scene in the park where they jump that kid. I mean, for me, growing up inside that sort of community, I've seen that that's exactly how things happen. I was wondering where your link to that was.

HK: Right when I moved to the city, I used to skateboard. All those guys in the movie, they were all my friends. None of them are actors. I wrote the script with those people in mind. For some reason, it's this strange thing, I can hear people's voices. I can hear cadences, how people say what they say. It was really simple for me, really natural for me to write it in that dialect. I was writing for those people, with them in mind.

Audience Member: Have you been influenced by documentary at all? Can you talk about a couple of scenes in *Gummo*—like the scene where the two brothers begin slugging each other, or the scene where they tear apart the kitchen—how did you arrive at scenes like that?

HK: Documentary is like anything else. If it's a good documentary, I like it. But I can never make documentaries because for me, even cinema verite is still a lie. There's still a manipulation involved. There's still a point of view. It's like fiction filmmaking. The movie doesn't get made on its own. For me, I never really had the patience to make a documentary, like a straight documentary. Those scenes in the movie—because the kind of storytelling I was trying to do was in a different direction, when you see those brothers beat each other up, it came from trust. I grew up with those kids. I grew up in that neighborhood and those were brothers I'd known since I was a little boy. That goes with this whole idea of setting up an environment and getting people to do things. It was kind of a—I use this word a lot—it was a "mistakist" art form, because it's like whispering something in one guy's ear, then whispering something in another guy's ear, two different things. I'd tell this one guy to throw the refrigerator at his brother and tell the other to, you know, spit on him. Then I'd walk out of the room and see what happens. With that, they just ran out of things to say and just started hitting each other. It wasn't scripted. (laughs)

Audience Member: Could you talk a little bit about your fight project? Is that ever going to be released? Is it a goof on *Fight Club* at all?

HK: No, no. I never even heard of *Fight Club* until yesterday. (laughs) I've never seen that movie so I could never goof on it. But I was in a strange frame of mind about eight months ago. I didn't really know what was going on with my life. I had this idea of making a really great comedy where I'd get in fights with people in the street. It would be a cross between Buster Keaton and a snuff movie. (audience laughter) I was really delusional, because I think I wanted the movie to be a ninety-minute feature, the funniest film ever made, like a really high concept comedy—almost like the sequel to *Caddyshack*. I'd have these camera crews following me around and the only rule was that I couldn't throw the first punch. No matter how bad I was getting beat up, unless it looked like they were going to kill me, nobody could stop the fight. I wanted to fight every demographic. I had to fight a lesbian, I had to fight a Jew, a Puerto Rican, a black. That was really important to me. I made it through about six fights and I got really messed up. My ribs were broken. I got both my ankles broken. The thing is, I also wanted to make the great tap dance film. (audience laughter) I just saw this whole tradition of tap going nowhere. I bought this pair of Capezio tap shoes. I took to it, it was really natural. I was inventing new moves. So I was making this film called *Tap* at the same time that I was doing this fight film. After my ankles were broken, it totally fucked my tap career up. My tap movie was screwed as well. I was really wrong when I started this movie because I'd forgotten how short a natural fight lasts. I mean, they're really brutal. So anyway, I fought like six times. The way I wanted to piece it together was that it was only the violence, no explanation, just one repetitive bone-breaker after the next. The most violent you could get. So I ended up in the hospital and arrested and stuff. Then I realized there was only about twelve minutes worth of footage. (laughs)

RP: So you made a short!
HK: Yeah, now it's a short. And I just don't think I have what it takes to go the whole ninety. So I don't know when it's going to come out. Or maybe I'll show it somewhere in a museum or something.

Split Screen: Harmony Korine

John Pierson / 2000

Originally broadcast on IFC in August 2000. Published courtesy of Split Screen/Grainy Pictures © 2000.

John Pierson: Good evening. I'm John Pierson and we're at New York City's Screening Room. Welcome to another installment of Split Screen, a series of twelve interviews associated with the excellent Faber & Faber publication *Projections*.
Harmony Korine: Shut the fuck up!

JP: (laughing) Keep rolling. The theme is film and filmmaking in New York. That was the voice of Harmony Korine, writer-director of *Gummo*, writer-director of *Julien Donkey-Boy*, and writer of one of the prototypical New York City street movies, *Kids*, which is why it's a little odd that you've actually abandoned this fair town, haven't you?
HK: Yeah, I can't stand it.

JP: Why is that?
HK: Well, I don't live here anymore, I'm not from here, and I've never liked it. To be honest with you, I don't even know why I lived here. I just think that for an artist or filmmaker, this city does things to you that aren't natural. I think it's because there are so many people on top of you all the time. At least, me, it was really difficult to concentrate. I was constantly distracted. I personally don't like being around lots of people.

JP: So let me ask you something. You're clearly really serious about your art and it's very good art. You're also extremely playful in how you've presented yourself since *Kids*. Your biography, back in the early days, was an incredible series of—please pardon me—fabrications.
HK: The thing is, a lot of people think they're fabrications but a lot of them are true. I did spend many months in the circus as a child and

Huntz Hall—well, actually, Huntz Hall wasn't my grandfather. That was something that I just threw out there because I was a big fan of his.

JP: However, I did see you up on stage at the press conference for *Julien Donkey-Boy* at the New York Film Festival and you did seem to be trying— I don't know whether you felt compelled to work harder to get people to see what you knew would be a challenging film for them, but you really did seem to be . . . behaving yourself, I guess.

HK: There's a difference between the films and myself as a person. With the films, I won't try and make it easier on the viewer, but I'll take that side very seriously. When it comes to myself, that's a different story. So insight into the work is one thing, but insight into myself . . . I mean, to me, the work is the ultimate insight into who I am. I've always said that if anyone cared they could learn more about me by watching the films and reading my writing than spending ten years locked in a room with me. It's true. A lot of the work I can't explain. There's no specific reason why it's up there on the screen. A lot of it is stuff that I'm afraid of, and that's why I put it up there, because if it scared me as a person or if it's something that I'm frightened of, then I know it's right.

JP: When you put somebody like Werner Herzog in your movie, somebody whose films I'm sure you grew up loving—

HK: He's a huge hero.

JP: He's kind of found a way to talk about his work that sometimes helps people enter it.

HK: Knowing Werner, I know differently, actually. I know that Werner cares very little in the end about explaining his work to anyone. He cares very little about even promoting his films. The idea is just to keep continuing, that it's his process that's important. For Werner—and this is one of the things we have in common—it's almost like going to battle when you make a film. It's a battle of discovery and obsession. The reason I make movies is that it's a process of discovery and creating some kind of chaos and beginning to sculpt that chaos into some kind of form.

JP: How much farther can that chaos go? In the case of shooting *Gummo* on conventional film, you could only shoot so much, but with *Julien*, because you were shooting digital with multiple cameras, you had a ton of material.

HK: Each film takes on a different structure. I love stories, I hate plots. That's basically the thing. I deconstruct my films. I'm interested in telling stories in completely different ways. I don't see things in a linear fashion, with beginnings, middles, and ends. I see stories just as I see life: Just existing.

JP: I'm sure you know that famous Godard quote . . .
HK: Of course, yeah.

JP: Well, you do it.
HK: I think it's, "All movies need a beginning, middle, and end, just not in that order." That one, right?

JP: Very early on in his career, before he actually made *Breathless*.
HK: Right.

JP: Let me go back to *Kids* for a moment. I'm going to be chronological if you can forgive me my conventional mind. Larry Clark directed that film. The way the story goes is that there's this element of him having "discovered" you. And I'm wondering how that, as a verb, makes you feel. Were you just waiting to explode anyway?
HK: I would've made movies regardless. I grew up watching films throughout my life. That was the one consistency throughout my life. I wasn't a child writer. I wasn't what you would call a prodigy. I just knew I would make films at a very early age. As far as *Kids*, what happened was that I never went to film school, I had never written a script before, and I was sitting in a park and Larry Clark came up to me and started taking photos of me. I had no idea who Larry Clark was. We started speaking and got in a conversation. He told me he wanted to make movies and that he was a photographer. And I said, "*I'm* gonna make movies." So he asked me to write this story for him. *Kids* was never a story that I was destined or born to write. I wouldn't have written it. For me, *Kids* is more of a commissioned work. It was very traditional. That was what he wanted. He wanted something very traditional, very narrative. It was almost transcendental. The story was very basic. So I went home and wrote that script in about a week, in seven days. I wrote one draft of it and that's what it became.

For me, the idea of it even becoming a film really wasn't even fathomable. I'd just moved up there that summer. These were the kids that

I knew. I had an ear for dialogue and cadence, things of that nature. So I could really remember how people speak in conversations verbatim. So it was very simple for me to write with that in mind. I wasn't interested in the plot at all. To me, the whole AIDS thing was a device. It was a way to sell the film, to get people hooked and watching the movie. I was more concerned with showing teenagers. I mean, I was a teenager at that point. But as soon as that movie was finished, I knew I never wanted to write films for other people and I knew that I didn't want other people to write films for me. With *Gummo*, I immediately began to write films in the way I saw and heard images. . . . I needed to leave Tennessee before I could go back and tell a story about it properly. Those were the kids I knew, a lot of the kids I went to school with.

[Clip from *Gummo* plays.]

There will be people that love my work and people that dislike it. That'll always be the case and that's fine.

[Second clip from *Gummo* plays.]

HK: I don't really consider myself a part of the American independent scene. I know that I've been somehow lumped into that, but I don't really feel that I have peers amongst so-called independent filmmaking. In fact, I don't even really understand the idea of independent filmmaking anymore. I think now the idea that a Miramax film is independent—Miramax is owned by Disney. . . . I've made every one of my films through a studio: New Line, Fine Line. . . .

JP: You've got Ted Turner back there somewhere supporting you and being horrified by it.
HK: Yes, so Ted Turner is in a way responsible for *Gummo* and *Julian Donkey-Boy*. For me, Clint Eastwood is as independent a filmmaker as John Cassavetes is. His vision is as dark and singular as any present-day independent filmmaker. And he's as much a hero of mine as someone like Fassbinder.

JP: It was surprising to hear you cite [as an influence], in an interview with Tod Lippy, one of the orangutan movies with Eastwood—
HK: Oh, *Every Which Way But Loose*. Yeah, but it's really true, if you think about how strange it is. You have this great American icon who, during

the seventies, made three films back to back with an orangutan. That's a really interesting conceptual thing.

JP: There does seem to be a spirit in the air with you of really enjoying certain acts of provocation, which isn't the same thing as a morality debate. Is this true?

HK: Definitely. I think my main purpose with me joining Dogme '95 and becoming part of the brotherhood was because it was at least in the beginning a great act of provocation. But I don't think of myself as a rebel or as a filmmaker who's naive in trying to create a new cinema. I've read that before. When I went to Europe, there were many critics who were saying that I'm the spokesperson for some kind of post-*nouvelle vague*. I don't see things like that. I see myself in the traditions of many filmmakers. I don't see myself as all of a sudden just coming out of nowhere and inventing something. There's a tradition of certain filmmakers, starting with Griffith, or even with Lumiere and Buster Keaton and Dreyer and obviously Godard and Fassbinder. And then you have Cassavetes, the great one. For me, I'd just rather be a part of that lineage than some poster child for some post-*nouvelle vague* cinema.

JP: Does it surprise you, for all the acclaim you get, when people start hating you?

HK: No, I want that, and I think in a lot of ways I deserve that. I consider myself a commercial filmmaker—commercial in that I want people to see my movies. In the end, the movies are made for the people. With *Fight Harm*, the movie I was making where I would go and have camera crews following me on the street, this was the ultimate provocation. I wanted to make the great American comedy. I wanted it to be a cross between something like Buster Keaton and a snuff film, where I would go up to people and do whatever I had to do to make them hit me, fight me. I would never throw the first punch. The only rule—I set up rules—the only rule was that no one was allowed to break up the fight unless it looked like I was going to be murdered. That was really the only rule. And that I couldn't throw the first punch.

I was a bit delusional and very mentally unhealthy when I was making that movie, because I wanted to make it ninety minutes long and just consist of one fight after the other—one brutal confrontation after the next. What happened was that I ended up in the hospital many times with broken ankles, broken ribs, and concussions. And that was fine, that was OK. But I was also thrown in prison a bunch of times. There's this thing called three strikes, you're out. I was told by the judge the last time that if I was arrested one more time for doing this, I would have to spend a lengthy time in prison. At this point I had something like nine true fights completed. But what I was delusional about was that I forgot how short a fight lasts when you're very small and you're fighting someone that's really big. At the most, a really good fight would last two to three minutes, sometimes even shorter. I was smashed in the head with a brick and that ended really quickly.

Then the worst was when I fought this bouncer at [NYC club] Stringfellows. This was where the comedy came in. I wanted to fight him, but it took me forever, because he was wearing a tuxedo, to get him to fight me. When I was young, my dad had this thing about never letting me be comfortable. I always had to be nervous. So when we were driving in a car to school he would always go like that [*punches in the air*] to me . . . somehow that just kicked in and I went like that to this guy. Nothing happened. I turned around and looked at the camera crew that was across the street. And I went like that [*shrugs*] and then next thing you know, you see the guy taking me by the hair and the back of my pants and throw me into the middle of the street. I got really excited by that. I was like, "Yes, come on, kill me, please, fucking kill me."

And I waited for the guy to come and run and hit me and there was a trashcan right there. What I was going to do was try and throw the trashcan at his face and try to smash his skull with it. But this is where the comedy comes in. This is true slapstick humor—and accidental slapstick humor. The trashcan was chained to a telephone poll. So when I went to throw it, it was stuck. It didn't go anywhere. So the guy punched me in the face and I fell back and cracked my head. My right ankle was on the sidewalk. In the film you'll see—when I show it—you'll see him run up and jump and crack my ankle in half. To me, that's a great comedy. The idea of comedy is that there's always a victim. It's the banana peel that would kill me. You know what I'm saying? You slip on the banana peel and crack your head. So I don't know. I had to abandon it for a while.

JP: Well, we, of course, would like to put ourselves at the front of the line to try and show this film. I'm sure there are others.
HK: It's a weird, because it's the most asked and wanted thing. So many people want to see me get beat up. It's the weirdest thing.

JP: It's funny because you can't help laughing a little bit even though it's a horrifying story. But you also can't help but think, like, "This can't be true."

HK: It doesn't even really matter if what I'm telling you is the truth; it's the idea, the concept. But it *is* true. I mean, there were plenty of people that witnessed it. And eventually I will show it. I think. And I think people will roar with laughter at my pain.

"I Was Dying but It Was Taking Too Damn Long"

Olivier Nicklaus / 2003

From *Les Inrockuptibles*, June 25, 2003. Reprinted by permission. Translated by Henri Behar.

A "black hole": For two years, not a word, not a sign from American film-making prodigy Harmony Korine. Only nasty rumors of self-destruction, breakups, and rehab. In conjunction with an exhibition of photographs and drawings of his, he agreed to talk about his "hellish journey to the far end of fear" and the return of "desire and appetite."

"Designer Charles Eames once spoke of 'unified aesthetic,'" he said. According to Korine, whether he shot a film on board a train or designed a chair, it was all part of the same vision. "For me, it's one and the same, whether I shoot a film, write a book, put a show together for a gallery, sing a song, do a tap dance routine, or just live my life. Whatever I can show, I can experience." Thus speaketh Harmony who, at the age of "almost" thirty, has largely diversified over the years.

After shooting two films, *Gummo* and *Julian Donkey-Boy*, he published two books, *A Crackup at the Race Riots* (French Publisher: Al Dante) and *The Bad Son*, directed Sonic Youth's "Sunday" music video, produced a record of sound doodles (*Ssab Songs*), played a part in *Ease Down the Road*, Bonnie Prince Billy's (aka Will Oldham's) country-folk album, and wrote the lyrics of Bjôrk's "Harm of Will" (on her *Vespertine* album). . . . Not to mention his fanzines with skateboarder-artist Mark Gonzales, fascinating cut-ups, drawings of Osama bin Laden, photographs of porn stars, and others of Macaulay Culkin, which are now on display at the agnès b. gallery. In all cases, Korine presents a cross-cutting, personal, and obsessive vision of humanity.

But why interview Harmony Korine today, when the only "event" concerning him is an exhibition at the agnès b. gallery—a show some may deem minor—while nothing seems to be happening in the field one would expect him the most: films?

Because, beyond his absence, the latest news about him has not been not very good: a break-up with his lover-muse, actress Chloë Sevigny, quarrels with his mentor, director Larry Clark, dope, drugs, rehab, sudden disappearances. It's that time gap that he discusses here.

Olivier Nicklaus: The last time we met, you told me at the end of the interview: "I realized my filmmaking was good when it began to scare me." Would you say the same thing about the drawings and photographs that are on display today?

Harmony Korine: The movies, the pictures, the drawings, they're all part of the same idea, the same vision. As for fear, over the past two years, I went through a kind of hell, all the way to the far end of fear. What interests me now is a form of objectivity: being able to get out of myself and feel things more globally.

ON: You talk about objectivity. Is it a matter of maturity, of pulling yourself away from narcissism?

HK: I've always been open to the world—up to a point. I started really young, at nineteen, and after those films, I felt creating was no longer enough. I wanted to live a life that was as strong as my films. For quite a while, I'd worked at such speed and with such intensity that I felt I was drying up. That's when it became difficult, I felt emptier and emptier, caring less and less about making films or writing books. It's important for me today to reconnect with life and experiment with new things, as I did when I was younger.

ON: So far, you've felt like a medium, an antenna around which themes and obsessions of the moment clustered, coalesced, and crystallized?

HK: Absolutely. The bulk of my job consists of extracting things I feel deep down and converting them into dramatic material. It's powerful, yet at the same time, it doesn't leave me unscathed. Whatever I put out artistically leaves me empty. Gradually, I ended up weakened. Carrying the world on one's shoulders is hard, particularly for someone as extremely sensitive as I am. Like a radar, yes, an antenna: that's a good image.

ON: When did you first feel that emptiness?

HK: I began to unravel after *Julian Donkey-Boy*. At which point can one talk of nervous breakdown? I began to find life way too dark. Nothing seemed important anymore. I wasn't particularly inspired. And I didn't like the people around me. Wherever I was, I felt uncomfortable.

I'd left New York and moved to Connecticut. I lived in a beautiful house in the woods, right in the middle of swamps. I had all my paintings with me. Then one evening, I'd just finished a script, I went out to dinner; when I came back, the house had burned down. I'd lost everything.

Two and a half years ago. I completely freaked out. I went to live at my grandmother's. Drifted aimlessly, didn't know what to do. Little boy lost. That house, too, burned down. My fault. I fell asleep with a cigarette in my mouth. The two houses I'd been living in: burnt down, back to back. Everything I had was gone: all my books, all my CDs, all my notes for future projects. Gone. Burnt to ashes. Strangely enough, hard as it was, it forced me to pull away from my projects and be a little more sensitive to what was happening outside my brain. I decided to leave my past behind me and moved to Europe. There, I developed an obsession with death. I must have moved a dozen times. Once people could locate me, I'd freak out and had to pack up and leave. I stopped calling people. I stayed in Paris, in London, in Germany for a while. I loved it, but at the same time, I was well aware I was giving in to self-destruction.

ON: Didn't you try to recover some of the film projects that had gone up in smoke?
HK: No, I wanted to live, instead of always trying to create. It was too violent for me, emotionally. Besides, frankly, I was totally unstable: I'd wrap myself in tin foil so as to contain my ideas. The fires were a symptom of what I was living, an anticipation of what was yet to come. I was spiraling down anyway.

ON: Between those fires and now, how did you manage to finally find your place?
HK: There was a whole period when I didn't give a damn about anything, so I decided to stop dealing in art, go back to my native state of Tennessee, and do nothing but mowing lawns. For the first time in my life, I didn't give a shit about anything. I was very sick.

ON: What was it exactly? Depression? Nervous breakdown? Temporary madness? Drug addiction?
HK: All of the above. But it became very violent. I wanted to do

something drastic, something definitive. I was like a tornado, I wanted to destroy everything I had created. To feel intact again. I was not trying to hurt people, at least not consciously; still, I ended up harming a lot of them in the process. Starting with me.

ON: Any specific regrets?
HK: I'm happy to have survived it all. Life is a process and I had to go through what I went through to be able to work again. I regret the harm I've done to others, but at the same time, I won't let myself drown in remorse. That said, while radically into dope, I was still conscious enough to realize I shouldn't shoot in that condition. I was clean when I shot *Julian Donkey-Boy*. It's afterwards that it all went awry. That's why I haven't made a movie since.

ON: How did you pull out of it all?
HK: The darkness had become too intense and life too dull. . . . I don't know why, I just couldn't die. I didn't live, I merely existed. I had just enough strength to get out of bed and take whatever substances would help me make it through the day. And that's about it. I lived in an apartment on the Rue de Rivoli, across the street from the Louvre. One day, it was snowing, I just stood there, thinking, "I've got to cross that street." I felt my teeth starting to fall in my mouth, my fingers tips and my toes were beyond numb, I had lost my sense of smell and my sense of taste. I was dying, but it was taking too damn long. That day, I decided to seek treatment in America, first in a hospital then in a string of institutions. I enrolled in a methadone treatment facility.

ON: Was there no one around to help?
HK: My family was there, and so was a circle of friends, but I had to choose to go it alone. People could be around, but not save me. It had to be my move. Many had given up, and I don't blame them, I just didn't let anyone get too close.

ON: Did the treatment work?
HK: Yes, step by step, I got off methadone. And about time, I'd say: methadone is great to get you off dope, but the problem is you don't feel anything anymore. So you must get off methadone if you want a chance to create again. It took me a while to come to terms with myself. I could have sat down in front of a typewriter and vaguely tried to describe my

emotions, invent them, imagine them, but it would have been fake and I didn't want that. The main asset of my work is its sincerity. For me, the ultimate sin is lying to oneself and pretending to be artistically sincere.

[Harmony interrupts the interview to go to the toilet. When he returns, he looks embarrassed.]

HK: I've never gone into such details with anyone. I don't know if it's a good thing or not. But at least by telling it all, I'm being honest. I guess one must be, occasionally. Besides, telling it is also a way of making it your past, not your future. No doubt about that. It's true I don't want to go back there.

ON: Would you then say that now you are cured?
HK: No, one is ever cured. I did what I had to do, I went through what I needed to go through. Now it's time for me to get back to work.

ON: What was your first step in that direction?
HK: Oh, it's very recent. Happened in the last few months. The Macaulay Culkin pictures shown at the gallery are about three years old. The rest was done at the end of last year. It's interesting if you want to know my state of mind at the time: very dark. Every single day, I didn't know if I'd still be around the following day.

ON: What drives your work?
HK: I have no choice. After living through it all, I feel like I'm starting again. And far more intensely. Appetite, desire are back! For different reasons, and probably in a different way.

ON: So where does "desire" lead you today?
HK: For the longest time, I knew how to make movies, but I didn't know how to tie my shoelaces. So, to start with, I'd like to find a balance between the two. Not to let work take over to the point of endangering my everyday life. I'm almost thirty, but I feel younger than I felt when I started out at nineteen. I'm ravenous again. I must shoot. Now.

ON: So what is that project about?
HK: It's a film produced by O'Salvation, the structure we put together with agnès b., who supports me financially. I'm going to mix known actors and amateurs, and the film will be shot with six hundred cameras.

We will build three walls, each with two hundred video-cameras, so I can edit in a mathematical way: camera 129, camera 372, etc. That's part of the experiment: there's a modicum of randomness and uncertainty, we'll see if it works. Maybe I'll end up with a basically "normal" movie. It's an experiment.

Under Glass

Jack Silverman / 2005

From the *Nashville Scene*, April 7–13, 2005. Reprinted by permission of the author.

As with kimchee, The Shaggs, or a Joel-Peter Witkin exhibit, nobody has ever walked away from a Harmony Korine film feeling neutral about it—one reason the Nashville-raised filmmaker counts directors such as Werner Herzog and Bernardo Bertolucci among his admirers. The same holds true for his *Above the Below*, screening 5:15 p.m. April 20 as part of an omnibus program entitled Beautiful Outsiders. Korine spoke recently about the film; Jack Silverman listened and took notes.

Jack Silverman: How did the David Blaine project come about?
Harmony Korine: Dave and I have been friends for a long time. Right when I got back from Europe we were brainstorming a stunt for him to do. Originally, we wanted to have him in a see-through oval . . . like an egg, hanging a few hundred feet above the Thames from a huge crane with a see-through wire, so it would look like a guy hovering in the clouds, and swinging back and forth, but it was impossible to do. So we did the next best thing: have him hover fifty feet over the Thames in a see-through box.

JS: How long have you known him?
HK: About ten years.

JS: How many hours a day did you spend filming?
HK: They sold the project as a stunt to Sky Television and Channel 4 in London, who gave us a budget. It was the show that was set to air the day he came out of the box. There was a live video feed inside the box twenty-four hours a day. So there's seven weeks of constant, twenty-four -hour footage of him inside the box, starving. He went seven weeks

without food. What became more interesting was the crowd's reactions, the people who were coming there every day.

JS: There were hecklers, right?

HK: Hecklers, yeah, but there was, at least in London at the time, it caused this really strange discourse with the public. It's not really a documentary and it's not really a television show. It's more like a visual essay or something.

JS: Are you narrating at all?

HK: There's no narration. There are bits and pieces of David speaking that we had recorded previously—things that I had written, things that I then laid over afterwards. There's no real narration.

JS: Did you expect hecklers?

HK: At the beginning we didn't quite expect as hardcore of a reaction right off the bat. A lot of people got really pissed at David, and saw it as a publicity stunt, or saw it as, "While there are people starving in so-and-so, how could you make a mockery?" People were reading in a lot of political connotations.

JS: That's ridiculous.

HK: It's ridiculous, but at the same time, I started to realize that it's working on some level, stuff that we hadn't thought out previously. The strangest thing we saw was this woman who was about eight months pregnant—it was about three in the morning—that was in the bushes, right by the box, forking her anus. A drunk woman, that would come, she came a few times, and she would sit there with a plastic fork, just shoving it up her anus. Stuff like that. It became a thing for her.

There was a younger guy who would come, who had seizures every day, but he knew he would have seizures at a certain time of day, and he would come and he would have these fucking seizures. He looked like Superman on the ground, flying. His body would kind of constrict, he'd swallow his tongue. So for me there was like a carnival atmosphere.

JS: Was there skepticism? Did people think he was cheating?

HK: Oh yeah, the whole time. There were news shows, people thought we had lined the box with salt, or there were minerals coming in through a water tube. There's still people who think so.

JS: Is this film the show that actually aired on British TV the day he came out?

HK: Yeah.

JS: Does it include any footage of him actually coming out and after he came out?

HK: The TV show did, and the DVD that came out in Europe has all that stuff—him coming out, saying a speech, then recovery footage of him in the hospital, doctors checking him out, Flavor Flav visits him, that kind of stuff. That's not part of the film though. But it's not just him in the box; we did stuff for a month and a half previous, different gags and setups and non sequiturs, different set pieces: him getting punched in the stomach by boxers, doing magic tricks for strippers. At one point he pulls his heart out of his chest for a girl on the street. You'll see.

JS: Is he holding a real heart?

HK: He pulls his organs out. You see him literally rip his chest open. You'll see.

JS: What's happening with the movie you're working on now?

HK: We start shooting in October.

JS: And you're going to film in Iceland?

HK: Iceland, Brazil, and some in Paris, but mainly Iceland and Brazil. Hopefully, if all goes accordingly, we'll start shooting in October. I'm here now writing another script that I'd like to shoot in Nashville when I'm done with that one.

JS: So what can you tell us about the film you're shooting in Iceland?

HK: At this point I'll just say that it focuses on a commune in Iceland.

JS: Can I be in it?

HK: Yeah, why not.

JS: So you're in Gus Van Sant's *Last Days*.

HK: Yeah.

JS: What kind of role do you have in that film?

HK: It's just a small part, this guy Jerve, a sycophantic . . . leper, kind of.

JS: You did a character named Jerve in *Good Will Hunting*, right?
HK: It's kind of an extension of that character . . . I just sort of run through it. (laughs)

JS: So is it a gag on the Internet Movie Database where it says you directed a film titled *The Diary of Anne Frank Part II*?
HK: No, I made that! It's funny, because other people have asked that. No one ever believes that's real.

JS: It sounds like a joke your friends would play on you. So what was that?
HK: It was an art video I did for a museum a few years back. It was a story told in these three simultaneous projected pieces, and it's like a sequel to Anne Frank's life.

JS: Is it serious? Is it tongue-in-cheek? Hard to say?
HK: Uh, you know. Yeah, it's hard to say. (laughs)

JS: Is it ever going to be released?
HK: I'm going to probably try to put out a DVD of a lot of the stuff that I did.

JS: Are you going to put out the *Fight Harm* movie?
HK: Probably some of the *Fight* stuff, and this other thing I did with Johnny Depp, in blackface.

JS: So is your ankle still hurting? Are you permanently injured from the *Fight* film?
HK: Not so bad. I can show you the bone that kind of came out of my leg. But the doctors did a pretty decent job.

JS: How old were you at the time?
HK: It was about six years ago, so I was about twenty-four, something like that.

JS: Seen any good movies lately?
HK: Jeez, it's been an awful time. I haven't gone to the theater in like two months. I just watch older films.

JS: Jim Ridley said he saw the Asia Argento movie, *The Heart Is Deceitful Above All Things*, and said he clearly saw your influence.

HK: Asia's been a friend for a few years. I haven't seen the movie. I saw her not too long ago, and talked about it with her.

JS: So you probably get sick of answering this, but what the hell were you thinking with the *Fight* movie? Was it just "what the hell, let's see what happens"?

HK: Kind of. To be honest, I really wanted to make the great American comedy. That's what I was striving for at the time. I was reading a lot of Milton Berle and listening to a lot of Henny Youngman, and there's always this victim concept—a guy slips on a banana peel and cracks his head. So I started to think, "What if I really slipped on that banana peel?" The first thing you think about as a director is, "Well, I could always find somebody who would probably be willing to go in and get themselves beaten up," but then I thought that wouldn't be nearly as funny as if I did it myself. I was just in a place in my life where it seemed like a really good idea, at that time, or it didn't seem all that strange.

JS: So David Blaine filmed that?

HK: Yeah, a lot of it. He did a really terrible job of filming.

JS: So do you identify with David Blaine? You both have reputations as provocateurs.

HK: I like Dave because he's willing to put himself in extreme situations and he's always been that way. The first time I met him he put himself in a pizza oven and turned it on, and stayed in there for half an hour. I always admired that.

JS: What's not to admire about that.

HK: Also, I really like magic. I like the idea of magic.

JS: So you're really a Henny Youngman fan?

HK: Yeah. In fact, I read his biography, *Take My Life, Please*. It was a really funny biography. In it, he said that his phone is not unlisted, and you can find it in the phone book, because he wants to be free to play bar mitzvahs. So I called information and got his number. When I called him, he was on his deathbed, I guess, and someone else answered, and I said, "Is Henny there?" and I made up this story about how I wanted to option his book. He asked me right off the bat how much I was paying, and said he wanted a lot of money. I think he died the next day. But I got to have this little conversation with him.

When I called him I was like, "Man, you're the greatest, Henny, you are my single greatest influence." And he goes, "If I had any blood, I'd blush." I was like, what the fuck! He's on his deathbed, and he's still doing one-liners. He also said, "My luck is so bad, aspirin gives me headaches."

JS: So I read you're a Marx Brothers fan too?
HK: Oh yeah. I've been a huge fan.

JS: So which Marx Brother got laid the most?
HK: Jesus . . . I don't know . . . Chico? They say he's named Chico because he used to chase chicks. But Zeppo was the handsome one.

JS: But he was also the straight guy.
HK: Right. But you never can tell what happens in private life. I think Harpo and Groucho were married really early on and had lots of kids. I don't know. If I had to guess, I'd say Chico.

JS: So it's pronounced "Chick-o"?
HK: That's what it's supposed to be. Everyone says "Cheek-o," but it is "Chick-o." He was also a compulsive gambler.

JS: What's your favorite Marx Brothers movie?
HK: I'm always partial to *Duck Soup*. *A Day at the Races* is good. And *Coconuts*.

JS: So you have a production company now?
HK: Yeah—O'Salvation. With agnès b.

JS: Are you looking for projects?
HK: Not really. It was basically conceived as a kind of venue for me to put out movies and books.

JS: Do you have any books coming out?
HK: I have one, a book of all the early fanzines I did all through the early nineties to like 2000, when I was living in New York, for different galleries at the time.

JS: So you just did the Bonnie "Prince" Billy video. Are you working on any more music videos right now?

HK: Maybe. We'll see. I get asked from time to time to do videos and I just always turn them down, because the people who ask me to do the videos, their budgets are never that big, so I can never make much money on them. For someone like Bonnie, whose music I love and who's a really good friend of mine, it's fun.

Harmony Korine at Home

Aaron Rose and Ari Marcopoulos / 2008

From *ANP Quarterly*, no. 9 (2008). Reprinted by permission of Aaron Rose.

It seems that anytime I mention Harmony Korine's name, it never fails that someone has some kind of reaction. Whether it's a strange memory, a funny story, or a strong opinion (good/bad) relating to the work that he's done, coupled with his ever-controversial public persona, it has always been clear that he is a creative personality who has had a massive effect on the cultural language of a generation. While Korine is best known for his work as a filmmaker, he is also a prolific writer, groundbreaking visual artist, and all around cultural icon. For the last fifteen years he has traversed our collective visual landscape like a true explorer—experiencing all the successes and failures that mark the journey of any truly genuine searcher.

I'll never forget the first time I met Harmony. It was the early 1990s in New York. Back then, Harmony and I hung around the same scene of skateboard kids. I had a gallery at the time and we were showing work by Mark Gonzales. One day Harmony walked in and proposed an exhibition. I think he was eighteen years old at the time and I was immediately struck by his brilliant and somewhat demented mind. I remember asking myself, "Who is this kid? Where did he come from?" He seemed to possess an intellect that was far beyond his years. He hadn't worked on any movies yet, he was just an unknown little punk studying at NYU, but I could tell immediately, even at that time, that he was destined for great things.

It wasn't long after that first introduction that Harmony met photographer Larry Clark while skateboarding in Washington Square Park. Clark was beginning production on a film he was going to direct and was so impressed with Harmony that he asked him to write a script. The film was called *Kids*, and the rest is history. Soon after that it seemed our entire scene became wrapped up in the production of that movie. It was shot in our friends' apartments and in clubs we used to go to. It was an exciting time to be young in New York. Although we never could have predicted it at the time, *Kids* went on to be a very important and critically acclaimed film. It created a massive uproar amongst parents and religious groups for its controversial (read: REAL) portrayal of youth gone wild. Being that Harmony was only nineteen at the time, the media grabbed on to him quick. It wasn't long before he was on the cover of international magazines and being interviewed on *David Letterman* (I highly suggest you look this appearance up on YouTube). Exhibitions of his artworks were mounted in Soho galleries and he began dating Chloe Sevigny, the female lead in *Kids*, and the two of them became a much talked about item around town. Harmony accepted his new role as media darling both with open arms and a dash of healthy cynicism, and his cocky remarks in interviews ruffled feathers from Los Angeles to London.

Even though he was being showered with attention for his role as the writer of *Kids*, it had always been Harmony's dream to direct his own films. Capitalizing on all his newfound attention, he immediately began hunting for collaborators to help him begin his career as a director. Harmony has always had kind of a Midas touch, so it wasn't very long after that he was in production. The result film, *Gummo*, released in 1997, was an absolute tour de force of underground cool. Set in Xenia, Ohio (but filmed in Nashville, Tennessee—Harmony's home town), the film was shot using a cast of local non-actors, including characters with Down syndrome, glue-sniffing, cat-killing, teenage heavy metal kids, and a black dwarf. The aforementioned Miss Sevigny played a white trash hussy who at one point rips electrical tape from her breasts to make her nipples "more perky." The film was a cut-and-paste montage of seemingly unconnected scenes set to a Norwegian Black Metal soundtrack. It personified youthful angst and decay in an America that seemed to be falling apart at the seams. Yet somehow, Korine coupled all this horror with a striking sensitivity . . . traits that have continued to run through all his work to date. Needless to say, *Gummo* became an instant art house hit, landed the Critic's Prize at both the Venice and Rotterdam film festivals, and impressed an influential handful of his cinematic peers, most notably Gus Van Sant, Lars Von Trier, and Werner Herzog, who called Korine "the future of American cinema." Accolades aside, though, in America, the film was met with mixed reviews. Janet Maslin, the influential film critic of the *New York Times*, called Korine a "nihilist" and dubbed *Gummo* "the worst film of the year."

While to outsiders, Korine's star shone brightly as ever, for those of us who knew him cracks were beginning to appear in the façade. Harmony was still only twenty-five and the stresses of all the attention he had been getting began to take their toll. He had begun to enter a dangerous place emotionally and at times the young, fresh-faced Harmony we had all grown to love seemed to be lost in a vortex of self-destruction. That said, within a year after *Gummo*'s release, he was back working on his next feature obscurely titled *Julien Donkey-Boy* (rumor has it that Harmony's friend/musician Will Oldham came up with the title). Starring Ewen Bremner as a paranoid-schizophrenic and Werner Herzog as his abusive and perhaps equally deranged father, the film was shot in New York City using spy-cams and various other handheld video cameras and then assembled into a degraded montage of psychologically striking scenes.

The release of *Julien Donkey-Boy* marked a distinct downturn for Harmony. While the movie were again a geniusly executed experiment in the possibilities of film, which may perhaps take years for people to fully appreciate, it received a much less favorable response at the box office than *Gummo*. Coupled with Harmony's continual downward spiral emotionally and chemically it was obvious that dark days had arrived. The following few years saw Harmony in exile, having moved out of New York City and instead sequestering himself in a small house in Connecticut. Though he continued to create work during this period, mainly via a string of gallery and museum exhibitions in Europe—and a mysterious, yet to be released, film project enigmatically titled *Fight Harm* in which Korine had himself repeatedly beaten up on the streets of New York—it was clear to those of us that knew him that he was struggling. He had reached the end of his physical and creative rope, a situation that culminated in tragedy in the form of his house mysteriously burning down and Harmony losing most of his worldly possessions in the fire. It was time to go underground, and that's what he did.

Cut to today. It's been eight years since *Julien Donkey-Boy*. At the time of this writing, Korine's third film, *Mister Lonely*, is about to be released theatrically worldwide. The film stars Diego Luna, Samantha Morton, and Anita Pallenberg, along with a cast of past collaborators including magician David Blaine, French director Leos Carax, and Werner Herzog. In true absurdist Harmony style, the film takes place on a commune of celebrity impersonators, intercut with a side story about a troupe of parachuting nuns in South America. While the premise may seem somewhat ridiculous, Korine has managed to direct what is perhaps his most accessible film to date. It revolves around a touching love story between

Michael Jackson and Marilyn Monroe, but focuses on the struggles we all have with identity, dreams, and personal connections. It is a film made by an adult—an adult who, by living through all the trials and tribulations of life, has chosen to take those experiences and turn them into something beautiful once again.

For the following interview, photographer Ari Marcopoulos and myself traveled to Korine's hometown of Nashville, where he lives with his wife, a local girl named Rachael, who is currently working on a country album and plays a role in *Mister Lonely*. He is healthy and clean. He spoke to us about his life, his work, and his dreams. It was an inspiring few days. While some people could have been irreparably damaged by the experiences Harmony has had, he is amazingly as full of life as ever. There is a creative glow around him that is infectious. He is excited for the release of the film and for his future. I think we all should be, too. The whole experience brought me back to that first time I met him. A time when I looked into the eyes of an eighteen-year-old kid and saw a person I knew would become one of the most important creative visionaries of our generation. This time I saw those eyes again . . . and they are as alive and vibrant as ever.

Aaron Rose: Let's start by talking a little bit about Nashville. Were you born here?

Harmony Korine: No. I was born in Bolinas, California, but I only lived there for a short time . . . just two years. Then my parents took off and moved to the outskirts of Nashville. It was a town that was famous for having the world's largest ball of string and a museum called "Famous Blacks in Wax." I actually moved into Nashville when I was eleven.

AR: What brought your family to the South?

HK: Originally they were from New York, but there was a small commune of their friends who had bought a place out in the country. My dad was getting involved with documentary films. He had a series on PBS called *South Bound*, which was basically like documentaries that explored Southern culture—things like music, moonshining. He was kind of like a folklorist, a video folklorist.

AR: Was he doing that before you guys came to Tennessee?

HK: No. It started a few years after we moved here. You know, kids in the rodeo. He made one about Uncle Dave Macon, who was one of the first stars of the Grand Ole Opry. Macon was a banjo player from Murfrees-boro; he was kind of like an early country-vaudeville guy.

AR: Were you ever around while he was making those films?
HK: Yeah. He made one called "Raw Mash," which was about a moon-shiner named Hamper McBee, who was also like a carnie. I remember spending the summers in these traveling carnivals. They would pitch a tent in like some small town in Florida or wherever, stay there for a few days, and then move around. I would sell goldfish. It was great for me be-cause I would have the run of the place. I could say, "I'm with the show" and they would let me on the rides and I would hang out with all these characters. It was one of those things that made me realize early on I had a real fondness for the chaos of a circus. It was also the first time I realized that there were men who looked like lobsters and women with rubber skin that walked the earth.

AR: That's funny because I remember reading interviews with you over the years where you had mentioned that you grew up with a traveling circus and I remember thinking, "Oh . . . he's bullshitting," but you weren't!
HK: No! It's true! In some ways I feel that I spent a large part of my life trying to re-create that energy and excitement that I felt in the carnivals as a kid.

AR: Just being around show people?
HK: Show people, performers, the strangeness of all the traveling, the chaos, the communal sense it provided . . . there was something about it that I just loved.

AR: You mentioned that your parents moved to a commune. Was it a commune in the 1960s "hippie" sense of the word?
HK: Yeah. I mean, it wasn't huge. It was maybe twenty people who shared all kinds of different responsibilities, did the garden stuff, took care of each other's kids, that kind of stuff. They breast-fed off the tits of many different mothers. I mean, I think my parents became disillu-sioned pretty early on with that stuff and ended up moving out and do-ing their own thing.

AR: What were your teenage years like here in Nashville?

HK: Well, because my dad was making documentaries, he would sometimes be away for three or four months at a time and I have a younger brother and sister, so it was hard for my mother, so at a certain point he stopped doing that. They moved into town and opened up a children's clothing store. When my dad was young his parents owned a clothing store in Manhattan that only sold children's fur . . . so he had experience. On his birth certificate, where it said his father's occupation, it only said "furrier." So anyway, there wasn't a big market for selling fur coats for children in Nashville so they opened a clothing store.

AR: Were you always a creative kid?
HK: Well, up until the time my parents had the store I never remembered them doing like nine-to-five jobs. So I never thought about growing up to be a worker in that way where I would "clock in and clock out." That reality was foreign to me. I didn't really know that world. My parents didn't really buy me a lot of toys so I would go out and play with sticks and things, you know, talk to trees and stuff. My father didn't like to play games. I couldn't get him to do things like throw balls and stuff, so I would go out by myself. I remember it was easy for me to get lost in my imagination. I started to dream things up, different scenarios and things. I didn't necessarily know that I wanted to be a filmmaker then; believe it or not, the first thing I really remember wanting to be when I grew up was a choreographer! When I was like six or seven years old I thought it would be great to tell people how to dance.

AR: Do you remember what spawned that?
HK: Well, I saw the movie *Tin Pan Alley* with the Nicholas Brothers and I just thought it was such a cool film. I don't know what it was about it . . . I just thought it would be really great to dance like that.

AR: Well, dance has been a theme in your work throughout your career. Almost all of your films have incorporated difference scenes of dancing.
HK: Yeah.

AR: When we met in the early 1990s, you were living in New York. How did you end up there?
HK: Well, my parents were from there and my grandmother lived in Queens, so when I was a kid my parents would let me go and spend the summers there. I always loved it . . . so I couldn't wait to live there. As

soon as I graduated high school in 1992 I moved into my grandma's house in Queens.

AR: Did you go there with a purpose?
HK: Well, yeah, by that point I knew I wanted to make movies. I had gotten a partial scholarship to NYU to the writing department.

AR: Wow! I never knew that!
HK: Yeah, I quit skateboarding when I was like sixteen and just started making short films in high school. I was taking a creative writing class in my junior year of high school, which is funny 'cause I was never really a big reader, but I had this fiction class and I wrote some short stories. I turned it in and this teacher really loved what I had written. She saw something in it. It was the first time I had ever had a teacher tell me anything past "you're a bastard" or that something was wrong with me. It was the first time I had ever heard someone tell me I was good at something. So she asked me what I wanted to do and I told her that I wanted to make movies. . . .

AR: Do you think that was directly inspired by your dad?
HK: As far as that goes, I think a lot of it comes from the fact that he loved movies. One of his things was to take us to the movie theater. I was always going to see films. We loved to go to Vanderbilt University and there was this theater called Seurat Cinema, which was like a retro/revival theater and the movies would always have some kind of thematic connection there . . . like they would program Douglas Sirk and Fassbinder on the same day and show W. C. Fields movies.

AR: So your dad took you see Fassbinder films?
HK: Yeah! The theater was right by our house and really cheap. Eventually, at a certain point I just started going to the movies alone or with a few friends after school. It was a great way to watch movies. So anyway, this teacher asked me if I could turn one of my short stories into a script. I was like, "I don't know, I've never made a movie before," and she said," What if I can get you two thousand dollars?" It was like a student grant or something. So I was like, "Sure! I'll give it a try." So she got me the money and my dad showed me how to work a 16mm camera and that was it. It was pretty decent actually for a high school kid. So I used that to apply for the scholarship to NYU.

AR: But you never completed NYU, right? Was that because *Kids* came along?
HK: Yeah. I was only there for one year. Pretty much in my first semester I met Larry [Clark] in the park and then I wrote *Kids*.

AR: Was that situation regarding meeting Larry and writing that movie really as serendipitous as it's been played off to be?
HK: Yeah. It's really pretty accurate. It was as simple as . . .

AR: You were hanging out with skaters in the park and he rolled up and you were like, "Hey, I can write movies!"
HK: Yeah, and I had something in my backpack. It was a script I had written for school that, just randomly, was about a kid who on his thirteenth birthday, his father, who was a taxi driver, took him to a prostitute and basically this kid was having sex in the backseat of the car and his father was telling him what to do. Like talking him through it. It was really awkward, you know? The kid was slightly autistic or something and the father, out of a sense of duty or fatherly love, was trying to give his kid a few pointers. So I handed that script to Larry and the next day he asked me if I wanted to write *Kids*.

AR: Was it a daunting proposition?
HK: Well, at that point I had never written an actual script before, so I didn't know how long it should take. So I figured, well, "a week is good," because I didn't have any reference. I figured if I wrote twelve to fifteen pages a day, at the end of the week it would be finished. So I locked myself in my room and my grandma would come in and feed me like cut-up fruit and I would just sit in there and write. I didn't know what I was doing! I didn't know what was going to happen at the end until I got to the end. Now it seems like that was a different person, like a lifetime ago.

AR: Well, it was.
HK: Yeah, it was. It was sixteen years ago, but talking about it now, it almost seems like I'm speaking about a different person, like it was a friend of mine. It's so strange. I feel very far removed from that person now.

AR: It's interesting because the basic facts around the creation of that film, you know, that you met Larry in the park and that you were nineteen years old, have been talked about quite a bit, but I had no idea you wrote the whole thing in a week. Did Larry dictate the story to you or did you come up with it?

HK: Well, the way the film originally happened was that somebody was giving like a million dollars to different artists to do a movie that had some kind of an AIDS theme.

AR: So AIDS had to be in it.

HK: Yeah, I mean that was not a movie that I would ever have written had it not been for the circumstances. That wasn't a story that I was dying to tell or anything. It wasn't something that I felt like getting out of my system. Also, the concept of actually having a movie made from this was so foreign to me. I wasn't even convinced that it was going to happen. I was just doing it because I had nothing else to do and I was getting a little money for it. There was nothing at that point that said that the movie was going to get made or that it was going to come out in theaters. It was just like, "I have this idea, can you try to write a script?" and I was like, "OK." I mean, the whole thing down to the way it was casted with all those kids, nobody had acted before, everyone was just kind of hanging out. At the time I remember it all seemed really natural. It seemed like a really obvious thing. It didn't seem so serendipitous. It didn't seem so outside the realm of what making a film should be. It just seemed like an experiment.

AR: But it is pretty incredible what happened with that movie.

HK: It's insane!

AR: If you look at your career since then, if you look at Chloe Sevigny or Rosario Dawson . . . none of you guys were professionals at that time. There weren't even any real aspirations at that point.

HK: No! Rosario, I mean, in some ways her story is the most amazing. I was like walking down Avenue C and we looked up and she was sitting on the stoop. It was like two days before shooting and we just said, "Hey, that's the girl!"

Ari Marcopoulos: And some people fell off, too.

HK: Well, then you can talk about the other extreme, because you have people went on to make it and do really well and then you have people that in some ways I thought were going to make it, people who had so much charisma, people like Justin Pierce and Harold Hunter, who didn't make it.

AR: I wonder sometimes if all of that attention that was forced upon those kids at such a young age somehow fucked them up.

HK: I think that might have been part of it. I also think that the reason why that movie worked for a lot of people, or resonated, was that those guys were living a life, maybe not exactly as it was portrayed in the film, but a lot those guys were living very hard lives. They were living lives where they were making it up as they were going along. So when you have people that are living like that, it's tough. Someone like Justin, I mean, he was so raw! He didn't have a base. He didn't have people telling him how to make the right and wrong decisions.

AM: There was precedent for that movie. There have been movies done that way throughout the history of filmmaking, but then *Kids* seemed at the time like the most contemporary manifestation of that kind of movies and it really hit a raw nerve with people.

AR: I think the AIDS thing struck a chord with people, too. Here you had a protagonist who was running around giving underage girls HIV!

HK: It's funny 'cause I didn't give a shit about any of that stuff. The AIDS thing was so uninteresting to me. For me it was just like throwing in a device to let the narrative unfold. I just wanted to make a movie, to write a film . . . and I remember the intent and I'm sure this was true for Larry, too: It was just to show these people doing these things in these places in a way you hadn't seen before. Now, saying that, there was definitely a precedent for this kind of film and there were other movies that I loved and that I used as models. Films like *Los Olvidados* or especially *Pixote* were huge influences for that particular film. So without those movies, *Kids* wouldn't have been what it was or maybe it would never have even been. It wasn't like I was a naïf, sitting up there making it up. I was using those other movies as models.

AR: When that film was being made, did you at any point wish that you were the one directing it?

HK: No. I was happy to be where I was because, for one, it wasn't a movie that I would have made. I still don't consider it *my* movie. I still think, for me, it's a movie that I wrote for somebody else. It's still not my film. The other thing is that *I* was a kid. It was great for me to watch somebody else direct a movie so that I could learn. I got a chance to be there through the whole process and see how it was done, to be there to see what was done correctly and where mistakes were made. Man, it was terrific! I wasn't ready to direct a feature film at that time. I was still figuring it out. I was only twenty years old. Also, by the time I was actually in a place where I had a chance to make a movie, I wanted to do something different. I wanted to play around more.

AR: It wasn't that long after the release of *Kids* that you started production on your first film *Gummo* . . . so you knew it was what you were going to do already.

HK: Oh yeah, I knew! I also knew at a young age, I mean, I really felt like if I wasn't making movies soon . . . I just knew I would be making films. I was going to make it happen. It had to! There was no other option. I needed to make movies. I needed to try things. I needed to go out there and do it. So *Gummo* came two years later when I was twenty-three.

AR: And by that point, your life had changed quite a bit.

HK: Yeah. By that point I had gotten a little bit of money. I had gotten some recognition. I would have never gotten to make *Gummo* had it not been for the success of *Kids*. It was great. That experience allowed me to make my films. Before *Kids*, if I would've handed in that script for *Gummo*, people would have just laughed at me. I wouldn't have even had a chance.

AR: At first glance, *Gummo* comes off as such an abstract and fragmented film. How did you go about writing it?

HK: It's funny because I didn't even have an order for that film. I would just write scenes and then start to paste them together. I would just have character and scenes that I wanted to see and then I would write them on cards and just start to kind of move them around and place them in a certain kind of order that I thought made sense. It was more kind of lyrical or something. At that time that was the way I was thinking things should be, you know?

AR: In prepping for this article, I was reading your collected screenplays and I re-read the *Gummo* screenplay. It's amazing to me how true to the original script that film actually is.

HK: I know! That's why I think when I turned that script in, the producers and money people just couldn't read it. People hand it back to me and say, like, "I don't even know what this is!"

AR: Was it hard to find financing for the film?

HK: Well, I think what happened was more like they said, "Here's a million dollars, go make a movie. I don't really know what the hell this is, but just based on the success of the other film . . ." I always felt, and even to this day feel, like a thief in the night. I'm always expecting someone to say, "Are you fucking kidding me? You're giving money to this guy who's going to do this?" And with *Gummo* I really felt that way. I was excited and as soon as I knew I had enough to make the movie we just went for it.

AR: You shot most of *Gummo* here in Nashville, right?
HK: Yeah, we shot it all here.

AR: Was any of it based on autobiographical experiences?
HK: *Gummo?* Almost of all of it. The whole film was based on characters or friends, some of whom are even in the movie, people that I knew from growing up here. The story was originally written to take place in Xenia, Ohio. I knew of it because the skateboard company Alien Workshop was based there. I had always heard stories about how strange it was and stuff and also about the tornados. So I went there thinking about shooting the movie there, but I didn't know anyone there and it seemed difficult and I realized that what I saw there was very similar to what I knew in Nashville. So the idea of Xenia became more kind of mythic than it was anything else.

AR: Was it cool coming to where you grew up, but this time with a big film crew?
HK: Oh yeah! I had only been gone like four or five years. But it was fun. My parents still lived here and what I would do is just give people cameras and stuff and just ask them to go somewhere and film stuff. I wanted images coming in from all directions and I wanted to make sense of it afterwards. I wanted to kind of piece it together. I thought of the movie as a tapestry or a feeling, more than it was any kind of straight-up narrative. But it wasn't a puzzle, either. I remember thinking that after the movie came out that people would maybe say, "Oh, I get it," or something, and I remember being afraid that I fucked up because I never wanted to make work where you would have to qualify yourself. I never wanted anything I did to be like something that you'd have to "get." Meaning that there was some kind of inside joke or something. The intent was to provide more of an experience.

AR: You weren't trying to be pretentious.

HK: Oh, definitely not. Also, I wanted to make movies the way I wanted to watch movies.

AR: What is it that you're looking for from a film? I notice the themes of comedy and sadness tend to run throughout your movies.
HK: Yeah, comedy and sadness, and I always thought it would be great if you could make someone feel both simultaneously. You know, if I could make someone feel guilty about laughing at something . . . I thought that was great! You know, mixed up emotionally or confused. Like it was just wrong to like it. *Gummo* was a lot about deconstructing and breaking down images and taking things that most people thought were horrible and beautifying them . . . you know, pushing an aesthetic on certain things. And then doing the opposite as well. Taking things that are not perceived as beautiful and breaking them down. I don't know . . . I was just playing. I thought it would be great to see a movie where there were just great scenes. Where you didn't have to wait through a whole film just to get to the moment that you remembered. You didn't have to waste time with a beginning and an ending to get to that great part in the middle. I was like, "What if I can just give you the great parts? What if I can just give you the most entertaining pieces and try to tell a story that way?

AR: That way you're also able to write non-linearly.
HK: Exactly. It freed me up because I always felt that if I was bored writing something, that the people watching it were going to be bored, too. So I thought that if I can laugh to myself, make it entertaining to myself while writing it, that it would have to translate that way to the viewer.

AR: It's interesting because as you were talking about spending time in the carnival and being interested in vaudeville when you were young, it seems like you took a very vaudevillian approach to writing *Gummo*. You know, one different scene after another in quick succession. . . .
HK: Yeah. Without question. I felt like if someone hated some scene in the movie it wasn't such a big deal because it would be gone and something else would pop up.

AR: So after *Gummo* came out, it seemed like really quickly you went into production on your second film, *Julien Donkey-Boy*. For the sake of length, I don't want to go into too much about that film, but one thing that I found very interesting at the time was your technical process on it. It was super unorthodox, right?

HK: Well, we actually shot that movie on lots of different types of video cameras.

AR: That was pretty early to be shooting video on a feature. . . .

HK: Yeah, well, Lars [Von Trier, director and founder of the Dogme '95 movement] had already made his film *The Idiots* and *The Celebration* had just come out, but it was pretty early to be using video. So we used a bunch of different types of video and then we transferred all the video to Super 8 film and then from Super 8 to 35mm film. I wanted this kind of swirled color.

AR: I remember you saying that you wanted it to look like color copies. . . .

HK: Yeah. Originally I wanted to make a movie that was just Xerox copies. I had this idea to shoot an entire movie on 35mm and then go back and transfer every single frame to a color Xerox and then re-photograph it. Almost like stop animation. It would be like a Xeroxed film. It would have been millions of pieces of paper, and at that point in my life I wouldn't have been able to pull off such a feat.

AR: Let's talk about that point in your life for a minute. You were, what, twenty when *Kids* came out?

HK: Yeah.

AR: Obviously, all that attention must have had a profound effect on your life. What are the pros and cons of that whole experience happening to you so young?

HK: Well, let's see. The pros are that I got to make films. It allowed me to make movies and to do things. You know, to write books and have shows. It gave me a venue to put things out and have fun doing it. I always had the knowledge that if I did something that was decent it would be seen somewhere. That was great! Terrific. It was fun living in Manhattan at the time.

AR: You were a total New York celebrity!

HK: Yeah, I guess. But I was making it up as I was going along. For those first few years I was enjoying it . . . but you know, at a certain point, I was starting to feel something creeping up on me.

AR: Was this around the time you made *Julien Donkey-Boy*?

HK: Yeah, it was also before that, though. I can't really put my finger on it exactly and it wasn't like it was any one thing. But as fun as all that stuff was, it seemed that once my anonymity was blown or once my cover was blown, I don't know, I didn't really know how to function. You know, I'm not going to say I wasn't ready for it . . . it was just that for me as a person, it wasn't necessarily what I wanted. I mean, I wanted to make movies, but I guess that everything that came with it at that time so quickly—maybe I wasn't prepared for it. Maybe it was stuff that I thought was for the most part phony? Somehow, I was just there, you know? I was just in it.

You know, I'd go someplace where I used to just hang out and sit on the edges and then all of a sudden I was like, "Oh man, I'm right in the middle of this hit now." I was just lost. Something happened. I wasn't having fun anymore or enjoying it and I started to feel like I was being sucked up. I didn't have anything to give anymore. Sometime around that movie, or maybe just after it, I just felt like there was this great disconnect and that started a whole other part of my life . . . a sort of downhill trajectory. Also, it wasn't that interesting, you know? It was scummy. I'd look around the room at the people I was hanging out with and I didn't like those people, but I would think to myself, "Fuck, well, I'm here, so there must be something wrong with me, too." I was like, "I gotta get out of this place." Forget making movies. You know, my movies are a reflection of my mental state and I know I was in a bad mental state then, so I wasn't in a place where I could make movies. In some ways *Julien* was kind of like a black hole. It was a dark state for me. I was fucked and I knew it.

AR: When you go back and watch that film, do you see that?

HK: Well, I don't even watch that movie. I don't watch any of my movies. I never do. In fact, I don't even own them! I don't have any of my movies, my books, nothing.

AR: Why not?

HK: I just don't feel like I need anything to remind me of what I've done. You know? I'm happy they exist and that they're out there . . . but I don't know. I just don't have anything.

AR: The reason I'm asking about this stuff I because I feel it's important for people to hear about the other side of celebrity. We live in such a celebrity-obsessed culture that I feel like it's almost a duty to possibly debunk the myth. Not because I think celebrity is bad or anything, but maybe just to warn people that in order to stay healthy and happy, that maybe fame shouldn't be the goal. That maybe in the end it should be about the work.

HK: Yeah, I understand. But at the same time, I also want to say that with all the drugs and all that shit I also had a lot of good times, too. I would be lying if I said that I didn't enjoy some of it. You know, I put myself in these bad situations, at least in the beginning, willingly. I didn't necessarily understand what I was getting into, but I was just out there. You know, sometimes it's hard when you don't have an emotional buffer.

AR: In life you don't always have somebody who's taking you along and saying, "Make this choice," or "Don't make that choice."
HK: Yeah, but even if I did . . . at that age, if someone would have been telling me what to do . . .

AR: You would have been telling them to fuck off.
HK: Yeah, for sure.

AR: I've always thought it was cool that you've managed to have your hands in many different creative avenues besides film. It's rare for a director. You've had exhibitions around the world, you've written books. Do you approach all those projects differently than, say, you would a film project? Is there a difference?
HK: I see them all as pretty much the same thing. They're all pretty much a unified aesthetic or unified thought. The thing about filmmaking that always frustrates me is the lack of spontaneity. It takes so much to make a film. You have to go and convince people to give you money and then you have to talk to actors and convince them to be in your film and there's always so much convincing and prodding and time . . . and then once a movie is done, you have to wait for it to come out. You know, it's just such a long process. So a lot of times, the other stuff, like the artwork or writing the books or whatever else I was doing, was born out of the frustration that I couldn't make films quickly enough to satisfy any sense of spontaneity. Also, I felt like with movies, everyone is so precious. You know, because it's so difficult to make one and so much money is on the line. Everything is so thought out in that world. I wanted to be able to make mistakes. I wanted to be able to try things . . . and if something didn't work out or if people didn't like it, it wouldn't matter. With film,

people have this life or death attitude, like if it doesn't make a certain amount of money, or if it's not championed by critics . . .

AR: Why do you think that is?

HK: It's so collaborative, and so much time and effort and money is spent. Even in films that are made for very little money, you know? It takes so much energy and it's so exhausting that I think people want big returns. Sometimes big returns mean selling out an idea or capitulating or watering down a thought. I didn't want to have to do that. So if one idea isn't going to work in a film I'd put it in a book or put it on a wall or take a photo of something and I would be just as happy with any of those things.

AR: I remember one of your first exhibitions in the 1990s was a display of fake suicide notes. What was the idea behind this?

HK: Oh yeah! I had this idea once of writing suicide notes that were like form letters. So, if someone wanted to kill themselves, but they weren't creative enough to write their own letter . . . I wanted to basically write as many of them as I could and put blank signature spaces on the bottom. You know? And even if one of my notes didn't fit exactly into your life, maybe there would be something that you could identify with emotionally in one of those and you could just sign your name on the dotted line before you hung yourself. In my mind it seemed really noble at the time. Like I was giving voice to all these suicidal illiterates.

AR: I remember walking into that show and people being like, "What the fuck is this?" I think it was around that same time, the mid-nineties, that you were one of the first people to tell me about Norwegian Black Metal. You were into that stuff really early! It's funny because that Black Metal imagery is so popular now, but at that time it was still super underground.

HK: Well, I used a lot of that music for *Gummo*. There was this girl Spider that used to work at Printed Matter in New York. She actually ended up doing the *Gummo* soundtrack because she was corresponding with all those bands at the time. I was familiar with like hasher kids, more like stoner kids, but I remember talking to her and hearing about these bands like Bathory or Mayhem and I would hear these stories coming out of Norway, you know, the murders and church burnings and all that creepiness. But for me, I just thought the music was so extreme. It was just like the least commercial music that a person could create. It was like something that, no matter what, would never be on the radio. It was exciting and scary. It was just devilish!

AR: Let's talk about your book *A Crackup at the Race Riots*. You called it a novel, but it's really a super abstract book.

HK: Well, it was a novel in the same way that *Gummo* was a film. I was just kind of writing things and putting stuff together. That was my process at that time. A lot of it was just having ideas and thoughts and bits of dialogue and fragments and pieces of conversations, appropriated text, and I just thought that maybe I could tell a story using all these different voices. You know, there were all these scraps of paper and different elements. It was a kind of randomness that I wanted to make sense of. I also wanted to write kind of like a joke book, you know? A book of homemade jokes that I was making up. So it was kind of like a joke book to me. I used to have tons of joke books and I just thought they were the best books. You know, the ones that are broken up into chapters and themes. I thought I could do something similar.

AR: Speaking of jokes . . . you wrote a screenplay called *Jokes*, right? What ever happened to that?

HK: It was a project I was working on with Gus Van Sant. The idea was that different directors would do each section. The only part of that film that was ever shot was the part that Gus did. It was filmed in Kentucky and called "Easter." You know, by that point in my life, I was so burnt that it was a wash. I couldn't tell if I was coming or going, so like the idea that I was gonna be able to make a movie . . . you know, it just wasn't going to happen. My brain had pretty much melted.

AR: Another of your movies that has been spoken about widely but still never seen the light of day is *Fight Harm*. What's up with that film? Does it really exist?

HK: That's the one thing I'm asked about all the time. You know, maybe one day I'll put something out. I go back and forth. There are only a few fight scenes that survived my fire. Is it even worth it? Is the idea and concept good enough? Is it going to be a letdown? People are going to see me get beat up. Is that gonna be good? I don't know. I'm not sure. Also, for me, there's something gross about going back and watching that stuff.

AR: OK, well, this seems like a good time to get out of the past. Here you are, living in Nashville, and you've just finished your third feature film, *Mister Lonely*. It has been eight years since your last film. Was it hard to get back into the creative process?

HK: I didn't know if I could! I didn't know if my mind would function in the same way. I felt like I had really pushed it to the limit . . . so I didn't know if once all that toxic shift was out of my system I would still be able to do anything. I didn't know, barely, how to put one foot in front of the other. But honestly it all came back pretty quickly once my mind was clear again. But I have to say that during that period I had no idea if I was ever going to make movies again.

AR: Where did the idea for *Mister Lonely* come from?

HK: It started with just images. I wanted to see nuns jumping out of airplanes without parachutes on bicycles and stuff and dancing in the sky. I just thought it would be nice to make a story about them. I thought it would be nice if it was something about, like, a test of faith. Maybe one nun would fall out as an accident and survive and the rest would jump out on purpose in order to test their faith. Then I also thought it would be cool to make a movie about a commune.

AR: You think that's because you grew up that way?

HK: Well, yeah, but I thought it would be even cooler if the people on the commune were all just iconic celebrity impersonators. In that setting, I could combine their myth with just kind of like the day-to-day activities of a working-class hippie commune. So you could watch Sammy Davis Jr. tend the sheep or Abe Lincoln on a tractor or Madonna washing clothes.

AR: Are you trying to make a comment on celebrity?

HK: I really don't think about it that much. A lot of times I don't know where it comes from or why I even do the types of things I do. I don't even really question it that much. I've never even gone into anything with an agenda to make statements like that. I don't know, I don't know even know if I'm smart enough to make those kinds of statements. I've always just wanted to project some kind of feeling . . . something that has an emotional connection, a resonance in a character, rather than some kind of grand statement. For me, everything is about people and characters—personal moments. So a lot of times when I'm doing something I don't even know why I'm doing it or what I'm trying to say. Even when

I'm shooting or even during the editing process, I'm still trying to figure it out. For me, it's best not to question things too much. I don't really want to know why I do the things I do.

AR: Did that make it hard when you were going out to finance this film?
HK: Yeah. Also, this last film was especially difficult because it cost a lot more money than my past films, it took place in a lot of different countries, it was a big cast, and on top of it, I hadn't made a film in so long. In some ways, *Mister Lonely* was like my first film again. It had been eight years, which is like a lifetime. I worked harder to get this movie made than I did on my first movie by far. But at the same time, I'm not one of those people who want to complain; maybe the whole thing about making movies is that it shouldn't be too easy. Who said that it should be?

AR: How would you say this new film is different from your previous work?
HK: Well, I wanted to make a movie that had a little more structure than the other films. I wanted to make a film that was more like an allegory. There are these two stories that run parallel, like one would serve as the poetic punctuation to the other. They never really intersect, but they both speak to the same idea or theme. It's a different type of movie for me; stylistically, maybe it's a little more classical than the other films. I just wanted to go with the image more than anything . . . I wanted to go with the beauty of the image. I didn't feel like I needed to damage the image or tamper with it as much. At the same time, it's still directly part of the lineage of the other films.

AR: Do you feel *Mister Lonely* is a more adult film?
HK: No, I don't know. I mean, all those films reflect your mental state at the time of making them, right? So I know as a person I'm a lot different at thirty-three than I was at twenty-three. I don't know. You tell me.

AR: Did you want to make a film that was more commercial than your previous films?
HK: I don't know if I wanted it to be more commercial, but I wanted to try things that I had never tried before. I also felt like the style of the film, the way it was made, suited the story in the same way that *Gummo* was made had a lot to do with that fragmentation. This movie wasn't like that. This movie has an arc to it. I didn't think it needed that whole

thing. I thought it would be nice to just try to tell a story differently than I had in the past.

AR: It's not like being a big Hollywood director has ever been the goal for you anyway.

HK: Definitely not, but at the same time I thought it would be nice to do something and at least have a few more people see it.

AR: Your films have always had very eccentric characters. I mean, a commune of celebrity impersonators is a pretty far-out premise for a film. What is it about those types of characters that attracts you? You know, freaks or people who are outsiders. There really is this very distinct "Harmony" way of looking at things.

HK: I guess I always just kind of admired people who live outside of the system. I have always had an admiration for people who are dreamers and able to invent their own lives. Like if they weren't happy somewhere they could step outside and create it. A lot of times I feel that the purest souls are the easiest to hurt. So those are the people that I've always found most interesting. People who invent their own realities and people with really extreme, obsessive natures. You know, lobsters boys, strippers with elongated tailbones, and one-legged tap dancers. I think sometimes there's an inherent tragedy involved in those characters.

AR: I guess a nice way to wrap this all up would be to talk about the future. Here you are, living in Nashville, a new feature film about to be released, you're married now to an amazing woman. Your life could not be more different than it was when you were shooting *Gummo*.

HK: I still feel like I have most of the same obsessions and I am attracted to the same types of characters that I was attracted to even as a teenager. The same things that made me laugh then still make me laugh now. So it's different but the same. I just want to get to a place where it doesn't take eight years between films. The filmmaking process is too precious sometimes. In almost every other art form you're allowed to experiment and make mistakes. I just want to get away from logic and sense. I want to live in the world of nonsense.

AR: So what's next for Harmony Korine?

HK: It's a secret.

Mister Lonely Director Harmony Korine

Eric Kohn / 2008

From *Indiewire*, April 29, 2008. Reprinted by permission of the publication.

Much time has passed since Larry Clark discovered Harmony Korine skateboarding in Washington Square Park and hired him to write *Kids*. In its wake, Korine exploded into the mainstream as a radical artist with a bad boy streak. His first two features, *Gummo* and the Dogme '95 entry *Julian Donkey-Boy*, divided critics and furthered his reputation as a fiercely independent figure. Just when his world seemed to be moving too fast, Korine left New York City for his native home in Nashville, got married, and made a new movie to reflect his comparatively happier state of mind.

Mister Lonely stars Diego Luna as a disillusioned Michael Jackson impersonator whisked off by a faux Marilyn Monroe (Samantha Morton) to a strangely fascinating commune of like-minded characters. In a separate storyline, Werner Herzog plays a priest whose team of nuns inexplicably learns how to fly. In e-mail exchanges over several months and during an interview last week in New York City (where *Mister Lonely* is screening at the Tribeca Film Festival prior to its May 2 release), Korine discussed the themes of the movie, his general filmmaking philosophies, and the dubious case of the Malingerers.

Eric Kohn: Have your expectations for the way the film is received changed since last year's Cannes premiere?
Harmony Korine: I try not to think about it too much. I have never been good at gauging reactions to my films. I remember thinking *Gummo* would be embraced by the public in much the same way as *Bambi* was when it first came out. I am always wrong about such things.

EK: There's a point in the film when the story gets significantly bleaker.

Did you always intend to have reality intrude on the movie's surreal sense of beauty?
HK: Yes, this is one of the central themes of the film. Reality always seems to trounce the dream. Nothing too good lasts too long. Fuck it and enjoy while you can.

EK: Are there specific surrealist filmmakers you admire?
HK: I do like [Luis] Buñuel, but there are not too many others who would fall into this category. Obviously, the Marx brothers are the great America surrealist act, and they have always been my favorite.

EK: In some interviews, you claim to have to have spent time in between your last film and *Mister Lonely* traveling with an Amazonian tribe called the Malingerers and searching for a mythological fish. Did you make this story up?
HK: Of course, this is the truth. In fact, I'm planning another trip back there soon. One of the members just gave birth to a twelve-pound baby with a fully grown tooth, and I am the godfather. Apparently, the child has been given my name.

EK: Isn't a "malingerer" someone who fakes insanity?
HK: That is correct.

EK: You haven't been telling that story as much these days.
HK: I figure everyone's already heard it. Actually, Rachel, my wife, she's the one that said I'm repeating myself too often.

EK: I think it's fascinating . . .
HK: What? A fantasy?

EK: No, I didn't say that.
HK: It's just a long story. It eats the whole interview. Enough people have read about it.

EK: Anyway, it's yet another example of your off-the-cuff nature as a storyteller. There's at least one scene in *Mister Lonely*, when Herzog talks to a man about his marital infidelity, that's clearly improvised.
HK: That scene was somewhat improvised around the man's actual story. He is referred to locally as the "village idiot." Herzog struck up a

close friendship with him. In reality, this man does wait every day for his wife to fly home to him. He spends seven hours a day standing on the airport runway with red plastic flowers. He has been waiting for three years now. I'm not sure exactly what he thought was going on while we were filming that scene with him, though.

The thing about the improvising is that, in some ways, the idea of it is misleading. Maybe it implies that you let actors stand there and they just make shit up. That's almost always awful. I try to create an environment where you encourage and hope for things to happen above and beyond what you imagined. For instance, filming the commune with all those people, you try to have all these people in costume always there, staying in character to some degree. I came up with things on the spot. The trouble with filmmaking that I always had was that it lacked this sort of spontaneity. I felt like everything was so thought out, because it has to be. I try to approach scenes in a more musical way, putting different elements together and riffing off them. I toss grenades into the scene.

EK: For example?
HK: I can't even say. It's everything.

EK: Do you coach your actors?
HK: I won't coach a performance if I don't like it, unless it's something like—most of the time I'll cut and start over. What I'll do is throw out ideas. I went to the Lincoln character and said, "Tell me that story about Vietnam. Tell me that story about the melting Jane Fonda dolls. Tell me that story about doing acid with Hanoi Jane." Then, he'll laugh and break into that story. Sometimes it creates a mood or an idea that hadn't existed before.

EK: I spoke to Herzog a few weeks back and asked him if he saw any parallels between the priest he plays in your film and the Michael Jackson impersonator played by Diego Luna. Herzog said, "Who's Diego?"
HK: [laughs] He had no idea about the other story.

EK: Did anyone else?
HK: Aw, that's a secret I don't like to tell. I don't want to get anyone upset out there. But, no, it depends on the actor.

EK: Woody Allen says he never tells his actors anything other than what their character knows.

HK: I don't go to that degree, but sometimes I give actors different screenplays. [laughs] Sometimes, I might have five or six different endings that I give to five or six different actors.

EK: Has Herzog seen the movie now?
HK: Yeah, he saw it like two days ago. We did something together in Los Angeles at the Egyptian. It was pretty funny.

EK: He said you view him as a mentor.
HK: I don't even know if "mentor" is the right word. I don't really need a mentor. Werner is somebody whose films make me believe. Watching his films when I was young, I felt very similar to the way I felt when I first saw Buster Keaton in *Steamboat Bill Jr.* I just felt there was something old and deep in what he was doing. Some kind of poetry that wasn't like anything I'd felt before. I couldn't imagine the mind of a person who would invent such scenarios. When I first saw *Even Dwarves Started Small*, I couldn't believe a human being could make that up. It seemed like it was coming from such a strange place. Who would have thought about crucifying the monkey? Why was that car rolling around in that circle for so long in *Stroszek*? There are moments where it's something inexpressible. It's something you can't say in words. It goes through you.

EK: You once said that you don't believe in "the idea of exploitation."
HK: There are degrees, like if you're filming someone who's blind and not telling them. As long as people have their faculties about them. . . .

EK: What about the guy on the runway in *Mister Lonely* confronted about his marital infidelity?
HK: He knew what was going on. I'm not, like, filming people that have been lobotomized. It's all up to interpretation, I never felt like I've crossed any boundaries. Actually, I've always felt like everything seemed justified and beautiful. It almost seems like the reverse is disgusting—like, why wouldn't you put these people in? They should be celebrated. Fuck it, life is too short. I'll let all the academics argue those points, but it feels right, I don't care what anybody says. I'm going to go there.

EK: Have you ever felt like you've had to compromise something in any of your films to guarantee a release?
HK: There are definitely times where I've felt like there's something pushing it, but it's different for me because it's never like sex or violence—the

normal things: "Oh, there's an erect dick in this picture," or "There's too many people dying." My movies don't really have that. It comes from something being too real. Usually, I'll go with that if it makes sense in the story.

EK: Are you comfortable with people reading *Mister Lonely* as an allegory for the transitions you've gone through in your life?
HK: Sure, why not? I don't think there's any right or wrong way. I've had the same reaction to almost every film I've done. It's like there's no middle. I hate being bored. I always wanted to be entertaining. I either wanted to make films that rose above or fell down below. However anyone reads it is fine with me. I'm sure a big percentage of the audience won't even care about reading it. They'll just want to walk out and think nothing about it. Hopefully, there are some people out there that will get a good laugh.

EK: This movie is opening the same weekend as *Iron Man*.
HK: What's that?

EK: A Marvel Comics character.
HK: Oh, right. [laughs] Is somebody worried about that? If I make as much as money as they'll probably make in concessions, I'll be happy.

EK: You do still have a connection to popular culture, right? In your book *A Crackup at the Race Riots*, you mention your affinity for celebrity journalism. The various people imitating pop icons in *Mister Lonely*—you've got Marilyn Monroe, Michael Jackson, and Charlie Chaplin in there—seem like your way of deconstructing these personas.
HK: That was something I was very conscious of trying to do when I was first writing this with my brother. I was definitely interested in them as icons. I was mostly interested in the obsessive characters underneath, doing the impersonations. Also, I thought it would be fun to take the mythology of these icons and have them bleed into the actual narrative.

EK: How do you collaborate with your brother, Avi?
HK: Well, I've written two scripts with him, this one and another we just wrote. We kinda take turns. We talk about it, and I try to stay loose. I'll write something, and he'll read what I write. Then he writes something. It's just a game we play. It's like acting. It's fun to write with him, and

then there are some things that are too hard to express to him that just require me sitting down.

EK: Do you have a timeline for finishing your next project?
HK: I've got this other, strange idea I'm going to write pretty quickly and hopefully I'll be making a movie by the end of the year. I'll work with any financiers as long as I have final cut.

Lasting Impressions

Michael Tully / 2008

From *Filmmaker Magazine*, June 2008. Reprinted by permission of the author.

In the mid- to late-1990s, while in his early twenties, Harmony Korine burst onto the scene as a screenwriter (*Kids*) and director (*Gummo, Julien Donkey-Boy*) of films that challenged, disturbed, and wowed viewers. But it wasn't just his work that earned him full-blown enfant terrible status. Fueled by substances and a reckless approach to life, Korine's personal antics were as written about as his films (dating Chloe Sevigny, dazing and confusing David Letterman, wearing gold fronts with Old Dirty Bastard, etc.). After burning down two houses and bouncing around Europe in a crazed, ragged state, he finally succumbed to exhaustion and confronted his drug-smoked demons. Eight years later, Korine has reemerged with a new wife, a new home, and a new film, *Mister Lonely*, which feels like the artistic blossoming of a precocious, tempestuous boy into a sensitive, mature man.

To describe it superficially, *Mister Lonely* seems like another one of Korine's practical jokes: A lonely Michael Jackson impersonator living in Paris is befriended by a Marilyn Monroe impersonator, who convinces him to join her in a Scottish castle and live a happy life with other impersonator friends (including her abusive husband Charlie Chaplin, her daughter Shirley Temple, Sammy Davis Jr., Little Red Riding Hood, Buckwheat, James Dean, Madonna, the Pope, and many more). Add to this a parallel, seemingly unrelated story of a priest in Panama (played by Werner Herzog, no less) who has discovered a group of nuns who can jump parachute-less out of a plane and pray their way to a safe landing. Yet somehow, amidst these potentially outlandish situations, Korine delivers an achingly personal and heartfelt meditation on our quest to find our true selves in such a sad, indifferent world. That he does it with such dazzling invention on so many different levels—visual, sonic, thematic—is what makes *Mister Lonely* such a unique and remarkable achievement. After screening in Cannes, Toronto, South by Southwest, Sarasota, and Tribeca, IFC First Take opens the film on April 30 in New York City.

Michael Tully: First of all, I was absolutely floored by the film. It has a rare magical gift of existing on a plane that's fantastical, grounded, dreamlike, and realistic all at the same time. Was this a balance you tried to strike through intellectual rigor, or were you working from a purely emotional, subconscious place?

Harmony Korine: A little bit of both maybe, but for the most part I try to abandon the need for too much plot, logic, or sense. I try to override that and try harder to investigate something that's more intuitive and that's more about guts. I have the script, I have the ideas, I have the dialogue, and it's kind of like riffing off of these things, you know? If it feels emotionally honest I'll start to play with it or take it in a different direction and kind of improvise.

MT: In other words, you have to take what you initially create, which is your screenplay, to another level?

HK: Yeah. I mean I have always wanted to make movies that go through you like an experience or something that you can't really, I guess, talk away, that you can't even necessarily explain—almost like music or something that is more felt instead of dissected and analyzed. I always felt like it doesn't really matter so much what I use to shoot these films, whether I use a video camera or a camera phone or whatever—it's just the subject, the ambiance, and the mood, you know?

MT: Along those lines, I am personally more drawn to artists who shun too much contextualizing and analyzing of their own work. You seem to align yourself with that camp but I do want to ask you to do a bit of that. *Mister Lonely* felt to me not like the work of a totally different person, but there is something about it that felt like a step up from your other films. Would you agree with that?

HK: It's definitely a step in some other direction—if it's up or to the side, I don't know. I hadn't really made a movie in nine years, and I went through this period where I didn't even know if I was going to make films again. All the movies—and everything I've done, really—reflects [my] mental state at the time. So I think [*Mister Lonely*] is kind of different but the same because I felt differently about the world and a little differently about film [while making it]. But at the same time, I'm pretty much attracted to the same type of subjects and the same humor as when I was a little kid and when I first started making movies. I didn't want to not make a movie for a long time and then come out with something that was very much the same or something that people expected. I wanted to push myself a bit.

MT: That early scene with Werner Herzog absolving the pilot in South America of his "philandering sinfulness"—how did that scene come about? Was it unscripted?

HK: Yeah, that scene is one of my favorite scenes in the movie. It's one of those strange accidents that can happen in a movie if you pay attention to what's going on in the environment—if you see what the world is like outside the frame. We were setting up the shot with the nuns loading food into the airplane at this little airport in Panama, and it was really hot. A friend tapped me on the shoulder and said, "Look at Herzog." I turned and saw Herzog standing under this umbrella with this guy. My parents live in Panama, and I had seen this guy before when I would come to visit them and, basically, what he says in that scene is very accurate. He comes to that airport every day with these plastic roses and waits for his wife to get off the airplane. I guess she left him two or three years ago, and he's kind of like the village idiot. Anyway I saw Herzog talking to him, I saw the guy crying, and I was thinking, "Oh man, what's going on there?" Herzog came up and he was like, "Put the camera on me right now, there's something very special!" There were also buzzards in the sky—I always feel like when there are buzzards in the sky it's a sign of something good. So we just put the camera there and did one long take.

MT: What about the scene with Denis Lavant, as Charlie Chaplin practicing his English—that to me felt like it could have been something that was born on the set as opposed to having been scripted. How do you balance those types of scenes with scenes that are more atmospheric or ephemeral with scenes that are more story-oriented? Do you say each day, "This is the script, these are things that we need, and if we get those covered maybe we'll allow for a little messing around on the set"? Or is everything just totally organic and in the moment?

HK: I guess I have the script as just an outline, but the script is just words on paper—it's just a start, a jumping off point, at least for me. Everything is about the feel and about creating an environment. What I try to do, and what I've always tried to do, is, in some ways, mimic [the characters'] story [in the filmmaking]. Create a kind of universe. These characters are like chemicals, and you want to take those chemicals, put them in a bottle, shake them up, and then document the explosion. I always try to create an environment where people can kind of lose themselves. Certain actors are better at it than others, and somebody like Denis was incredible because he lived in the castle as the Charlie Chaplin [impersonator] for the entire [shoot]. He used to wear these leather socks, and he would unicycle naked down the hallways late at night. I guess he knew that I would pick up on these things, and so even in scenes that didn't include him, he was always kind of on the periphery acting out, showing me these things, and that scene is one of them. He was practicing his English, and I just saw him in this chair and told Marcel, the cinematographer, that there was something pretty about it, there was something just, I don't know . . . solitary. It made sense with the story. I don't know, I think those are the moments that people . . . like when I watch movies, I never really think about plots. Or I never really think about, you know, that kind of specific narrative, it's always more just characters and scenes and moments. And I try hard to populate these films with lots of those moments.

MT: It's really hard for me not to read a lot about a movie I want to see before I'm able to see it. I'm just a nerd that way. But one criticism I have read that is in keeping with what you just said is that, maybe midway through *Mister Lonely*, we sort of abandon the Michael Jackson character and the film turns into a dreamy poetic slice of life about all of these people coming to grips with themselves in their own world. Is it that you're not just not interested in following these kinds of "central narrative" through lines? Are your films more about individual situations and scenes providing the drama and the humor within themselves?

HK: Yeah, it's just that I don't really give a fuck. I never do, and it's like in the end, I make a specific kind of film, a film that I will feel strongly about. I thought the reactions to this one would be slightly different, that it would maybe be more palatable for some people, and while maybe the subject matter isn't as rough, in the end the reaction seems pretty much the same as with [the other films]. I'm starting to realize that when you play with narrative, or conventions of storytelling, it upsets a certain type of person. Which I understand, you know, because you become used to watching things with a beginning, a middle, and an end. Things that don't necessarily shift in tone. But I don't really make those types of movies. There are so many other people who make those types of films. You know, I understand if people don't like it, it's not that I ever expected something otherwise.

MT: About your personal life, you had some dark times there for a while and it's pretty clear that *Mister Lonely* is a very personal film even if it doesn't appear that way in the superficial sense. This isn't merely a story about a fictionalized Michael Jackson impersonator. This is a story about you. I'm wondering if the actual story, the initial kernel, was born during that foggy haze, or did it spring to life when you emerged from that cloud and were able to start thinking about writing again?
HK: Yeah, well, I'd written a script about a pig when I was really messed up in the head. It was called *What Makes Pistachio Nuts*. And like, it was a really long script, one of those epic movies, about this guy and this pig named Trotsky. He used to ride it up the sides of these walls—he'd get this special adhesive and stick it on the hooves of the pig. And when I was writing it, I thought it was a great epic. It seemed like it could be the greatest story ever told. Then my house burned down, and I lost the script. I lost almost everything with it. It basically sent me on a kind of spiral. I moved to Europe and got lost there and then met these people, and it's a long story, but when I was coming out of it, I started thinking about nuns. I don't know, I always just usually think of things in terms of visuals, pictures, images—I let myself kind of daydream. I'll see someone standing by a window with bloody knuckles and curlers in her hair and I'll start imagining a movie behind that picture. I started doing something similar with a Michael Jackson impersonator. I thought, wow, that's a strange idea, the idea of someone living as Michael Jackson, trying to sustain a living based on Michael Jackson's dancing and singing. Where does one identity begin and the other end?

MT: In addition to many other things, *Mister Lonely* winds up becoming, I think, a profound meditation on celebrity culture and personal identity. Did that happen in the scriptwriting stage, or was it even later in the process, during production or even post-production, that you even realized what you were trying to say in the film?
HK: I don't really know. I would be lying if I said I knew whatever I was trying to say. Like the thing with the nuns, the nun story kind of predates the other story. I guess always the thing was that the [two] stories were never connected in a concrete way, but I felt like they are both the same thing. They were both speaking to the same idea. The two stories

were kind of dancing with each other. Or they would comment on each other, sort of like punctuation or something. I just don't know if I'm smart enough, or if I have this kind of defect, but I just don't ever set out to say any one thing. In some ways [the movie] just says nothing, or it says a lot simultaneously. I don't know. I didn't set out to make a statement on pop culture, but if things happen accidentally, I'll take credit for them. That's always been my belief. I just like these characters. I've always been attracted to obsessive characters—people who live outside the system, or create their own world.

MT: As far as editing, I'm interested to hear how your process works, specifically with regards to feedback. Do you screen for friends and outsiders or trusted eyes? How does that work for you?

HK: Not generally. I mean, I had my wife Rachel come in and watch it every once and a while. And Chris Cunningham would come in from time to time because we were editing in London and I trust his opinion. There are certain people I'd ask certain things, like, "Does this scene work better with this or that?" But sometimes I actually enjoy getting lost in [the footage], enjoy the creating so much it's almost like I think the mistakes are what make it unique. Does that make any sense? You know like the mistakes or the awkwardness of it is actually what I want people to cling to. In doing that there's something nice about it being totally your own.

MT: As far as being done, is that also a similar gut instinct? Do you prefer to have a deadline like a festival premiere?

HK: How do I know when it's finished?

MT: Yes. Does a deadline at some point get you into gear?

HK: Yeah, deadlines are good. I also get sick of the material. I get so bored watching the same thing over and over again. I never feel like anything's ever perfect but when it feels like it's pretty much there I like the idea of just putting it out there and walking away.

MT: You seem to work with really, really great top of the line technicians and cinematographers: Jean-Yves Escoffier, Anthony Dod Mantle, and now Marcel Zyskind. How do you make these professional and personal connections?

HK: It's always been the same. It's like when you hear a musician who's really great but it's more than them just being a virtuoso—it's about their personality coming through. I feel that way with cinematographers.

Certain cinematographers, you know they know the truth, you know they're in there to find something deeper. Escoffier was like that and the same with Anthony and then Marcel. A lot of times you can cast the cinematographer like you can cast an actor. At a certain point personality is more important than technical proficiency because [cinematography] has a lot more to do with how you view the world and how you see people and relate to things than what lens you are using.

MT: You've recently gone into making commercials. Are you able to gain anything from making commercials that might help when it comes to features?

HK: I'm not going to lie, I just started doing them last year and it wasn't something that I really thought about too much. But I hadn't made a film in so long, and it's hard to sustain a living by making one film in eight years, especially the types of movies I make. So when someone approached me about doing ads it was mainly for money. I needed to eat and I got a lot of ho's [laughs] with bad teeth, I got lots of dentist bills and shit, so I needed to take a step into that world.

MT: But given that you are a very personal filmmaker and you've never experienced filmmaking by committee, how did you adapt to the commercial world?

HK: It's interesting to me because I did come from a place where I could do what I want to do and make images I want to see. I've been lucky in that way, but shooting ads was totally different. You're a worker for hire, but then there was something I found comforting in that. It was hard for me to learn how not to care—not that you don't care, you want everything to be good—but you can't get too emotional about shooting a fucking douche commercial or it's just not going to work. So that part I like and there's so much money that you can try things and get access to equipment. To be honest there's certain commercials and ads that I find way more interesting than most movies. There are certain [commercials] that are as valid as long-form features.

MT: And that ties into your videomaking. Those short pieces also provide opportunities where you can experiment and then bring that to your long-form features.

HK: You know what, it doesn't even matter. I never really did care where [work] comes from, whether it's a picture on a piece of paper, or a Polaroid, whether you're singing into a micro-cassette recorder or whether

I'm doing a tap dance or getting myself beaten up. It's all the same thing to me. It's a unified aesthetic. It's all storytelling. There are certain clips on YouTube that are to me just as amazing, poignant, and touching as a great film. I try not to have any snobbery when it comes to that stuff.

MT: I don't know if you've even seen the one of a burglary gone wrong. It's like a modern-day Buster Keaton.
HK: Oh yeah, and there's one called "Saudi Skates" where these guys in Saudi Arabia are being pulled by a car. They're wearing slippers and they're skating on this wet road, and to me it's like, it's the greatest image that I've ever seen. It's just strange. I enjoy watching the stuff.

MT: So I heard you're a happy homeowner?
HK: [laughs] Yep.

MT: Having a home and a stable relationship—has that helped your creative process?
HK: Yeah. I needed it because I lived like a tramp for so long—I was fucking disgusting. I had just lost myself and had burnt down two houses. I lost everything, had nothing left, so it was important to me that when I came out of it that I moved back home to where I grew up in Nashville. In some ways this town anchored me and gave me something even before I met my wife. And it's nice to have at least some kind of family life. It's good because the other way was too crazy. [laughs] And that's not to say I don't like to travel and do things and go places but it's nice to go back to Nashville.

MT: Are you still into eating up pop culture and old cinema and music like you used to?
HK: Yeah. Definitely. It's still pretty much the same. I'll never have a time in my life where I'm as actively watching films as I was in my early twenties. That's when I was so voracious and seeing everything for the first time. Now it's just re-watching movies that I love and going back to certain things. But I still get a lot of energy and excitement from things people are doing.

MT: Do you have anything new in the works?
HK: I've written this one script and then I have this other thing. When I was a kid some of my friends and I got involved in this strange avant tap dance scene here in Nashville. We used to steal these cement curbs from

sidewalks and put them on patios and do this dancing called curb dancing. You'd barbecue and some of the guys would drink cough syrup and
we would dance on these curbs for hours. So, I've tracked down some of
my curb dancing friends and have been making a film on the history of
curb dancing and the guys that were really innovative.

MT: Do you wear tap shoes or is there a specific urban shoe for this?
HK: Just black Capezios a lot of times, but the thing is, no one is allowed
to wear shoelaces. It just adds to the style of the whole thing. We got
some amazing footage, we got this one woman from Haiti who lives outside of Baton Rouge who does this kind of curb dancing called "Above
the Ankles, Below the Waist," which is kind of voodoo tap dance. It's a
series of moves that she does that if you watch hard can put you into a
trance.

MT: Will that transfer through the screen?
HK: It will, but from what I understand the risk is that if it takes you too
far the only way to undo it is to do the same series of moves but in reverse,
and that has so far proved to be more difficult. This lady's husband, by
the way, turned himself into a goat. Not that I ever saw it, but . . .

"I Need to Believe in Something to Get through the Day. That's My Own Thing."

Ali Naderzad / 2008

From *Screen Comment*, June 26, 2008. Reprinted by permission of the author.

There's a weariness about Harmony Korine as he stands against a urinal in the Soho Grand Hotel. I suggest to him that we have the interview out in the garden since the hotel's lounge is as hot as a proofing oven. He straightens himself up and says, "Fine, man, whatever."

Life for Korine has been swirling downward after *Julien Donkey-Boy* came out in 1999. After the meltdown he walked away from filmmaking and bummed around Europe before ending up in Paris.

Korine is back to work with a new film. *Mister Lonely*, which he wrote with his brother Avi, is all poetry and bliss—bringing Fellini, Wim Wenders, and Matthew Barney to mind. American cinema hasn't looked this original in a while. Diego Luna plays a Michael Jackson for-hire impersonator making a living in Paris. In a strangely predictable way Michael meets a Marilyn impersonator (Samantha Morton) who takes him to a commune where other impersonators put together their own variety shows.

Korine's early work (*Kids, Gummo, Julien Donkey-Boy*) about folks living on the wrong river's edge seemed to follow the same enraged narrative. With *Mister Lonely*, repression is out. Although Luna's character suffers from bouts of melancholy, the commune of impersonators he joins has a definite lust for life. Korine talked about his tribulations, faith, and an ever-corruptible younger brother named Avi.

Ali Naderzad: You totally disappeared after *Julien Donkey-Boy*. What happened to you?

Harmony Korine: I went traveling and ended up in France after I burnt out all my other countries. I started falling apart, I wanted to live a life that was separate, and I didn't want to have anything to do with movies anymore. I ran out of money, I ran out of friends, and I ran out of hope.

AN: How long did you spend in France? Do you even speak French?
HK: [Smiles] No. I wasn't listening. I spent just under a year there. During that time I only left my apartment four times, I think.

AN: So the inspiration for *Mister Lonely* came in part from your experience there? How did you enlist your brother Avi's help in writing the screenplay?
HK: Yes, partly. Avi was living in Philadelphia in someone's attic. He was only eating Chicken McNuggets and watching boxing matches. It'd been long since I had written anything and I figured I liked the stuff that he had written, especially the less pornographic stuff. So I asked him if he wanted to come down and do this with me. His only special condition was that I find him the special honey that had been discontinued from McDonalds. So I tracked down this farm and got a bunch, and he came down and we just sat in a room for three months and came up with the concept.

AN: Are you very close to your brother?
HK: We hadn't been so close physically because he's so much younger and I was out of the house a lot when he was growing up. But we have a lot in common—we share the same kind of humor, find the same characters interesting.

AN: So what was the dynamic like between you two?
HK: I had images and ideas and specific characters, and we started riffing, talking about different things, what about this idea, etc. Usually, if we'd both laugh at it, then it was good to keep. It took about a month of talking about it and writing our little notes, and then another month of actual writing.

AN: Are you very picky when it comes to the finished screenplay?
HK: I usually write just one draft. As soon as the script is finished, I'll reread it and clean up the dialogue a little. I don't know what a perfect script is. I don't ever spend too much time to get a script perfect, I just don't really care if it seems OK.

AN: There are two plots in *Mister Lonely*: the impersonators and the fly-ing nuns. Do you think that some people might have a hard time con-necting the nuns to the others?

HK: They're not there just randomly. The nuns represent a different way of saying, "Look at this estranged group of people." I felt like that even though the stories didn't intersect in a concrete way, they spoke to the same idea, it was allegory showing how the characters paralleled each other. They were both groups of marginalized, displaced dreamers that were living outside of the system. And in a way the nuns have this hope that if you believe strongly enough in something you can survive. You can ride bicycles in the clouds and do tricks and land and survive.

AN: A little like these impersonators believed they could become the greatest stars the world has ever known.

HK: Right. Just like that, just like these impersonators believed that you could be someone else. There's an emotional sense in there, but I never really cared about making perfect sense. I've always wanted to make movies that were nonsense.

AN: Could Diego Luna and Samantha Morton's characters (Michael Jackson and Marilyn Monroe, respectively) thrive in the real world?

HK: Well, all the characters are show people and they really come alive when they perform. Performance is everything. And dreamers that they are, they hope that the whole world will come to see the show.

AN: But they're in for a surprise. . . .

HK: Right, reality always has a way of intruding on dreams and the truth of their situation becomes obvious. There they are, living in a remote commune in the Scottish Highlands. They are delusional, but I think they had a beautiful dream, a pure dream, and sometimes the purest dreams are the ones that get hurt the most.

AN: Do you believe in God?

HK: Belief is an important part of my life. I won't say too much about this, but I need to believe in something to get through the day. But that's my own thing.

AN: Do you believe in agnès b., then?

HK: [Laughs] Well, I have a production company with agnès b. She had been waiting for me to get my act together. When I was ready, I called her up and told her I had a script, let's go. That's where it came together.

AN: Now that you live in Nashville, do you miss New York City?
HK: Not really, no. That's part of the past. My life in Nashville is great. Moving there was my saving grace. That and meeting my wife Rachel [who plays Little Red Riding Hood in *Mister Lonely*]. It's been terrific. When I get off the airplane, my heart rate goes down, you know you're in the right place. I can just drive around in my car and dream up scenarios.

AN: You're not a very prolific filmmaker. Are we going to have to wait a decade for your next movie?
HK: I hope to god it won't take me a decade until the next film. I've already written another one. My mind is in a better place. I won't be so precious about things. I'd like to make a movie by the end of the year.

In Conversation: Harmony Korine

Amy Taubin / 2008

From the *Brooklyn Rail*, July 16, 2008. Reprinted by permission of the publication.

Harmony Korine, best known for his screenplay *Kids* in 1995 (written in a matter of weeks when he was twenty-two [Editor's note: He was nineteen.]) and the experimental provocation of *Gummo* from 1997, and *Julian Donkey-Boy* in 1999, has made his third feature *Mister Lonely* over the course of ten years. One afternoon in mid-May, Amy Taubin caught up with the filmmaker at French Roast Café in the West Village to talk about the making of the film.

Amy Taubin: How was the making of *Mister Lonely* different from your first two features, *Gummo* and *Julien Donkey-Boy*?

Harmony Korine: I had a very kind of definite idea of the way I wanted to see movies when I made the first two. I wanted to make a collage with images coming from all directions—sight and sound, a kind of tapestry. This idea was very appealing to me, and still is—kind of making sense of chaos and of moments. With *Mister Lonely*, when I started to think about these characters, in some ways they were less of an assault. I felt like I just needed to go with the images. I wanted to just make beautiful pictures. Visually, the way we photographed it is a little bit different from some of the other films. But in terms of the filming, the way we directed is pretty much the same. We just set up situations and encouraged and allowed things, and I kind of hoped that things would go in a certain direction. So you create an environment where you allow mistakes or a sense of awkwardness, for life to seep in, and then for the actors and the cinematographer to take it in some other direction. So it's the same, I think.

AT: Concretely, did you have scripts going into all three of them?

HK: Yeah, to varying degrees. *Gummo* was like 50/50, in that there was a script, and 50 percent of what you saw on screen had been written. Then the other 50 percent was maybe completely improvised around an idea or something that was still connected to what was written. *Julien* was twenty pages long and had almost no dialogue written—it was more like a synopsis of what could happen. "Improvise" is a weird word because people have this idea that it's like you have these actors and they just start talking and it just works. But it's never like that. You spend a lot of time figuring out the character with the actor—how they speak, how they move. It's just basically understanding the characters, who they are. I don't like to over-rehearse. But once we've decided that this is the way they should be, this is who they are, then . . . there's no right or wrong. Once they go out as that character in a specific setting and the camera is there, there's either a good moment or a bad moment, but there's no real right or wrong; it's like life, you know, in that way that they just are.

AT: Is there a difference between working with professional and nonprofessional actors?

HK: Yeah, when you're casting a nonprofessional, it's more about bringing out that personality, allowing them to be free, but also not really making a documentary. Even when I'm casting for the person, I'm kind of twisting it a little bit. I'd almost say it's like science fiction, like the real world but where things are just slightly tweaked. Most of the characters have this sense that the real world isn't enough, or science isn't enough. They push it that extra step, not too much but just enough so that you can believe it, really, that they exist the way they exist. And then with real actors it really depends on who they are and how they work.

AT: So perhaps *Mister Lonely* is a metaphor for what you're saying about actors—they find the characters, and then they go out into the world as them.

HK: Sure, show people, performers, yeah.

AT: Whereas most people who work with actors would want to get under the skin of what they show.

HK: I'm just interested in show people, a person that can go out and change themselves in front of an audience and then go back to their house and turn it off. There's just always something that I've found beautiful about show people. I guess actors are show people too. . . .

AT: Any particular show people?

HK: Show people, like W. C. Fields or Buster Keaton or Al Jolson . There's a poetry or almost a strange insanity to what they did. When I was a kid, I would see their films, and I almost couldn't figure out how they existed . . . it seemed like they hovered above reality. Does that make any sense? Some of those characters were so strange to me and so compelling and so funny. I was really attuned to that sensibility.

AT: Do you mean in the sense that the Marx Brothers were always the Marx Brothers no matter what situation they were in?

HK: Yeah, but also it was almost like they were inventing their own reality. When I was a kid, things in my life seemed so linear, and then I watched the Marx Brothers and it just changed my perception of the rules. I realized there doesn't need to be a beginning or ending, that things could just be funny, or things could just be touching on their own, you could just build whole movies out of moments. Which is always what I loved about films, and life as well. It wasn't plots—I never wanted to be around people that plotted life out . . . in my life, at least, I never felt like anything began or officially ended. I just felt like things just happened, existed, it was more like an abstraction. Keaton or the Marx Brothers in some ways expressed that in their films, I think.

AT: So it's like Keaton falls into a particular situation and has to figure out on the screen what to make of it?

HK: Yeah, and also the thing about Keaton . . . it was almost like everything was a vignette. You were watching the scene on its own, waiting for the laugh, but you were almost never cognizant of the fact that there was a story, that there was some kind of narrative. You know in *Steamboat Bill Jr.*, you have this sense of doom, but it's like you're not paying attention to it because you're watching scenes individually, like slapstick.

AT: And do you think that the kind of thing that you're describing is possible outside of comedy?

HK: Maybe. When I started making those first films, narrative for me was like when you're looking at a book of your parents' photos, and you would have this randomness, like there's a picture of you standing next to your grandmother in Greece next to a picture of you being bathed by your mother when you're three years old next to a picture of your father drinking a beer. On their own, they're almost meaningless, or maybe just these moments, but in some weird way at the end of this photo book, there's a narrative, there's this inherent drama in the story of this family. But it's also that if you peeled off the picture and took it on its own, maybe it would be its own moment. . . . I've always wanted to make movies where you could just blindfold yourself and pull out a scene on its own and get something from it. I didn't care about the middle parts, I just wanted the above and below. Movies that consisted entirely of moments and characters. So yeah, I guess it is possible that it doesn't always have to be comedy.

AT: What's your life like now?
HK: It's surprisingly good. I get almost nervous when things seem so comfortable for me, which isn't that often [*laughs*]. I got married, I found a really great girl, and after all that craziness, I left New York, which is good, moved to Tennessee, got a house and a yard.

AT: And do you have animals?
HK: Just got a little dog [*laughs*]. It's one of those designer dogs, like a stuffed animal or something, it's the first animal we've ever had. [*Laughs*].

AT: Are you going to have kids?
HK: Yeah. I think it'd be nice—I don't want to have kids and be an old man. You know those families where it's like the dad is like a grandfather?

AT: Like Jonas [Mekas]?
HK: Yeah that's true. When I first saw Jonas I couldn't believe it.

AT: But Jonas defies age.
HK: Yeah, he's an enigma, he really is. So, yeah, I'd like to give it a try.

AT: And you spent time in Nashville when you were young. So is it like going home?
HK: Yeah, actually I live one street away from where I was when I was going to school there. It feels good, I have some friends there. . . . I like to drive around the streets and just listen to the radio, and I just see characters all the time. The South changed since I grew up there as a kid, but there's still a few streets that are really special, and great characters. Like the other day I saw this woman with curlers in her hair and boxing gloves, and she was punching herself in the face, she was walking, a black lady, and it was spectacular, the kind of thing I live for. And the other day I saw this black guy dressed up as a dollar bill, just walking down the street, it was like a stuffed animal but a full dollar bill. So that's the kind of thing I do. I'll see a character or a person like that and I'll just

imagine what their house looks like, and maybe they have kids, and I just start to embed a backstory. It's good, that's how I make movies.

AT: Have you ever thought about why you're so interested in American eccentricity, or American Gothic?

HK: I actually don't spend too much time on introspection. I just kind of go with it, but I got into this discussion with a friend of my dad—when I was growing up my dad made documentaries, he had a series on PBS in the late seventies, called *Southbound*, and it was about moonshiners, kids who ride bulls, people who make music with their mouths, I guess you could call them eccentrics. One of them, "Raw Mash," is about a moonshiner who lived in the mountains and in the summers worked at these carnivals, so I spent summers at the carnivals in Florida and traveling around. In some ways I was happiest there that I've ever been in my entire life. I would go around and I'd tell people "I'm with the show," and I'd go on all the rides for free, I would hang out with the lobster boys, the fire breathers, the tap dancers. There was an energy at the carnivals, this strange chaos, that I was so drawn to, there was a mystery to those people. How they would do special things under the tent, how they would unpack and then pack up each day and travel with each other. And there was a lot of dysfunction and strangeness, alcoholics, and generations of carnies and stuff, but it was fun for me, it was a world that was different from my reality. So in some way I feel like I'm always trying to get that back. Even when we're shooting, I'm trying to create a similar kind of sense where special things are always happening.

AT: Where did you go to school?

HK: For elementary school, my parents sent me to a private school, and it was awful. Everyone was white and Christian and there was one black girl and her last name was White, which I always thought was amazing. I didn't feel like a freak there; it was more that I was bored. I would make things up and I would get into a lot of trouble because I was constantly trying to entertain myself. Then in seventh grade, I got into this really good private school, but I was thrown out the first day for jerking off a hot dog. I jumped up on this table and started wanking this hot dog—I don't know what happened, I just got inspired. So I got sent to public school. I was twelve years old. I walked through the doors; it was all black and Puerto Rican kids. It was a different world and it was one of the greatest days of my life. In some ways, that's when my life began. That's when I felt that life was in color.

AT: And it really was.

HK: And it was. And immediately, I made new friends. At that point in Nashville, there were a lot of strange kids. It was like life was changing. The greatest thing ever was getting kicked out of private school.

AT: And so when did you get to be a movie freak?

HK: My dad just loves movies, not in any kind of a snob way, and my mom too. When I was little, if a good movie came to town, foreign or whatever it was, they were excited to take us. And I also would watch my dad and his partner editing—sitting together in little rooms and not agreeing on what they were doing. You just pick up on it. I was thirteen or fourteen when I actually got the thought that it might be something I'd like to do. Before I wanted to be a tap dancer.

AT: I remember when I first talked to you when *Kids* was about to come out, you mentioned your parents getting movies for you to watch on a VCR at night because you couldn't sleep.

HK: Yeah, and a satellite dish. We lived out in the country so they were one of the first to have one. Then when VCRs started getting popular, he would get movies from his film friends. I was a nervous or an anxious kid so that was a big thing—staying up watching movies.

AT: The other night you said something about how people were going to make movies in the near future. You first saw movies on the big screen and very quickly you moved to movies on TV and then on an editing table. So you are logically a person to entertain all those possibilities.

HK: Well, always the big screen is the ultimate. There's no substitute. But I've also had great experiences watching them on television, even though there's something underwhelming about TV. But I feel a lot of people are scared right now. They don't really know which direction it's all going in—movies, digital, and computers. I think it's exciting; it's nothing to be scared about. In the end, whatever form it takes, it's still about stories, it's about characters, it's about feeling something, being moved.

AT: Do you watch a lot of stuff on YouTube?

HK: I definitely do. There are certain clips on YouTube that I think are better than 99 percent of the movies out there, or at least that make me laugh or that I find oddly poignant. You obviously don't watch them the same way you'd watch a film, but in a lot of ways, if you look at *Gummo*, there's a kind of similar sensibility.

AT: You could take a lot of *Gummo* and make YouTube clips of it.

HK: Because that's how we were making it at the time. The idea was to give cameras to as many people as I could. Give a Super-8 camera to my sister; give a Polaroid to my best friend, and just tell them this is what I want, this is what I'm aiming for—just go out there and shoot it, bring it back to me and I'll make sense of these moments. That was what it was about. It was like a tornado—images falling out of the sky. I didn't care where they came from, or how long they were, or who was in them, as long as I felt like they made sense within this collage of filmmaking. We shot most of *Mister Lonely* on Super-35, but I would shoot on a camera phone, if I had a story or subject that would make sense to shoot that way. It's all just technology, it's all just machines, what's interesting is the people, the characters, the images.

AT: Gus Van Sant says he keeps wanting to go back to making movies with just two or three other people, that he can't bear having big crews around him when he works. Did you feel that the scale of the production of *Mister Lonely* was encumbering?

HK: For sure. Directing, when I was making it up with my camera and the actors were there, was terrific. But everything else was horrible. That was one of the reasons why I stopped making movies. It was hard for me to reconcile all the shit that you have to put up with. I felt like I couldn't figure it out. I was always trying to get to some moment, to reach something that resembles spontaneity in cinema. And it was such a challenge, because everything you had to deal with—and I'm not talking about the money—the logistic, the egos, the bureaucracies, the whole thing was taking all the fun away. I wanted to go out there and just invent it as I went. I wanted to have fun. I never understood directors who work with storyboards and who stick to the scripts. It's like the suburbs, all your houses look the same, and I'm sure they're comfortable, but I don't wanna fucking live with you. I don't want to live in such neighborhoods. I wanted to throw some grenades in there and make things exciting. *Mister Lonely* was difficult to put together logistically—four countries, lots of actors and stuff. But I remember having a discussion with Herzog once and he said "Who said filmmaking should be easy? Maybe it should be hard, maybe that's part of it." Now I'm starting to understand that a little more, or maybe come to terms with it. But still, if you ask me how I'd like to make a movie, I'd always like to make a movie with as few people and as little involvement with the outside world as humanly possible. I've always been jealous of musicians that just could pick up an instrument and start to play. I want to be able to play with a camera like that. *Julien* was like that in some ways. I wanted to be able to riff on cameras in the same way good musicians experiment with their instruments. Instead of detuning a guitar or piano I wanted to detune the camera.

AT: So, did you ever think that in Nashville, you could just get together or a group of people would be there all the time?

HK: Yeah, that's the idea now. We started a production company, just a couple months ago. We started to buy our own equipment, to get to a point where things aren't so precious, where making movies is about just . . . or it's not even just movies. I just like to make things—essays, images . . . and to get to a point where if I have an idea we can act on it. Also, I want to feel free to fail as well. There's so much attention on having big openings for your movies, on making money and getting great reviews and this and that. So nobody tries anything anymore. By the time most directors get to make a movie they're so scared that they want to make it really appealing. I don't care. I would rather try something and fail rather than not try.

AT: So how did you start working with agnès b., who is one of the most amazing people in the world?

HK: When I first lived on Prince Street, when I first met you, remember, her store was there. I would walk by her store and see all the posters in the window—the best poster collection ever! And I would go in and try to steal, well, I would ask for the posters and they would shoo me out. And every once in a while I'd try to go in and rip one off the wall. Then I actually met her at the Venice Film Festival at the *Julien Donkey-Boy* premiere. She just liked the movie and she'd flown in. I talked to her, and she was, like you said, just amazing. She's incredible. I can't even put into words how great I think she is. I mean she's a great designer and she's been around. She's a self-made woman, she's a poet, she has an empire, and she's never sold out. But there's also just more to her as a person, there's something very special about her. She does all that stuff but at the same time she remains really beautiful. You know what I mean? She has a heart in herself. Also, she loves movies as much as anyone I know. Immediately we started talking about how it would be great to make things—make films, make books, make videos. And that's how it happened. But around that period, I was very fucked up. She helped me during that period when I was flat on my back and nobody else would, when I was just totally drained, when I was living like a tramp. When I was pretty much debased.

AT: You were a fucking drug addict!

HK: Yes, I was a drug addict, but also, I was pretty much like there was nothing left. I felt I was completely disconnected from everything. Maybe the drugs were, in some ways, a way for me to slow things down. Living here in New York at that time I wasn't equipped, I wasn't ready. All I ever wanted to do was make movies but somehow my reality changed. And I looked around and I thought everyone around me were phonies, I thought everyone was trying to pick my pocket. And I thought, man, there must be something wrong with me. It just seemed like things were too fast for me. The day just kept going and I couldn't figure out where the time was. So I just wanted to slow time down and get a little peace in my life. But boy did I do it the wrong way. [*Laughs*]

AT: Well, you nearly burnt a lot of bridges.

HK: Some I'm sure, I know. I burnt houses too.

AT: I heard all about that. And I always thought it was a metaphor for burning bridges.

HK: Could be.

AT: So is this like a collaboration you have with agnès or does she function like a producer?

HK: She's pretty hands off. She kind of gets things going and she steps back. She shows up on the set a couple of times, and she's always checking in, to see how things are going. You know, I think she wants to make a movie herself.

AT: She's told me about that. She says she's going to shoot it next spring.

HK: Well, can you imagine trying to make a movie on top of everything she does. . . .

AT: How will she ever have time to focus on it? When you look at any of your movies now, do you feel like you made them? Or do you feel like they're separate from you?

HK: I don't look at them. It's not like I have an aversion to my own films, but at a certain point the last thing I want to do is watch my own movies. I just like to put things out there and then walk away. I don't have my own posters in my house. I don't even own my own DVDS or books that I've written. I don't have anything. You would walk in my house and you wouldn't see anything that reminds you of me except pictures of myself and my family. I never understood going to director friends' offices and it's just covered with their works. It's like living in your own asshole. I feel like you can get really caught up in some kind of history, or living in the past. I know I put myself into those movies, my ideas, and they exist almost like your children, a child would exist. But there's something nice about putting them out there, leaving them to their own devices, and just going out there and making up something else new. I've been talking about this movie for ten months, so I'm so happy it opens today so I can fucking go on with my life and make something new.

AT: Because the idea of celebrity is such a cultural big deal—that we're a celebrity-mad culture, that our obsession with celebrity is what's wrong with the culture—there are certain expectations people might have about *Mister Lonely*. But you don't go near any of that stuff. Did you ever feel like you needed to engage all those issues about what is celebrity, or why you, yourself, became a celebrity so fast?

HK: It was never even a thought on a conscious level. When I'm making movies it's never about making sense, it's about making perfect nonsense. With this film, you can say, maybe, that those characters or the celebrities or pop icons are metaphors for something greater, that it's an allegory. But really, it was just the characters that I loved. It was the idea of Sammy Davis Jr. in the morning waking up and tending the sheep, or James Dean and the Pope washing dishes. Or Buckwheat. . . . In all my films, what I really loved are these characters that are obsessive, that are inventing their own realities, inventing their own languages, making it up as they go. They're dreamers. It's the same thing with the nuns in the film—the real world is not enough. They have to make it a little more exceptional. And if you believe strongly enough that it's possible, it's possible. And I guess at the same time there is a kind of inherent trauma in these obsessive characters. They can get so far removed and isolated that they forget that the world is waiting.

AT: There is a moment of enormous pathos in the movie when they realize that there's no one in this world that they can perform for because there's nothing but performance in the world they've created. And that, as far as I'm concerned, says a great deal about celebrity culture. So what kinds of ideas are kicking around in your head now?

HK: I might do something smaller, something that I can do a little bit quicker, where I could move around, probably just shoot something in Nashville. Something, you know, with probably not such big actors. It's like a feeling. You know, you did this, now I'd like to do something that's the opposite of this. Then maybe after that I'd like to do something again that might get a few people angry.

His Humps

Eric Kohn / 2009

From *New York Press*, September 30, 2009. Reprinted by permission of the author.

"It's all just one long game," rants a demonic reprobate in Harmony Korine's *Trash Humpers*, which screens at the New York Film Festival on October 1. That's actually Korine talking, under the guise of a monstrous geezer—one of several populating this hauntingly immersive, knowingly fragmented work—as he unleashes a detailed rant on suburban domesticity. At this point, it should come as no surprise to anyone familiar with Korine's eccentric output that he plays by his own rules. After Larry Clark discovered him skateboarding in Washington Square Park at age nineteen and hired him to write the breakout sex drama *Kids*, Korine went down a chaotic path of media overexposure, emerged as a major radical artist and provocateur, then promptly flamed out. But his strongest tendencies stuck around when he reemerged.

Korine's first two directorial efforts, *Gummo* and *Julien-Donkey Boy*, sympathized with social pariahs and emphasized morbid imagery. But then came the arrival of an older, happier Korine with the gentler, life-affirming *Mister Lonely* in 2007.

The movie follows a depressed Michael Jackson impersonator whose life turns around when he encounters a commune populated by other costume-wearing recluses. *Trash Humpers* also features masked outcasts, but they bear a much darker presence. Predominantly shot on VHS and edited with VCRs, the movie cycles through the lives of these elderly-looking creatures as they engage in twisted versions of leisurely activities: Singing, dancing and, yes, fucking garbage (or "fornicating trash," as an enthusiastic humper puts it at one point), they appear to embody Korine's darkest fears and deepest aesthetic interests at once.

When I sat down with Korine last week before the world premiere of *Trash Humpers*—which he shot on a whim four months ago—at the Toronto International Film Festival, he hadn't done any interviews about it yet, and admitted that he wasn't quite sure how to express his intentions. So we hammered it out together.

EK: It sounds like you reacted to a few sources of inspiration here.
HK: There's a law in Nashville that everybody has to put their garbage dumpsters in these specific alleys. Sometimes, I would dream about these garbage bins, or I would look at these garbage bins and some of them had fallen over or propped against a tree. There was something vaguely human about them. Then I started thinking about when I was a kid, and I saw a group of old people that were like peeping toms. It just brought back a lot of memories. I was thinking, "It would be interesting if these trash cans looked human," and then . . . these people started humping on them.

EK: There are a few startlingly effective monologues in the movie. Did you script any of the dialogue?
HK: I wanted to make something that was more like an artifact, something that was found or unearthed. I just wrote down a series of loose scenes, but there was no written dialogue. I figured out how to do it in a stealthy way. Once we started shooting, it took on its own logic. By the time it was shot, it was done. The experience was as close to free-form improvised painting as filmmaking can get. We were moving as quickly as we could think it. Once I figured out the characters, I did a lot of tests beforehand, going to these locations with people in costumes late at night and taking photos. I was just exploring certain ideas. I would look at these photos I'd taken, and this lo-fi footage—there was something haunting about it. Everyone's always looking for the most pixels, the greatest beauty. I thought, "Maybe it would be nice to use the absolute worst."

EK: Any cinematic influences?
HK: The only movie that I was actually thinking about as a reference was the William Eggleston movie *Stranded in Canton*. It has this liquid home movie photography and an accidental narrative. He just walked around filming his friends in black and white video. It's very fluid.

EK: Once you had the look of the movie, how did you work out the narrative?
HK: It's a universe where people only do bad things. They enjoy killing, fucking, and burning, but they do it in ways there are transcendent,

poetic. They take sadism to a new level, turning it into an art form. They suck out of the goodness until it's just true horror.

EK: We're watching crazy people do crazy things, but the images are less disturbing than bizarre and poetic.

HK: To me, the most beautiful thing in the world is an abandoned parking lot and a soiled sofa on the edge of the parking lot with a street lamp off to the side. America seems like a series of abandoned parking lots, streetlights, and abandoned sofas.

EK: Throughout the movie, we hear you chanting, "Make it! Make it! Don't take it!" What's up with that?

HK: I knew this guy who was in a cast for six months, but he kept lifting weights with his left arm. When he got his cast off, his right arm was like a twig, but his left arm was insanely muscular. I could never get that out of my mind. He would sit there coaching basketball and go, "Make it! Make it! Don't take it!" But sometimes he would do it with his strong arm, and sometimes with his twig arm. I never forgot that.

EK: In contrast to so-called "torture porn" horror, you don't glorify the violence in *Trash Humpers*, but you do seem to appreciate the perpetrators of it.

HK: It's kind of like an ode to vandalism. There can be a creative beauty in their mayhem and destruction. You could say these characters are poets or mystics of mayhem and murder, bubbling up to the surface. They do horrible things, but I never viewed them as sad characters. They're comedic, with a vaudevillian horror element to what they do. They dance as they smash things and set them on fire. They're having a great time.

Q&A at New York Film Festival for *Trash Humpers*

Dennis Lim / 2009

Recorded at the Film Society of Lincoln Center, October 2, 2009. Printed by permission of the Film Society.

Dennis Lim: Your film inspired my favorite sentence ever in a *Variety* review. The review ended, "Across the board, technical credits are appalling, in a good way." Maybe you can start by talking a bit about those technical credits.

Harmony Korine: It was shot mainly on VHS and edited on VHS. I got so tired of hearing everyone talk about pixels and picture quality, how beautiful everything was. I wanted to work with the worst cameras possible, the absolute worst, and achieve the same thing. The idea is that it was a found tape, so the only thing I had to stay true to was this idea that it was a VHS tape that had been rerecorded on over and over again, so it made sense. We just used really crappy machines.

Audience Member: Since there is obvious vandalism in the film, did you have any trouble with the authorities?

HK: Yeah, I mean, there were a few guys we paid off. (laughter) No, really, it was very strange, actually. One of the things I found bizarre was that it was almost impossible to get arrested. Not just that—people really didn't even seem to mind. It's strange, because for me, it was like an ode to vandalism. I couldn't believe everyone was so kind. For instance, I remember doing a scene—I don't even think it's good to call these scenes—but we were recording something, and it was these guys, some of the humpers, were really humping these trash cans, and this guy had walked out in his backyard and there was a spotlight over it, and he said, "I just called the cops. They will be here in five minutes." I said, "We're filming a movie." And then he goes, "Oh, do you want my lights on? No problem. Do you want me to move the cans for you?" It's a strange world, you know? I think it's probably easier now to kill somebody than it ever was. (audience laughter)

DL: So you never encountered the cops while making this film?
HK: When we were filming the dead body and the guy's testicles were hanging down, a cop did come by and looked at that. Besides that, it was pretty easy.

Audience Member: Where was the film shot?
HK: It was mainly filmed in Nashville, close by where I live.

Audience Member: Where did you find the cast?
HK: My wife is the female humper. Travis and Brian are friends of mine. The rest of them are pretty much people we knew or admired there. Basically the way you saw it is how we made the film. At a certain point we just lost ourselves in this film and we would walk around with these cameras in character, hanging out under bridges and in backyards. We would spend days and nights just tearing shit up. You would knock on the door of someone you knew who could tell a funny joke. Maybe it didn't have a punchline. Then things would get good.

Audience Member: Where did you find the fat hookers?
HK: Craigslist. (audience laughter) No, a lot of those old hookers are really just family friends. High school buddies.

DL: You did actually use Craigslist, right?
HK: I can't give that way.

Audience Member: What motivated you to do this film after *Mister Lonely*, which was a much more expensive, elaborate production?
HK: The making of that movie was really nice, but all the things that surrounded it were awful. It was an experience I never want to go through again. It took too long, there were too many people involved. In moviemaking, you can lose your excitement for things, and the actual making is very nice when you're actually being creative. But I don't like sitting around and waiting. I'd like to get to a point in my life where it's like painting or something where you can almost move as quickly as you can think. I used to just walk in these alleyways behind my house and look at these trashcans and sometimes they would've fallen over or someone

would've propped them up against a garage and they looked mildly human. Some of them looked like they'd been molested. I'd just close my eyes and dream up these scenarios. I dressed up my assistant for a couple of nights and went out late at night with disposable cameras and took photos, using that as the template for this movie. It's different but the same.

Audience Member: You might be right that this isn't even a movie. So why is it important for us to watch it as a movie? Why not upload it to YouTube?

HK: We watch lots of things that aren't movies. This is a movie, but when I say it's not a movie, I mean that it's not like it's a movie that we're used to seeing. I think movies are changing—some of them are becoming other than what they were. It is what it is: an experience. All the films that I make I just try to give you something you've seen before in a way that's different. It's a movie that I probably will throw away someday.

DL: When you were making it, did you envision showing it at a movie theater?

HK: Honestly, I envisioned this playing at shopping malls. I mean, I think it could.

Audience Member: At first, with the picture flickering, it's really hard to look at because it's so degraded. But after a while, when I got confident about your intent, I started to see it, like you said, as painting. As you were editing it, did you get into the texture of the movie?

HK: I didn't think about it at all. I literally wanted to make something that appeared to be taped over many, many times. I used to collect these tapes. Two years ago somebody handed me a cassette tape they found in a thrift store and told me to watch it. I used to throw a lot of that stuff away because I'm scared of what I'll see on it. About six months later, my wife asked me to put on a DVD and as a joke I put on this tape. It was just these kids driving around the countryside—you know, teenagers—playing trumpet, and they'd hit each other and wrestle. One of the guys was deep-throating something. After like fifteen minutes, my wife and her friends were like, "Turn it off, turn it off!" And I said, "Why?" And they said, "Because someone's gonna get killed." I thought that was interesting. There was nothing that implied that was going to happen but they felt something ominous creeping up there. I thought that was a nice kind of idea for a film and the only thing I was trying to stay true to. It was a kind of anti-aesthetic: I didn't pay attention to composition so much.

DL: Do you think there's something inherently menacing about the quality of decomposing video?
HK: There is. There's something that forces you to look more. The picture is not clear so you're scared of what you can't see. It's forcing your eyes to work. It's a horror film in the way you might say that the feeling it gives you is horrible. The tone of it is horrible. I guess some of that comes from the graininess.

Audience Member: How important was performance to you with this film and why did you decided to appear in it?
HK: Well, this movie didn't make sense without me in it because it wouldn't make sense not show who's filming it. I felt like if I was in it, it would be better for everybody.

Audience Member: What was your shooting schedule?
HK: It took a couple of weeks. There was no schedule. We just did it. There was nothing. It was very much the way you saw it was the way it was done.

DL: And you shot this not long ago, right?
HK: Yeah, just like four months ago.

Audience Member: Were there any drugs involved?
HK: There's always drugs involved. (laughter) Not necessarily by me, but it's just a fact of life.

Audience Member: Will there be sequels?
HK: I would like to take these guys to Hawaii. (laughter) I was thinking about this the other day. You know that movie *Field of Dreams*? I was really thinking about this. You know in that movie where they have that line "If you build it, they will come"? Well, this is the opposite. With these guys, it's, "If you destroy it, we'll come on you." (laughter) Anyway.

DL: Is that the tagline?
HK: I just thought it was connected to that movie somehow.

Audience Member: What do you want from a movie?

HK: You know, movies are like moods. Honestly, that's the way that they're made for me. I'll feel a certain way, I won't think about it too much. I just want to be moved in some way. What do I get from the best movies? Something I can't speak in words. Those are the greatest experiences—the things that transcend description. It's something I always strive for personally. It's why I could never be a critic. It's very difficult for me to put in words a lot of times why I love something. I would probably write one sentence like it was great.

Audience Member: Who was the guy who recites the trash poem?
HK: He's actually a very famous songwriter. He wrote a couple of hits for Glenn Campbell. (laughs) I just thought it made sense. I felt like it needed the poem.

DL: Was that his poem or did you write it?
HK: It was something he basically wrote.

Audience Member: Do you see yourself as an American filmmaker? And do you see the film as a kind of comment on America?
HK: Yeah. I'm like a really uniquely American director. I would almost say I'm the most American director—except for Clint Eastwood, maybe. I really mean that. This is a very American movie. I love America. I grew up in these areas so there's nothing I love more than abandoned parking lots, soiled couches, and that kind of stuff.

Audience Member: Why are they humping trees?
HK: Because the trees look good.

Audience Member: Do you prefer *Gran Torino* or *Trash Humpers*?
HK: I actually liked *Gran Torino*. He's very grumpy in that movie.

Audience Member: How does the film stand apart from viral videos like the ones on YouTube?
HK: I don't know. You tell me. It seems like it does but I think it can also fit in there.

DL: Do you watch a lot of stuff on YouTube?
HK: Yeah, yeah. I'm a big fan. Just not everything. There are clips people send me that I don't like. They assume I like the really disgusting stuff, but . . . yeah, I think it's great. In a lot of ways, I liked that before it was

even there. My friends and I would make tapes, trade tapes, that were very YouTube-like. For me, it's terrific.

Audience Member: Can you talk about why you wanted old person masks?

HK: I just thought they were creepy. There's something strange about that grouping of three men and one woman. I knew I couldn't get old people to do these types of things and not have something bad happen to them. I just like the idea of people who look like that doing those types of things.

Harmony Korine on *Rebel*

Gwynned Vitello / 2011

From *Juxtapoz Magazine*, May 11, 2012. Reprinted by permission of the publication.

In April 2011, MOCA approached *Juxtapoz* with a unique project that they were producing with James Franco: *Rebel*, a multi-faceted, mixed-media, collaborative art installation and project loosely based on the making and legacy of James Dean's famed film, *Rebel Without a Cause*. In July 2011, *Juxtapoz* published a cover story examining *Rebel*, interviewing James Franco, Harmony Korine, and Aaron Young, about how the project came about.

While initially supposed to premiere at the Venice Biennale in the summer of 2011, this May 15, 2012, MOCA will be presenting *Rebel* at JF Chen in Los Angeles. The exhibition will feature James Franco's conception along with works by Douglas Gordon, Harmony Korine, Damon McCarthy, Paul McCarthy, Terry Richardson, Ed Ruscha, and Aaron Young. Here is our conversation with Mr. Korine in the summer of 2011.

Gwynned Vitello: You were born in Bolinas, California, so that has to have a connection with why you're named Harmony, doesn't it?
Harmony Korine: Yeah, that's right.

GV: Have you spent much time in Bolinas recently? It's so beautiful.
HK: I haven't been back in a while, I was born there, in a . . . I don't know if it was a commune but . . .

GV: Well, it's sort of one big commune.
HK: Yeah. I was out on the beach when I was born, somewhere with a lot of people chanting.

GV: And now you lead a life of no boundaries. Can you tell us how you got involved with this project?

HK: I had been talking to James Franco for a while about making a movie. And for the last couple years we would always toss ideas back and forth, and then about six months ago he came to me with the concept for this thing for the Venice Biennale, based on *Rebel Without a Cause*. He specifically wanted me to do something that was rooted in the violence of that iconic gang fight at the observatory in the movie. When we talked about it in the beginning we talked about using real gang members, and ended up having un-simulated knife fights.

GV: Maybe he was thinking of that documentary you started to make, *Fight Harm*, perhaps?
HK: Yeah, I think some of that came from there, too, the *Fight Harm* movies where I would provoke people into fighting me.

GV: You must have actually suffered physically. . . .
HK: Oh yeah, that's why I stopped. I was really out of my mind at that point. I wanted to make what I thought would be the greatest American comedy of all time. Something that was an extension of Buster Keaton or the Three Stooges; something that was just really vile and base and rooted in the lowest, purest form of humor, which I always thought was violence. You know, like someone slips on a banana peel and cracks their head open.

GV: So that's how he approached you—the violent aspect, but there was more to it than that, because of the focus on youth. . . .
HK: I think that he's specifically interested in the mythology that surrounds that film: James Dean, Sal Mineo, and the director. . . . Something that I hadn't really spent too much time thinking about myself, but I thought was interesting, and I liked those concepts, and I also liked the other people that were involved in the project. So it was exciting.

GV: I haven't seen *Rebel Without A Cause* in an awfully long time, but it seems like you've watched a lot of films throughout your life. Obviously you re-watched the film before you took this on. Did it look different to you than when you had seen it when you were younger?
HK: I guess so. It almost seemed like a comedy, so melodramatic. I always liked how most of the teenagers looked like they were in their thirties.

GV: That's what they did then. Natalie Wood was supposed to be sixteen!
HK: Yeah, so that adds a kind of humorous element to the whole thing.

There's something that was always kind of astonishing about James Dean—it's hard to believe he was ever was really a person. He inhabits this other domain. It's hard to believe that he wasn't just a cartoon or a figment of my imagination.

GV: Or a poster in a dorm room or something . . . he didn't get old and fat like Marlon Brando, so he's always James Dean. So tell us a little bit more about your film.

HK: I just lived with it for a couple months, I took all these different elements that I thought were related to gang culture and put them together. It's difficult for me to articulate exactly where it comes from.

GV: But James gave you free reign. You're the director and he said, "Do whatever you want to do."

HK: Yeah, definitely. He conceptualized the whole project. It's his in that he put all these things together. The idea is his.

GV: He wanted you to focus on gangs and violence, so did he give the other artists certain scenes to explore?

HK: Yeah, from what I understand that's how it happened. The other artists dealt with different scenes and elements of the film, and the backstory.

GV: Were you aware of what the other artists were bringing to the *Rebel* installation? Did you get a briefing, or was it like you didn't need to know?

HK: I knew that Paul McCarthy was building certain things . . . not a lot of detail about what other people were doing. I didn't really think about it so much. I think everybody's still making things. Even mine's not finished yet.

GV: Would it matter if it was in Venice or someplace else? When I think of Venice, some of it looks kind of decayed, while some of it looks like Disneyland.

HK: I made mine keeping in mind that it was part of an installation that's in Venice, but I also thought about how the film segments would exist separately from that. So it's made for this location, but it will work as well on its own.

GV: How will it be screened there?

HK: It will be projected on this island off of Venice, there's this decayed house . . . I can't even explain really what it is.

GV: I was thinking about the mansion in *Rebel Without a Cause* . . . thinking there's some kind of connection with Venice there.
HK: Maybe so, I'm not sure.

GV: Are there women portrayed in the gangs?
HK: Yeah, it's all women! It's only female gangsters. We did all the castings out of South Central and Compton. We did a lot of clips where I live. It's broken up into two gangs, Sal Mineo's gang and James Dean's gang. And then also East Coast–West Coast, Tupac–Biggie, it's like a BMX slaughter in downtown L.A.

GV: Right, which we saw in the trailer, the scene in the parking lot. So how did you cast? Was it the same way you usually do your casting, where you just go on site and round 'em up?
HK: Mostly girls that had been paroled, just getting out of prison. And people that I had heard about—infamous neighborhood girls.

GV: Was the concept of using all women something that was part of the blueprint of *Rebel*, or was it something that developed along with the concept?
HK: It was just something I thought about. It just made sense—I liked the idea of these girls with machetes on bikes. It just seemed like a natural thing to do, it was exciting. Most of them don't have their clothes on.

GV: Well, that comes out of the original *Rebel* because from what I understand that was one of the first films that blurred gender roles, the men were way more sensitive than they were usually portrayed. So it's interesting to have women fulfill a more masculine role in your film. I understand there's also a prominent musical element—what kind of music did you choose?
HK: Well, it's scored to the film. Also, all the voiceovers were taken from the original film, from the scene that preceded the gang fight and the slideshow that they give in the scene before—that discussion on the cosmos and how small man is in relationship to the stars. I re-did that text with somebody else's voice and added a lot of other things, I peppered it with ebonic-type slang and then I screwed it all. I pitched it all down so it's totally fucked up and screwy.

GV: Well, that's so different then than *Rebel Without A Cause* because even for its time it was using stilted gang talk, so this is a little more real.
HK: Yeah, this is next level shit.

GV: And you let the girls kind of talk their own talk. . . .
HK: There's actually not even any dialogue.

GV: It's all action and music?
HK: It's all slow motion. It's all shot at really, really high-frame rates, so yeah, it's pretty slow.

GV: The original *Rebel Without a Cause*, although it was groundbreaking, was such a sugarcoated depiction of rebellion. As you are using real gangsters, real people, did you decide to take it to a whole other level of a ridiculous take on the notion of rebellion?
HK: I don't even really think about it too much like that. I just honestly don't even think about things like that too much. It's more about just like when you close your eyes. . . . I just allow myself to dream and go to a certain place that's difficult for me to explain. If the feeling's right, if I'm being pulled and the sway is right, then I don't question it, I just make it. And that's how it was with this. I just dreamt it up based on this idea that Franco had, based on simulated gang wars.

GV: When an interviewer asks questions we frame things in a way that boxes you in to answering a certain way, and I know from your filmmaking, that it's very linear . . . a slice of life.
HK: It's also that sometimes I just feel like the best things don't exist in words. It's like something that's post-logic. I don't ever care about making perfect sense, it's like making perfect nonsense. It exists outside that. I've never had any other kind of motivation other than to see something in a specific way that no one else is showing me.

GV: It's very much like skateboarding. You don't go out and skateboard to score a certain amount of points, you're just out there.
HK: Or if you're gonna use a skateboard analogy, you could say it's almost like Mark Gonzales, like the first time I ever saw Mark Gonzales skating on his grip tape and I was like, "Wow" . . . you realize that there are no rules, that you can do anything.

GV: So you still live in Nashville?

HK: Yeah, I didn't live there for a while, but I moved back a couple years ago.

GV: So you were there, and then you went to New York City (because everyone's gotta go to New York City for a while) . . . and you've got a child now.
HK: Yeah, I've got a kid.

GV: Are you in the country?
HK: No, no I live in the city. I live right by Vanderbilt University.

GV: So back to the project. What are you finishing up on the film right now?
HK: I'm just doing the sound, mixing it, which is great. It's really almost done.

GV: You're doing just the film or are there other projects related to the installation?
HK: The movie, of course, and then I'm making these other little loops, these images that are repeated. And then I'm taking all the props from the film, including the severed James Dean head, the prosthesis and put it in vitrines, and then the BMX bikes will hang from trees. And the Tupac and Biggie shirts everywhere, it's all part of a whole.

Harmony Korine Talks *Spring Breakers,* Casting Selena Gomez, and How Her Mom Is a Fan of His Work

Eric Kohn / 2012

From *Indiewire*, September 10, 2012. Reprinted by permission of the publication.

Harmony Korine's *Spring Breakers* marks a significant shift in exposure for the thirty-nine-year-old filmmaker, but nobody can accuse him of selling out. The movie, which premiered in Venice and made its North American premiere in Toronto last week, stars Selena Gomez, Vanessa Hudgens, and Ashley Benson as a trio of young woman who rob a diner to fund their trip down south. After a series of depraved party experiences, they eventually encounter the absurdly self-involved gangster Alien (James Franco), who manages to seduce most of the girls with his materialistic obsessions.

If there's anything tame or familiar about the spring breakers' initial exploits, Korine tears it apart with a gloriously surreal deconstruction of pop imagery. Having secured distribution with Annapurna Pictures (but still attracting interest from larger studios in the wake of its positive reception), *Spring Breakers* has already brought Korine onto a level of popularity that the director never could have achieved in the day of *Gummo* and *Julien Donkey-Boy.* Even the filmmaker had a hard time believing it when he dropped by *Indiewire* HQ on Sunday to discuss the movie.

Eric Kohn: You've said this was the hardest production of your career. How did the experience differ from your other movies?

Harmony Korine: It was the most difficult shoot in the sense that I had very little time. The look of the film was very central to it, so there were certain things I needed, like various equipment and cameras, so I could make the visuals the way I wanted them. I had to compensate for that, which affected the schedule, which affected the pace. And then you had these girls shooting on location, mostly in real places with people around them who weren't actors. We put them in an environment they weren't used to being in. Obviously, very quickly people found out about that. Sometimes there were more paparazzi than crew members. It can get weird very quickly. It was a whole set of problems I had never dealt with.

EK: Nevertheless, it's not like you sold out and made a conventional narrative feature. Where did the concept for *Spring Breakers* come from?
HK: Early on, I had wanted to make a film in this style, and had been trying to develop in other ways—through short films and advertisements—this idea of microscenes. The movie to me is closer to electronic music. My idea for the film is more music-based than cinema-based. Music now is mostly loop and sample-based. A lot of stuff I like is more tracey and physical. I was hoping to develop a film style with this movie that could mimic that in some way. That's where the liquid narrative comes from, this boozy-jazzy thing.

EK: It's an incredible soundtrack that combines compositions by Cliff Martinez and Skrillex, but sometimes you can't tell which is which.
HK: That was the idea. I love them both and wanted to take a certain element of what each does best and have them merge. I wanted the music to have a physical presence.

EK: There are also a number of big pop songs. How on earth did you get the rights to Britney Spears music?
HK: The movie was always meant to work like a violent, beautiful pop ballad, something very polished that disappears into the night. Everyone was really cool about it. I've gotten to a point in my life that's pretty cool where musicians are accepting and wanting to be part of what I do.

EK: Even more impressive is the cast. What did it take to cast these young women, who are best known in teen-oriented fare, in a movie so subversive?
HK: When I was thinking about the cast, I was thinking about who could play these parts, and was wondering who the girls are in this generation that best represent a certain ideology. There was something intriguing about the idea of using girls primarily known from a Disney-type reality.

Immediately, instinctively, I said it would be great if Selena Gomez would do this. It's pretty crazy that they were all pretty receptive to it.

EK: Why do you think they were receptive?
HK: A lot of them knew my films, which always surprises me. I got an email that Selena was going to hop on a plane and come to my living room in Nashville to audition, and that her mom was coming with her, and that she would be there the next morning. It was pretty crazy. Her mom is younger than I am and she had grown up watching my films and said she had been a fan of them.

EK: So you now have an audience that grew up with your work.
HK: Yeah, it's pretty weird. I still feel like a kid, but really I've been making movies now for almost twenty years. It's nice also knowing that you're accepted by the culture in some way. When you're out in the wilderness making movies, sometimes you don't know where you live. It can be difficult to gauge who knows what, who sees what, and I try not to think about it too much.

EK: And yet every time you make a new movie, the media focuses on how it reflects your public persona.
HK: That's the other thing. I'm not sure I like that. Sometimes, when I read things, I feel like my narrative or whatever the fuck it is, becomes too prominent. Every film is not a stealth move. It's not a game of chess. I make films because I have ideas about certain characters or images. It feels like it's part of the moment. This movie felt like something intangible, difficult to articulate, but I had to pluck it out of the air.

EK: Do you think you would work on this scale again?
HK: Monetarily, it wasn't that big of a film. But I only want to go harder and bigger. I only want to push myself and make things more spectacular. It's exciting for me to try to do things I never thought I would do and go places I never thought I would go. I want to experiment. At the same time, making movies is so hard that it can feel like warfare. A lot of the energy of the battles are fought about things that have nothing to do with the creative element.

EK: Do you think this is your angriest film?
HK: I don't know if it's angry, but it's certainly the most aggressive. I

wanted to make a film that feels like there's no air in the room. I never wanted the audience to be comfortable or complacent. I never even wanted it to seem like they were watching a movie in the traditional sense. I wanted it to be something different. So there's not that much dialogue. Words get in the way. I wanted the film to have a very physical presence.

EK: What's your overall take on the idea of spring break?
HK: Spring break is a rite of passage, an American pastime. In the film, it's more metaphorical, the idea of losing yourself. I don't feel like the soul is gone in this country but that it has morphed into something else. Everything is experienced thorough screens and through views and technology. Sometimes the act of watching is like nothing. I just wanted to show how it's all the same.

EK: In the opening montage, a spring break beach party starts out like some kind of terrible reality show before it turns increasingly depraved and tribal.
HK: And I also wanted it to involve a kind of gangster mysticism. Everything has become so corporatized and boring so real outlaw culture or criminal culture feels like the last vestige of American rebellion. These girls have grown up on world star hip-hop and Gucci Mane.

EK: How did you decide on the structure? The story itself is pretty thin.
HK: I wanted to run all through the idea of clips, like YouTube stuff, through a filmic filter. I wanted it to seem like the images were just flying or falling from outer space. I wanted to develop a new vernacular, at least for myself. It was an appropriation of images and ideas that were familiar and iconic to people, but I ran it through this fucked-up filter that spit them out in a new way. The movie is about energy more than anything, a feeling, what happens when you get lost. It's not about spring break; it's about when you drive a couple of miles away from spring break and you're out on the boardwalk by the beach in this weird, fucked up, drunk place. It's like beach noir. I really wanted the film to be about surfaces. I told [cinematographer] Benoit [Debie] at the beginning that I wanted it to look like candy—like he had lit the movie with Skittles. It was about this dance of surfaces. The meaning is the residue that drips down below the surface.

Interview: Harmony Korine

R. Kurt Osenlund / 2013

From *Slant*, March 14, 2013. Reprinted by permission.

A singular filmmaker inspired by the likes of Fassbinder and Cassavetes, and championed by modern masters like Herzog and von Trier, Harmony Korine is one of cinema's most defiantly pure and unpredictable artists, toying with genre, technique, and narrative conventions ever since penning 1995's *Kids* and helming 1997's *Gummo*, his near-indescribable directorial debut. Other highlights of Korine's mercurial career include *Julien Donkey-Boy*, a Dogme 95 effort about schizophrenia, among other things; *Mister Lonely*, a picturesque fantasy about a commune of celebrity impersonators; Trash Humpers, an ultra-divisive, documentary-like curio; and the script for Ken Park, another hot-button collaboration with *Kids* director Larry Clark. Evidently galvanized, Korine now returns with the paradoxical party thriller *Spring Breakers*, a film that, despite its maker's serial interest in untethered youth, is sure to shatter expectations, and, at this point, may just be 2013's best American movie.

Effectively deflowering the public images of Disney and ABC Family princesses Selena Gomez, Vanessa Hudgens, and Ashley Benson, *Spring Breakers* is a techno-fied riff on the seaside mythos popularized by MTV, telling the tale of a quartet of thrill-seeking coeds (the fourth is played by Korine's wife, Rachel) before morphing, in a dreamlike descent, into a neon-gangster mind-fuck worthy of Tony Montana. It's a watch-and-watch-again work of culture-skewering pop art, made all the more potent by the ostensible stunt casting it deftly transcends.

Korine—who, with a full, unruly beard, torn jeans, and scuffed sneakers, still shows shades of the skateboarding twentysomething who wrote what's perhaps the most controversial film of the nineties—joined me in a private New York hotel room to discuss Spring Breakers, its headline-friendly cast, and a structure he compares to pop music. Before he even takes a seat in the ornately wallpapered room, Korine makes note of the faint "unce-unce" pumping out of the house speakers. "It's like porn music," Korine says. The scene, as they say, is set.

R. Kurt Osenlund: *Spring Breakers* is one of few hedonistic crime movies that very successfully balances the glorification and the sharp critique of its subject. What drew you to this subject in the first place?
Harmony Korine: I don't know—it was more of a feeling, I guess. It was the idea of starting a film as a spring-break movie that was kind of celebratory, and then having it veer off into something that's more of a crime film—something slightly more sinister that exists more in the shadows. I just thought it was an interesting idea.

RKO: While the movie retains an individualism and a certain experimental tone, one could say that it's your most accessible title to date. Is that something you thought about while you were making it?
HK: Yeah, I thought about it. Because, obviously, you have these actors who have all these fans and fanaticism and chaos surrounding them, and who bring all this other stuff that I knew would follow the film. But also, I was mostly just drawn to the characters and the storyline, and I guess all that other stuff just happened because of that.

RKO: One of the reasons I ask is because I spoke to James Franco last year, and he said that you had advised him to keep a balance between his esoteric and commercial projects, so I was wondering if *Spring Breakers* represented a bit of that balance for you.
HK: Yeah. I think, at its core, the film is linear and, in some ways, a very simple story. Then all around it is something that's kind of like a tone poem—hyper-poetic, almost like a pop song. I wanted it to be able to speak to both high and low in an interesting way.

RKO: In the film's marketing, Franco's transformation seems like one of the biggest draws, and yet, while he certainly nails the role, the performance isn't some novel distraction that leaps out from the piece. It's just another part of the film's fabric. With so many gonzo elements like that, was it tough to maintain the movie's cohesion?
HK: It was about an energy. His character and the film itself are kind of cultural mash-ups, but you want it all to be based in something pure, something that's raw and has a heartbeat. So, yeah, I always just tend to follow my gut with the films and with the characters when I'm shooting.

And if it feels legitimate, or feels like an intimate reinterpretation of that, I go for it.

RKO: And then there's the casting of the girls, of course, which is sure to launch just as many point-missing controversy articles as it is to draw unsuspecting teen fans to the theater. Clearly you're aiming for some provocation here, but these girls are running this show and, for better or worse, owning everything about themselves, making *Spring Breakers*, for me, an unlikely feminist film. Do you see it that way?

HK: I won't say. I'd rather hear you say it. For me, I try not to speak too much on that kind of thing, because I'd rather let you interpret it in a way that's very personal or specific. But, I mean, obviously, these girls transcend anything that you've seen other girls do. They transcend anything that the guys in the film do. They almost become spirits—like gangster mystics.

RKO: "Gangster mystics"—I love that. And you worked with your wife, Rachel, on this film, just as you worked with former girlfriend Chloë Sevigny on films like *Gummo* and *Julien Donkey-Boy*. What are the benefits—or, perhaps, drawbacks—to directing your significant other?

HK: Well, the drawback is that you can sometimes drive each other crazy. It's harder for her than it is for me, because I become super-obsessive and all I can think about is the movie. That can be very difficult for people who are around me. But at the same time, the benefit is that there's a trust there. And, of course, you want to work with someone that you, you know, love.

RKO: The one thing that seems a bit more literal or typical than what we usually see from you is Selena Gomez's Faith and her spiritual plight. Even her name is right on the nose. I'll assume this element, and its execution, are all part of the film's yin-and-yang irony.

HK: Sure. And also, there's no irony to her character. Her character is completely earnest and literal. I wanted to go with a name and a core that were completely honest and straightforward. Because the other girls are much more abstract and wild. Always, from the beginning, the characters were conceived and thought of as one single entity—one being. Faith's character is the first to leave and she's the morality. So once the morality is stripped, you're left with something wild and dangerous, and what happens in the film becomes the result of that. And when Cotty [Rachel Korine] goes, it gets even more wild and dangerous.

RKO: So you see them as representing tiers of moral responsibility?
HK: Definitely.

RKO: The film's look merges neon decadence and crisp, seaside vistas with lower-tech aesthetic choices that recall some of your earlier work, like the use of surveillance footage, for example. I wanted to know specifically, about the sand art–like distortion effect that's used when the girls were arrested. How was that achieved?
HK: Well, we were shooting everything on 35mm film, and then I was experimenting with these Japanese novelty cameras called power shovels. And, basically, we'd just buy tons of them and make what were sort of like totems, attached to the main camera. And they were all switched on to different functions. So we were filming in black and white, and sepia tones, and whatever you'd call a 1970s look, all simultaneously. I wasn't sure how I could use the cameras, or if I could use them, in a way that wouldn't be annoying, so my assistant editor came up with these sort of composite, morphing-image shots, and started playing around with them on an Avid. And then I thought they looked perfectly trippy, like hallucinations, and I liked them for the drug sequences. They serve as almost hallucinatory punctuation, and they look like melting film.

RKO: The way the narrative unfolds visually is also quite remarkable. There's a lot of cross-cutting and chronological manipulation. Can you briefly describe that technique and the reasons behind it?
HK: Well, again, I wanted to make something that was very experiential—something that was like a liquid narrative, with micro scenes, like something you'd see in electronic music. I thought of it like loop-based music, where you'd have certain things that would repeat, and come back—refrains. I even thought of pop music, where you have courses and mantras, which, in the film, almost become like catchphrases and hooks and earworms and things. So I always thought about the movie more in terms of a very physical music experience—something bombastic, with images and sounds falling from the sky. You could even say it's something that's close to like a drug experience.

RKO: Is there something, visually, that you're itching to do next? Because the palettes of your filmography are very diverse. There's a lot of DIY; *Mister Lonely* is very painterly; and, now, this film is a whole new beast.

HK: I don't know. You know, for me, it's all about pictures, and images, and textures, and the way things look and feel. I'm just constantly obsessed with that and trying to find new techniques and new ways to make movies. I've been interested in that ever since I was a kid. So, how do you take something out of being just a film and make it more inexplicable, and transcendent? A lot of that comes from experimenting, which is why I do a lot of short films—they inform what I do in longer form. So I don't know. I'll think I'll just keep messing around and trying new shit.

RKO: Most auteurs, even those who frequently experiment with genre, are generally able to be somewhat defined through their work. You, however, have continued to do a pretty good job of defying definition. How would you define yourself as a filmmaker?
HK: I just want to be great. That's all. And live beyond all those types of descriptions. I don't want to be contained in any way. As a person and as an artist, I always feel restless. I don't ever feel comfortable set in a specific style or function. I always want to try something even if it doesn't work. If people consider something I do to be a failure or a mistake, I'm fine with that. Sometimes there's beauty in mistakes, and the most interesting things sometimes come out of what people consider to be . . . awkwardness.

RKO: The soundtrack for *Spring Breakers* features Nicki Minaj's "Moment 4 Life," and the girls speak often about holding on to great moments in the film. Is that largely what this movie is for you? A fantasy about the impossibility of clinging to a moment?
HK: Yeah, man. Wow, definitely. That's definitely one of the big things the movie speaks to, for sure.

RKO: Is that something you feel often yourself? Wanting to capture a moment in time?
HK: Sure. That's why I used to do drugs a lot. I just wanted to isolate the moment, slow it down, and examine it. I always felt life moved too quickly. But that's the way life is.

Nashville. Harmony's House. Present Day. Part III.

Eric Kohn / 2013

Interview conducted March 30, 2013. Previously unpublished.

Eric Kohn: How do you feel about the way *Spring Breakers* was perceived?
Harmony Korine: I've been so happy about it. It really reached a lot of people. The fact that the film exists the way it does and was seen by as many people as it was makes me really happy. I think more people saw this film than any of my other films combined already.

EK: It grossed more in its opening weekend than any of your previous movies in their entire theatrical runs.
HK: Yeah. Probably in the first day.

EK: Does that feel like a validation?
HK: I mean, I don't know really need validation, but I feel happy that a lot of people got to see the film and that it'll make things easier going forward when I want to make movies. I think there's value in that it seems like, for the first time, a different audience saw the film, and was introduced to different types of images and a specific kind of storytelling. That's exciting to me. It's exciting to me that a lot of teenagers saw it.

EK: Were you surprised by the teen reactions to the movie?
HK: I had heard that a lot of them were sneaking in. That makes me very happy. Somehow it infiltrated the mainstream.

EK: Teen reactions on Twitter were pretty fascinating—they were all over the place.
HK: I think a lot of them thought it was going to be a certain type of film and then the actual film was completely different. But I knew that was

208

going to be the case. That was part of the desire. It's so much a part of the total concept of the film. In some ways, you never want the film to end; you just want it to go on. How could I not be happy about that?

EK: Do you have enough distance from the movie to view it outside of the intensity involved in making it?

HK: I don't know how much thought I even want to give it. I haven't really even started analyzing it that way. I don't think I will. That's the thing—you always want your films to be successful, for people to love them in some way. You want some type of reaction. But I never really know what the hell's going on. I make the film and once it's out there I just walk around.

EK: You're savvier than you give yourself credit for.

HK: I'm thinking it through. This film was made like a piece of pop, so I wanted it to work in that way—in a popular context. It would only really succeed if it was introduced in that way. From the beginning, it was a piece of pop art cinema.

EK: It certainly seemed to be achieving that when Britney Spears tweeted that she was excited to see the film.

HK: That was ridiculous. That's something where you live a long time and then something like that happens . . . a tweet from Britney—that's like an Oscar. (laughs)

EK: The reception may have marked a new period of success for you, but you're still being perceived in light of your earlier career antics—Selena Gomez and James Franco appeared separately on *Letterman* to promote the film, and in both cases, they addressed your nineties appearances on the show. How do you feel about that stage of your life still chasing you around?

HK: I'm not trying to shed anything. I'm still connected to that. The only time it's annoying is when it overshadows the film. But what are you going to do? I don't really care. I just do what I do. I was living adventures. All that criminal shit was part of the films. All that criminal behavior was part of what I needed to make the art work. At the same time, I just needed to satisfy that side of things for me. I don't really want to shed that, or distance myself from that. That's an important part of who I am. At the same time, I'm still not at the point where it's something I want to talk about now.

EK: What do you mean by "criminal shit"?

HK: The assumption is that criminal behavior is bad. I think that violent behavior toward other people is obviously bad. But criminal behavior for a writer-director is a good thing.

EK: Literal criminal behavior?

HK: Yes. Of course.

EK: Can you elaborate?

HK: Criminal behavior can mean a lot of different stuff. The criminal has a different way of thinking, a different way of aligning himself. A criminal has a different mentality that's outside the box in some ways. Obviously, I'm not talking about violent behavior. I'm talking about the concept of criminal ideology that I think is helpful for directors. I don't think that it's bad. There are a set of circumstances you can put yourself through, a mentality, a mind frame that can also help you as an artist. You just don't ever want to become complaisant, an upright citizen. You just don't ever want to be swimming with the stream. It's easier that way—you do less personal damage to yourself—but it's much less rewarding, if you know what I mean. It can mean a lot of different things. Even having to pay for criminal behavior is OK. The pain and comeuppance you go through can help you.

EK: The language you're using sounds awfully similar to the way recovering addicts talk.

HK: In some ways, depending on the type of addiction, it can be similar. Addiction is something sadder to me—that you're dependent on something. But a righteous criminal can make it happen. You get to where you need to go and there's a kinship in the directing process, a connectedness to that.

EK: When did you start talking about this idea of the criminal artist?

HK: No, I don't think I've ever said it to anybody. You've probably never heard me say this before or found it anywhere. But it makes sense to me. It's a different way of thinking. It just means that you have to be creative.

EK: Earlier, we spoke about how you rejected early opportunities to work in the industry. Now, you've figured out a way to navigate that world.

HK: I was a kid then and didn't understand the way things work. Also, my desire, what I wanted to do at that time, was specifically different from what I want to do now. I want to make different types of films and I know how to make things happen now in a different way. A lot of my energy has been spent just fucking the system headfirst because I didn't know any better. It's a hard way to create. You're spending a lot of time trying to create. The soul is the same but I have to figure out different ways.

EK: How important is it that you make a living on your films, rather than making money on commercials or other sources?

HK: It's very simple. The more successful your films are the easier it is to make films in the future. Anyone who doesn't want that is affecting the time it takes you to raise money. That doesn't mean it's all I'm thinking about; the fact that the films exist is a victory. The victory is in the creation.

Additional Resources

Books

A Crackup at the Race Riots
Drag City (reprint edition): April 16, 2013
Originally published by Mainstreet/Doubleday in 1998, this debut novel
from an underground filmmaker uses print, photographs, drawings,
news clippings, handwriting, a poem, attempted diagrams, and clip
art to enhance the text, which primarily tells of a race war that happens in Florida, where the Jewish people sit in trees, the black people
are run by MC Hammer, and the white people are run by Vanilla Ice.
Or as the author himself described it front of a national television
audience, "I wanted to write the Great American Choose-Your-Own-
Adventure Novel." In actuality, it is a collection of hard-luck stories,
off-and-on-color jokes, script scraps, found letters, free rhymes, drug
flashbacks, and other missing scenes, all exploring the world of show
business with fingers prying in the cracks and feet set lightly in the
black humors of the real world. With chapters about books found in
Monty Clift's basement and Tupac Shakur's ten favorite novels, and
a set of eleven suicide notes with room included for the reader's signature, the book is a one-of-a-kind post-postmodern examination
of the dangers of public life from a unique voice in independent culture, one that might make William S. Burroughs sigh and turn the
page at least. (Synopsis courtesy of Drag City)

The Collected Fanzines
Drag City: November 18, 2008
These eight limited-run fanzines were originally created between 1992
and 1999 and were sold out of the Alleged and Andrea Rosen galleries in New York City. Collected together for the first time, all of the
original content is represented—low-concept, hilarious juxtaposi-
tions of words; scribbles and doodles; lists; monologues; free verse;
jokes; innuendo; and both fake and real interviews. They blur the

lines between fantasy and reality, and are often prankster in nature and laugh-out-loud funny. With weird musings, fake celebrity gossip, and hastily drawn art, this collection is a must have for fans of the authors and lovers of pop culture. (Synopsis courtesy of Drag City)

Collected Screenplays: "Jokes," "Gummo," "Julien Donkey-Boy"
Faber and Faber: April 8, 2002
This collection of three screenplays—*Jokes, Gummo*, and *Julien Donkey Boy*—displays Korine's unorthodox approach. (Synopsis courtesy of Faber & Faber)

I See Poetry in Everything, Even You
Karma: 2013
This stunning publication is a collaboration between artist Dan Colen and Korine—in which the paintings of Colen and poetry of Korine are randomly collated, forming an abstract and lyrical conversation between the two artists. *I See Poetry in Everything, Even You* is a limited edition of 500 unique copies. (Synopsis courtesy of Karma)

Pass the Bitch Chicken
Holzwarth Publications: July 2, 2002
The result of a collaboration between filmmaker Harmony Korine and painter Christopher Wool, this series of experimental images tests the limits of the pictorial and the abstract, pushing the boundaries of visual and textual narrative to extremes. Korine's photographs form the basis of an intense process of layering, drawing, overprinting, and photocopying. Passed back and forth between the artists, these images are eventually reduced to ghostly shadows beneath a barrage of scumbled dot screens, random patterning, and symbolic blurs and drips. Gradually, the fragmented, distorted images serially mutate, attacked by a combination of mechanical and human processes. Yet despite the violence exerted upon it, a vestige of narrative always survives. (Synopsis courtesy of Amazon.com)

Pigxote
Nieves: 2009
Consisting of forty-nine photographs from Korine's private archive, *Pigxote* reveals a largely unexamined side of the artist's creative process. It depicts a mysterious young girl moving through a televised

landscape of intuitively arranged "experiential moments," and offers further insight into the poetic mind of one of Nashville's finest sons. (Synopsis courtesy of Nieves)

Shadowfux
Swiss Institute/agnès b.: March 31, 2012
Separately renowned in their respective mediums of film and painting, Harmony Korine and Rita Ackermann meet in their mutual affection for unorthodox, mischievous beauty, and more specifically in the creation of psychologically jarring figures amplified through fragmented narratives. *Shadowfux* documents the artists' first collaboration. Taking Korine's recent film *Trash Humpers* (2009) as its point of departure, it features large-scale works in which Ackermann and Korine have collaged, painted, and drawn over stills of the film's beguiling young bodies with old faces. Generated through a call-and-response method, *Shadowfux* illustrates the importance of cutting to both artists' works. Additionally, it presents short texts by Korine, as well as previously unpublished deleted scenes from *Trash Humpers*. (Synopsis courtesy of Amazon.com)

Websites

Harmony-Korine.com
http://www.harmony-korine.com/news/
Unofficial fan site has been main online resource for news and background on Korine for several years. Includes filmography and roundup of other works.

Harmony Korine on Facebook
https://www.facebook.com/harmfulkorine
Facebook page is an unofficial repository of news pertaining to Korine's latest work.

Harmony Special K
http://www.angelfire.com/ab/harmonykorine/
Unofficial fan site hasn't been updated since 2001, but includes detailed timeline, photos, and other biographical information.

Harmony Korine on Wikipedia
http://en.wikipedia.org/wiki/Harmony_Korine
Wikipedia page is extensive and kept more or less up to date.

Harmony Korine on YouTube
http://www.youtube.com/channel/HCg6NTBSrJWoo
Automatically generated list of YouTube videos pegged to Korine, including all three fabled appearances on *Letterman* as well as dozens of other interviews and short works.

Additional Interviews

Butler, Blake. "Tupac, Neck Braces, and Suicide: An Interview with Harmony Korine." *Vice*, April 23, 2013.

Elliot, Nicholas. "A Visit with Harmony Korine" (French). *Cahiers du Cinéma*, March 2013.

Fuller, Graham. "Harmony Korine: Directing on the Edge of Madness." *New York Times*, October 4, 1999.

Goldman, Andrew. "Harmony Korine's Spring-Break Intentions Are Pure. *New York Times Magazine*, March 8, 2013.

Herzog, Werner. "Gummo's Whammo." *Interview*, November 1999.

Heimlich, Adam. "Harmony Korine's Real-Life Fight Club." *New York Press*, December 1999.

Knegt, Peter, and Smith, Nigel M. "John Waters Talks to Harmony Korine: Highlights from Their Conversation at the Provincetown International Film Festival." *Indiewire*, June 26, 2013.

Lim, Dennis. "The Return (and Reform?) of Harmony Korine." *New York Times*, April 27, 2008.

Lim, Dennis. "Venice Film Festival: James Franco and Harmony Korine on *Spring Breakers*." *New York Times*, September 7, 2012.

Longworth, Karina. "*Trash Humpers*: Talking Tall." *L.A. Weekly*, May 13, 2010.

Michael, David. "Interview: Harmony Korine." *Fashion*, May 16, 2013.

Mitchell, Elvis. "Harmony Korine." *Interview*, May 2008.

Simonini, Ross. "Interview with Harmony Korine." *Believer*, March/April 2010.

Staskiewicz, Keith. "A Fourth-Dimensional Interview with Val Kilmer and Harmony Korine." *Entertainment Weekly*, April 25, 2012.

Swanson, Carl. "Harm Reduction." *New York*, April 13, 2008.

Index

CPSIA information can be obtained
at www.ICGtesting.com
Printed in the USA
BVHW080049080120
568860BV00005B/47/P